the power of
Experiential Learning

a handbook for trainers and educators

Colin Beard & John P Wilson

**KOGAN
PAGE**

First edition published in 2002

Kogan Page Limited
120 Pentonville Road
London N1 9JN
UK

Stylus Publishing Inc.
22883 Quicksilver Drive
Sterling VA 20166-2012
USA

British Library Cataloguing in Publication Data

A CIP record for this book is available from the British Library.

ISBN 0 7494 3467 8

Typeset by Saxon Graphics Ltd, Derby
Printed and bound in Great Britain by Biddles Ltd, Guildford and King's Lynn
www.biddles.co.uk

Contents

Contents

Acknowledgements

This book owes its existence to numerous sources of inspiration and support. In particular, we wish to recognize the invaluable contribution of Dominic Irvine of Epiphanies Limited (Dom@epiphaniesltd.com; www.epiphaniesltd.com) who has shaped our thinking and contributed to the concepts developed here. Notably, he continued to advise and cajole us with regard to the importance of this book having a practical application – an essential ingredient in experiential learning.

The book was also given colour and texture through case studies provided by Peter Dehnbostel and Gabriele Molzberger for their work on DaimlerChrysler; Mike Hopkins of Rolls-Royce plc; Rosie MacIntyre for her insights from her twins into the influence of hereditary experience, Harry Matlay of the Knowledge Management Centre, University of Central England Business School for Pegasus Transport; and David Wilcock of Liberating Potential for his contribution on Gestalt.

Other influences include: Pauline Attard for the role of acting on learning; Ann Marie Cooper of Linklaters and Alliance; Roger Greenaway for his contributions to outdoor development; Lena Jones on ethics; Outward Bound Singapore for exploring and challenging some of Colin Beard's theories; and Joan Butt, Toby Rhodes and Jon Waller.

We are also learning from our experience with this book and *Human Resource Development* that Philip Mudd's demonstration of patience and encouragement as Editor is a powerful means of support.

Last, but by no means least, special thanks to Maggie Lovatt and Catherine Wilson for their spiritual support.

1

Unlocking Powerful Learning – A new model

> *Experience is the child of Thought, and Thought is the child of Action –*
> *we cannot learn men from books.*
> (Benjamin Disraeli, 1826)

INTRODUCTION

If you follow the advice of Benjamin Disraeli's quotation above you would not proceed any further than the first page of this book before returning it to the shelf! However, don't go away; bear with us as we explain how this book will offer a new way of thinking about and organizing the development and delivery of experiential learning.

Disraeli was using his skills as a political orator to polarize the debate about theory and practice and draw attention to the need to think and learn through experience. The argument that 'we cannot learn men through books' is an unsustainable one but Disraeli's underlying message has a kernel of truth. Traditional learning with the teacher or trainer spouting facts and figures and pupils or participants regurgitating the information without deeper involvement is a very ineffective form of learning. A much more effective and long-lasting form of learning is to involve the learner by creating a meaningful learning experience.

Experiential learning is a client-focused, supported approach to individual, group and organizational development, which engages the young or adult learner, using the elements of action, reflection and transfer. *The Power of Experiential Learning* will enable you to see new ways to unleash some of the more potent ingredients of learning through experience. It has much to offer in the search for greater learning efficacy. In order to free the spirit of learning and let it emerge from its chrysalis, whether it be in management education, corporate training, youth development work or schools, as providers we all agree that we need to explore in much greater detail the nature of the learning 'experience'.

Whilst there are no easy answers, there are significant areas of yet untapped knowledge about many of the ingredients that can be used to create new recipes for learning. In this chapter we illustrate this with a model, in the form of a *learning combination lock*, which comprises a series of tumblers each designed to illustrate the almost infinite range of ingredients that can be altered in order to enhance learning. Using the learning combination lock the potential number of learning permutations is more than 15 million and it can be further expanded to an almost infinite number. Whilst we are on our guard to avoid simplistic mechanistic thinking, we do believe it is robust material and we discuss the theoretical basis of our thinking, as well as offering many practical examples to illustrate the value of learning from experience.

Experience pervades all forms of learning; however, its value is frequently not recognized or is even disregarded. Experiential learning undoubtedly involves the 'whole person', through thoughts, feelings and physical activity. The recognition of this 'whole environment', both internally and externally, is important. Experiential learning can take on many appearances in life, such as recreational or leisure activities, exhilarating journeys or adventures, experimentation or play. It can also be in the form of painful events. Heron (2000: 316), in writing about the facilitation of learning, used a 'whole person' approach. He believed that the perfect life was was never complete, but often torn and damaged. People, he said, were engaging in a form of action enquiry throughout their everyday life. 'This consciousness-in-action involves, intentionally, both participatory and individuating functions: feeling and emotion, intuition and imagery, reflection and discrimination, intention and action.'

Providers, too, are increasingly required to understand in greater depth this process of action learning, establishing with great care what it is that clients want or need. In order to respond to these requirements it is necessary to create the best environment for learners, one that will enable them to focus on *their* key issues. The best environment includes the best places to think and learn, and that includes both natural and artificially constructed environments. In order to achieve effective and long-lasting learning it is necessary to address the three areas of cognition, behaviour and emotions. The use of experiential learning as a vehicle enables us to combine all of these elements together rather than addressing them individually.

The Power of Experiential Learning explores both the historical roots of experiential learning theory, and practical applications, and it provides numerous signposts leading to other sources to draw upon. We, like other professionals, have ventured into, borrowed and learnt from many other disciplines in order to facilitate learning and change. We include ideas and integrating features from fields such as psychotherapy, psychology, education and training, people development, adventure and leisure. The book suggests numerous ways to stimulate people's senses, and so stimulate deeper thinking and learning. We offer methods that help people to see and understand things as if for the first time, even though they may have undergone the experience before. We also offer methods to revisit past experiences and view them in a new light. Both of these methods we call *retrospective learning*. Moving from the past to the present, we consider methods to improve immediate learning, which we call *concurrent learning*. Finally, we investigate the possibilities of learning through imagination and projecting ideas into the future; we call this *prospective learning*.

The book includes methods that enable people to make sense of their experience, as well as methods to develop and practise new behaviours. The techniques include mood setting, drama, creative writing, art, meditation, environmental modification and routine rituals. We also help you as developers, educators and trainers to focus on the design of new ideas and we explore ways to improve professional practice and ethical responsibility through self-monitoring and feedback techniques. Many of the theories and practical methods presented in this book apply equally to providers; as practitioners, we too are learners, and good practice emanates from our ability to learn from our experience.

In order slowly to build our learning combination lock, we first explore simple dichotomies and the need for providers to incorporate the concept of *balance* in learning activities. The balance may be of energy–tension, challenge–support, task–process, male–female, indoor–outdoor, natural–artificial environments and real–simulated activities, illustrating some of the key factors that contribute to the millions of opportunities for learning.

We also develop many simple models that take the form of *waves* or circles, and these are important in our thinking throughout the book. Waves of energy underpin the daily experience and these waves of activity influence the basis of experiential programmes. We nurture and prepare people, energize and engage people, help to support, provide for or create their experience and then relax people. There are surface waves and deeper ones, short ones and long ones.

> A novel can be likened to an ocean. The little waves we see lapping the shore are in fact carried on the waves that are nine ordinary waves long. These waves are themselves carried by waves that carry nine of them and these larger waves are similarly carried by waves that carry nine of them. Some waves in the ocean are miles long.
>
> (Buzan, 2000: 200)

The Learning Combination Lock

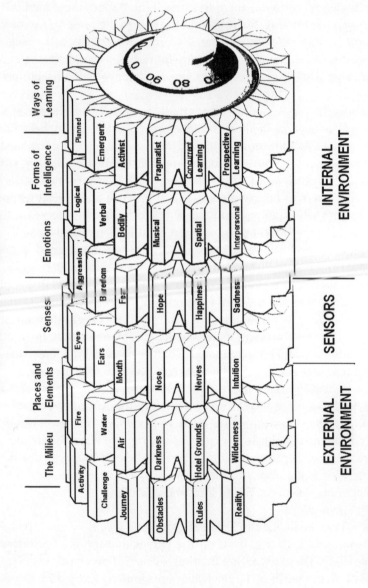

Figure 1.1 The learning combination lock
© Colin Beard

So let us now look at this learning combination lock, a new conceptual framework (see Figure 1.1).

For the first time ever, to our knowledge, all the main ingredients of the learning equation have been brought together in the learning combination lock. In the past only some of the elements have been discussed in the literature, and then often in isolation, which therefore gives only a partial picture of the learning environment. The following chapters will address the various tumblers that make up the learning combination lock; however, we will briefly discuss each of these main categories to provide an overview and enable you to dip in and out of the book in order to find strategies and answers that apply to the circumstances in which you find yourself.

The learning combination lock in its elementary sense is based on the notion that the *person* interacts with the *external environment* through the *senses*. However the learning combination lock is presented as six tumblers to represent visually the complexity of the many possible alternatives. Beginning on the right of the combination lock the tumblers show the ways a person learns, ie the theories, and also the forms of intelligence. These two tumblers should inform the choice and selection of other tumbler options, so as to avoid a random, one-armed-bandit approach to selecting the ingredients for experiential learning activities.

The next group of tumblers, located in the centre, is concerned with senses and emotions. These are where we perceive and emotionally respond to the stimuli from the external environment, in other words we internalize the external learning experience.

The final group of tumblers, on the left of the learning combination lock, consists of places and the natural elements that provide the external stimuli, as well as the milieu of activities.

As you read through the book, you may well identify new elements to add to the contents of individual tumblers, and perhaps even add completely new categories of tumblers. In this way you can create your own personalized learning combination lock to answer and respond to your own obstacles and challenges.

THE TUMBLERS

The milieu

Most outdoor and indoor learning exercises consist of a number of basic ingredients in which the participants are involved. These normally involve some form of physical and intellectual involvement that may provide a challenge to test mental and physical endurance, eg building and using a raft or operating a virtual organization. Sometimes the activity involves a journey, which may be geographical, imaginary, chronological or even the life cycle of a company.

Most, if not all, activities involve obstacles that must be overcome by the participants. These may be real or imaginary, and require those involved to operate within an agreed set of rules. New obstacles may be introduced, rules altered and targets changed depending upon the learning aims and objectives. These basic ingredients are discussed in Chapter 3.

Places and elements

The environmental surroundings can strongly influence the emotions and attitudes of course delegates. For example, involving the participants in an orienteering or treasure-hunt exercise over windswept moorland in winter will produce a very different atmosphere from one that involves people sitting and watching the sun setting from the comfort of a warm beach.

The primal elements of earth, air, fire and water may also be incorporated within the learning activity to help delegates explore within themselves, discover new things and create personal enlightenment. Other elements, such as darkness and silence, tend to be less commonly used within education, training and development exercises but can prove to be very powerful channels to encourage learning. These tumbler dimensions are explored in Chapter 5.

Senses

The more senses we use in an activity the more memorable the learning experience will become because it increases the neural connections in our brains and therefore will be more accessible. The greater the involvement of the participant in the learning activity the deeper will be the participant's learning and therefore the greater the effect on future thought and behaviour. Thus, as many senses as possible should be used in the learning experience to support long-lasting learning that will result in better individual, group and organizational performance. This optimization of sensual learning is discussed in Chapter 3.

Emotions

The root of the word emotion is the Latin *movere* meaning 'to move', and the prefix 'e' qualifies it to mean 'to move away'. Emotions therefore suggest a tendency to act based on the feelings the person is experiencing. In developing learning experiences we need to consider the emotional baggage people bring with them and also the emotions that are likely to emerge as the programme progresses. Goleman (1996), in his book *Emotional Intelligence,* argued that, although intelligence or IQ was important, it was emotional intelligence (EQ) that was more likely to determine a person's achievements in life. Chapter 6 will investigate the power of emotions on the learning experience.

Forms of intelligence

In the section above we mentioned the concept of emotional intelligence, which, to a considerable extent, developed from the work of Howard Gardner. Gardner's (1983) book *Frames of Mind* proposed that there were seven forms of intelligence: linguistic; logical/mathematical/scientific; visual/spatial; musical; bodily/physical/kinaesthetic; interpersonal; and intra-personal. Moreover, he maintained that there were other forms of intelligence and stated that, 'We should spend less time ranking children and more time in helping them to identify their natural competencies and gifts and cultivate those. There are hundreds and hundreds of ways to succeed, and many, many different abilities that will help you get there' (Gardner, 1986).

Another form of intelligence is that of spiritual intelligence (SQ). Zohar and Marshall (2001: 9) suggest that Gardner's forms of intelligence are basically composed of IQ, EQ and SQ, and that SQ is 'an *internal,* innate ability of the human brain and psyche, drawing its deepest resources from the heart of the universe... Spiritual intelligence is the soul's intelligence. It is the intelligence with which we heal ourselves and with which we make ourselves whole.' This particular tumbler, looking at forms of intelligence, will be considered in Chapter 6.

Ways of learning

Some of us learn better in the morning, others in the dark hours of the night, and if we are aware of our preferences we tend to use this insight to plan how to organize our learning. In effect, this is personal learning theory and it can be very influential on our behaviour. More general theories of learning have developed over the millennia, and a vast array now exist that would require several volumes in order to give justice to their importance in influencing learning strategies. The three main types are behaviourist, cognitivist and humanist, and these are included in a table in Chapter 9, which identifies and briefly describes the main aspects of key learning theories.

One of the main theories that we discuss is Kolb's learning cycle, which led to Honey and Mumford's (1992) learning styles inventory, which focused attention on the manner in which people learn, ie activist, pragmatist, theorist and reflector. These learning styles are linked together in a circle, and add to the considerable number of learning theories that use a circle. These are discussed and challenged in more detail in Chapter 2.

There are also numerous other theories about the manner in which people learn. Three of these – retrospective, concurrent and prospective learning – are developed and discussed in the next chapter. In addition, action learning, developed by Revans, and reflective practice (Argyris and Schon) are brought together in Chapter 9 to illustrate the practical value of taking time out from busy schedules to think and reflect about work patterns and behaviour and thus lead to improvements in performance.

AN OVERVIEW OF THE CHAPTERS

Few books other than novels are designed to be read from cover to cover, and this book is based on the pick-and-mix principle. You will have your own particular requirements and should, therefore, dip in and out to select the areas that have most value to yourself. Below we have provided a brief description of the chapters to support your personal learning and investigation.

Chapter 2: Exploring experiential learning

Experiential learning, while superficially a relatively simple concept, becomes more complex as we probe the subject more deeply. Through this investigation the various dimensions of the experience are revealed, and one of the most fundamental is that experience can be considered as a synonym for learning. We look at how to create positive learning environments and also how even negative experiences can have a powerful impact on learning. The distinction between formal learning and experiential learning is also considered in order to encourage more involved forms of learning. A number of the basic models of learning are provided to illustrate how experiential learning has evolved, and we also consider experiential learning from the perspectives of the past, present and future. Finally, to provide balance, we critique the notion of experiential learning and Kolb's learning cycle.

Chapter 3: The design milieu

This chapter creates a basic 16-point typology for use in the design of experiential activities. Each of the 16 ingredients receives attention, and practical examples and case studies are provided. The chapter briefly examines a milieu of dichotomies: stories and journeys, planned and unplanned learning, reality versus simulation, writing and drawing, objects to help and objects as obstacles. Sequencing, pacing and the management of challenge and support are all covered. The typology provides an important checklist as well as forming the first of a set of tumblers in the learning combination lock. The main theme of this chapter is that there are many new and emerging trends that provide endless possibilities for experiential providers to enhance the delivery of any educational, training or developmental event.

Chapter 4: Exploring reality

In this chapter we consider the many facets of 'reality' as one of the most important ingredients of the first tumbler, and so it forms a chapter on its own. We explore how altering the level of reality provides further opportunities to unlock greater learner potential. Learner perceptions of reality can be applied to many aspects of experiential learning, including the learning process itself, the activities provided and the location in which they take place. In this chapter we explore the nature of the real experience and the degree to which experiences are perceived as real. We show examples where reality can be manipulated as a key consideration in the design and delivery of experiential learning, including the use of play, circus, radio, drama, sculpture, art and fantasy.

Chapter 5: Places and elements

Experiential learning can take place inside or outdoors, in natural or artificial environments, and in urban or rural locations; place is the basis of the external stimulus. This chapter examines the empathetic and combative use of different locations for experiential learning, and explains how to use the natural environment to maximum effect using natural rhythms, diverse habitats and the teeming diversity of living things. This forms the second key tumbler of the learning combination lock. The natural elements of the environment, such as wind, rain, snow and other natural phenomena, are perceived by our senses, which are found in the adjacent tumbler. Natural rhythms are known to affect our bodily rhythms and moods, and the curative powers of the environment now receive renewed attention from researchers worldwide. Artificially constructed environments on the other hand can be created as highly regulated forms of the natural environment. Artificial caves, ski-slopes, climbing walls, concrete white-water rafting courses and other artefacts can reduce the pressure on natural locations and they are found most often in urban locations where the majority of people live, thus reducing the need to travel. They are not just a substitute when the natural environment is inaccessible, for they provide important places for learning in their own right. The phenomenon of adventure travel as learning is described as an expanding niche market. Knowledge of the environment is essential territory for the experiential provider in order to understand the significance of the 'place' to maximize learning.

Chapter 6: The emotional experience

Emotional experiences and emotional intelligence underpin learning yet many educators and trainers have only recently given more attention to emotional competency. Emotional intelligence is at the core of all success according to Goleman, and experiential learning is largely experienced as an emotional state. This chapter begins with an examination of how emotions and moods underpin experience learning. The concept of emotional intelligence is examined and set in context with other types of intelligence. The chapter examines types of emotional waves and troughs, with balance as a central theme: different waves, different sizes and different frequencies all create the essential roller-coasters that form the emotional self. Emotions also form the root to our identity, and we examine the role of emotional blocks to learning such as fear and risk taking. The positive and negative aspects of emotional engineering are considered. We provide ideas to access the emotional being through the use of objects, metaphors, stories drama, fantasy, trilogies and emotional mapping of emotions to change inner scripts of the mind. We also briefly touch on spiritual intelligence (SQ).

Chapter 7: Working with emotions

In this chapter the learning combination lock shows how the senses form the basic conduit for an external experience to be translated into an internal stimulation. The stimulation of the senses creates a significant affective response, one that is a powerful determinant of subsequent learning. Helping people to be conscious of this emotional experience can allow them to manage and intensify their own learning. This chapter offers more ways to read emotional signs and to work with emotions as part of experiential learning. We offer methods to access the roots of emotion and ways to surface feelings and challenge emotions, and we further explore how humour, metaphors, trilogies and storytelling can be used to access and influence the emotional connection to learning. Helping learners to sense, surface and express both positive and negative feelings rather than to deny or censor them requires great skill and care in group work. It enables the colour and richness of the feelings of learners to be expressed and considered in a controlled way so as to maximize learners' understanding of the learning processes.

Chapter 8: Good practice and ethics

At the start of the chapter we explore what is meant by good practice and take a close look at the process of facilitation and responsibility within the profession. Real codes of practice are presented for scrutiny, and we also examine the vast range of ethical dilemmas that face experiential providers and create a *hierarchy of responsibility* involving individual, organizational, professional and governmental roles. We offer case studies addressing incompetence, bad behaviour and lack of awareness, and pose ethical questions such as, 'What would you do in this situation?' We explore the ethics of emotional engineering as well as the provision of emotional scenarios. Lastly, we look at *principle ethics* and *virtue ethics*, and offer a step-by-step approach to the resolution of ethical dilemmas.

Chapter 9: Ways of learning

To select the most appropriate elements from each of the tumblers in the learning combination lock requires that we have an understanding of the basic theories of learning. The final tumbler provides a brief description of the main theories, all of which are linked through the notion of experience. The fundamental message of this book is the importance of linking action with thought or reflection. This is a key element in the work of Kolb (1984) and is equally seen in Revans's (1982) action learning. This chapter demonstrates how action learning can be used within organizations to improve performance for individuals and groups. It also investigates the strategies employed in reflective practice (Schon, 1983), which are increasingly being used to develop the performance of people involved in professional practice. Practical case studies from Pegasus Transport, Rolls-Royce plc and DaimlerChrysler are used to illustrate the value of encouraging effective learning through practice and theory.

Chapter 10: Imagining and experiencing the future

It is not only through considering past and present experiences that we can learn. It is also possible to imagine multiple futures and rehearse alternative scenarios in our minds. This gives us the possibility to minimize the potential for failure and increase the chance of success. Thinking about future possibilities tends to develop the neural connections in the brain and further increase the likelihood of success. Furthermore, we look at how the conscious part of our brains can interfere with the subconscious to undermine our performance, and use the game of tennis as an example.

To find that point, that reason for our doing and our being, it helps to build on three senses – a sense of continuity, a sense of connection and a sense of direction. Without these senses we can feel disoriented, adrift and rudderless… We shall need all the help we can find to recognise our place and role in it. These senses are the best antidote I know to the feelings of impotence which rapid change induces in us all.

(Handy, 1994: 239)

CONCLUSION

The Power of Experiential Learning is a practical book that addresses the main factors to consider when developing and delivering learning exercises for yourself, employees, youth groups, schoolchildren, in fact all people who wish to learn more deeply and effectively. The activities can be delivered within classrooms, training rooms, hotels or residential centres. Equally we encourage you to develop exercises that make use of the wider outdoors environment, whether it be at the top of a mountain, deep in a cave, in a river, lake, sea or ocean etc.

The number of permutations for creating a learning environment is almost limitless, and we will present you with some of the main ones. Also, we strongly encourage you to add to the learning combination lock and develop your own personal learning combination lock that will help to solve your own obstacles and challenges and add to the vast range of options. We wish you every success with this process and we hope this book is a small contribution towards helping you to find a new sense of connection, a sense of continuity and a sense of direction.

2

Exploring Experiential Learning

> Experience is the name everyone gives to their mistakes.
> (Oscar Wilde, *Lady Windermere's Fan*)

INTRODUCTION

Learning from experience is one of the most fundamental and natural means of learning available to everyone. It need not be expensive, nor does it require vast amounts of technological hardware and software to support the learning process. Instead, in the majority of cases, all it requires is the opportunity to reflect and think, either alone or in the company of other people. In spite of it being a natural means of learning it is not always consistent nor effective for a number of reasons, such as a lack of time, a lack of awareness of other modes of operating and thinking, and the absence of other people to act as sounding boards to assess and evaluate our prior experiences. In order to improve, we need to utilize effectively the powerful potential of learning from experience.

All too often theories of learning, education, training and development are developed in isolation from one another and thus there is no overall coherence. The great strength of experiential learning is that it provides an underpinning philosophy that acts as a thread joining many of the learning theories together in a more unified whole. Yet, this philosophy, while appearing relatively straightforward, is in actual fact rather complex and forces us to consider the nature of who we are and what we mean by experience. In this chapter we will investigate experience in more detail and we encourage you to relate what you read to your own personal experiences so that your learning becomes deeper and more applicable.

DEFINING EXPERIENTIAL LEARNING

When a word or concept is examined in order to write a definition, it soon becomes apparent how elusive its meaning is, and the closer we look, the more indistinct and vague it can become. The word *experience* is no different in this respect; however, reaching for a dictionary can provide some help, and the *Oxford Dictionary* describes experience as, 'The fact of being consciously the subject of a state or condition; of being consciously affected by an event; a state or condition viewed subjectively; an event by which one is affected; and, knowledge resulting from actual observation or from what one has undergone.'

These definitions provide an initial starting point, yet John Dewey (1925: 1), who wrote extensively on the subject of experience, and also gave us the library book indexing system, stated that, 'experience is a weasel word. Its slipperiness is evident in an inconsistency characteristic of many thinkers.' An indication of this 'slipperiness' can be illustrated by looking at our own experience. Take an incident that jointly happened to you and another person, eg a road accident or perhaps a memorable event, and describe to the other person what happened in detail. Next, get the person to describe the event as he or she saw it. While many things will be very similar, there will be parts that either of you or perhaps both do not remember at all, and there may be interpretations of the events that you both see differently. You would both agree that although the event was experienced by both of you its impact was in many respects different.

From the road accident example above, it is evident that no two people experience the same event exactly the same way. More startlingly, and perhaps disturbingly, this not only casts doubt on the accuracy of our memory but also what we mean when we say we experience something. If the accident happened to someone else without our involvement, ie had an existence beyond ours, then we can only assume that the various interpretations we can put on the accident are mental constructions and only interpretations of the event. This line of reasoning, or philosophy, is called existentialism and this helps us to appreciate the complexity of experience. Plato, for instance, discussed the difficulty of accurately explaining what we mean by the word 'bed'. Likewise, another example of how we experience things differently is illustrated by Dewey (1925: 4–5), who stated:

> When I look at a chair, I say I experience it. But what I actually experience is only a very few of the elements that go to make up the chair, namely, that colour that belongs to the chair under these particular conditions of light, the shape which the chair displays when viewed from this angle, etc. The man who has the experience, as distinct from a philosopher theorizing about it would probably say that he experienced the chair most fully not when looking at it but when meaning to sit down in it precisely because his experience is not limited to colour under specific conditions of light, and angular shape.

This difficulty in accurately and precisely pinning down the meaning of experience is further complicated by the fact that previous experiences and a consideration of the experience alter the interpretation of the event and therefore the experience itself. Boud, Cohen and Walker (1993: 7) explained:

> For the sake of simplicity in discussing learning from experience, experience is sometimes referred to as if it were singular and unlimited by time or place. Much experience, however, is multifaceted, multi-layered and so inextricably connected with other experiences that it is impossible to locate temporally or spatially. It almost defies analysis as the act of analysis inevitably alters the experience and the learning that flows from it.

The definitions of experience provided by the *Oxford Dictionary*, as we saw earlier in the chapter, connect both the action and the sensing or thinking about the action. Indeed, Cuffaro (1995: 62) emphasized: 'Action and thought are not two discrete aspects of experience. It is not to undertake an activity and then at its end to contemplate the results. What is stressed is that the two must not be separated, for each informs the other.'

Dewey is, arguably, the foremost exponent of the use of experience for learning, and the word occurs in a number of titles of his books including *Experience and Nature* (1925), *Art as Experience* (1934) and *Experience and Education* (1938). Cuffaro (1995) explained that Dewey used experience as a lens through which he could analyse the interactions of people and their environments. In this way Dewey was able to connect opposites or dualities eg person and nature, subject and object, knowing and doing, and mind and body. In this way these polarities become connected and the concept of experience creates an organic whole of continuity, process and situation.

It becomes clear that experiencing something is a linking process between action and thought. Dewey (1916: 144–45) argued: 'Thinking, in other words, is the intentional endeavour to discover specific connections between something which we do and the consequences which result, so that the two become continuous. Their isolation, and consequently their purely arbitrary going together, is cancelled; a unified, developing situation takes place.'

These musings about the nature of experience are not merely an academic exercise with no real application in the learning environment. It is only by considering what we mean by experience that as trainers, educators and developers of human potential we can gain insight into one of the most powerful means to learning that currently exists. What we are actually doing right now by attempting to get closer to the term *experience* and by relating our experiences to these discussions is to create a coherent understanding where theory and practice relate to each other. And, while we might never reach the absolute truth about a person, an experience or a chair, we can at least try to understand and achieve a degree of enlightenment.

Figure 2.1 represents the relation between theory and practice. Our theories are abstract conceptualizations of how thoughts and external objects relate to one another in a consistent manner. They inform and guide us in our practice, and enable us to gain insights into the various events in which we are involved. If our practical experience does not match our theory of how we think things should be then we often revise our theories or sometimes revisit the experience in order to see if it can be fitted into our *Weltanshauung* – our way of seeing the world. Thus there is a continual interaction of theory and practice in which each informs the other.

The link between experience and learning is a strong one, and has been described by a number of writers. Wilson (1999: 8) defined learning as 'a relatively permanent change of knowledge, attitude or behaviour occurring as a result of formal education or training, or as a result of informal experiences'. Similarly, Kolb (1984: 38) explained, 'Learning is the process whereby knowledge is created through the transformation of experience.'

Experience and learning would thus appear to be closely intertwined and almost inseparable. In many respects, experience and learning mean the same thing and thus experiential learning is a tautology or repetition of the same idea. We can define experiential learning as *the insight gained through the conscious or unconscious internalization of our own or observed interactions, which build upon our past experiences and knowledge*. Experiential learning is, in essence, the underpinning process to all forms of learning since it represents the transformation of most new and significant experiences and incorporates them within a broader conceptual framework. A similar view is held by Boud, Cohen and Walker (1993: 8), who stated:

> We found it to be meaningless to talk about learning in isolation from experience. Experience cannot be bypassed; it is the central consideration of all learning. Learning builds on and flows from experience: no matter what external prompts to learning there might

Figure 2.1 The relationship between theory and practice

be – teachers, materials, interesting opportunities – learning can only occur if the experience of the learner is engaged, at least at some level. These external influences can act only by transforming the experience of the learner.

In summary, we are saying that the foundation of much learning is the interaction between self and the external environment, in other words the experience. Rogers (1996: 107) took this concept further and stated, 'There is a growing consensus that experience forms the basis of all learning.' Whatever the exact relation between experience and learning, and there is also an argument that experience in the form of genetic memory is passed down from parents to their children, there is no doubt that it probably provides the most coherent theory of learning. For the moment we will leave the final word to Kurt Lewin who developed the T-group training method (T = training). He drew upon the relationship between theory and experience to produce the well-known quotation, 'There is nothing so practical as a good theory.'

A MEANINGFUL EXPERIENCE

When we undergo an experience, this does not always lead to new insights and new learning. For example, if the experience only serves to confirm some already held beliefs it will be interpreted as supporting the existing cognitive status quo and little attention will be paid to it. If we do not pay attention to it the opportunity for new learning will not happen.

Experience may underpin all learning but it does not always result in learning. We have to engage with the experience and reflect on what happened, how it happened and why. Without this, the experience will tend to merge with the background of all the stimulants that assail our senses every day. There are stimulants around us all the time but our awareness of them and our sensitivity to them is dependent on how 'loud' they are, our degree of interest in them, what other stimulants are also competing for our attention, etc.

The average person is confronted and assailed with hundreds if not thousands of advertisements daily. Not only are they to be found on the television and radio, advertising hoardings, buses, newspapers and magazines, but also in the logos and names on many of the items we interact with, including clothing, pens, packaging of foods and our computer.

If we compare this number of appeals to our attention with the almost infinite number of stimulants around and within us, there is the possibility that we could become overwhelmed with the avalanche of information.

Our brain, like a computer, might shut down as a result of overloading. Take just a minute to look out of the window and see the variety of objects and interactions happening between people. You can interpret each item you see at different levels of involvement in order to understand it. Pirsig (1976) in *Zen and the Art of Motorcycle Maintenance* suggested that one method to achieve understanding was to analyse a brick and all its subtle shapes and textures. Through the use of a mental magnifying glass we are able to bring into focus varying levels of detail. However, to look at everything at this level of intensity would be overpowering and our brains would not be able to cope; in other words, there would be paralysis through analysis.

In order to prevent this overloading and stop it working effectively, the brain filters these stimulants to allow only those elements that are perceived to be of relevance to be mentally processed either consciously or unconsciously. Thus, we selectively choose what we believe to be of importance and, consciously or unconsciously, ignore other elements. It is these cognitive filters, which are part of our mindset and disposition, which can create mental blind spots. For this reason we may not be able to see things even when they are right in front of our eyes.

Despite cognitive blind spots our brains are always scanning the environment in what might be called the 'cocktail party phenomenon'. At a party we might be talking to a person and concentrating on what is being said, oblivious to everything happening around us. However, this focus may only be happening at a very conscious level; subconsciously, we would appear to be taking in other things that are happening. For instance, despite high levels of noise we may suddenly pick out from the cacophony the sound of our name being spoken and then immediately tune into that frequency to hear what people are saying about us!

Thus, perception and interaction are insufficient in themselves, and we must interact in a meaningful way with external stimulants if we are to learn. Experience is a meaningful engagement with the environment in which we use our previous knowledge (itself built from experience) to bring new meanings to an interaction.

LEARNING IS PERSONAL

We all have our own theoretical frameworks with which we interpret and cast illumination on our interaction with the world. Our own genetic make-up, experiences and disposition play a significant role in making each experience we undergo unique to ourselves. No one else sees the event in exactly the same way as we do ourselves; no one possesses the same experiences that influence our interaction with the event; and no one else perceives and processes the information in quite the same way.

All learning experiences are personal and unique to us. Boud, Cohen and Walker (1993: 10) explained, 'Each experience is influenced by the unique past of the learner.' They maintained that a person is aware of some elements of the world and is oblivious to others. Furthermore much of this process occurs without us being remotely conscious of what we choose to pay attention to and what we do not.

Perception is learning

When we perceive a stimulus, either external to us or even within ourselves, this can be regarded as a form of learning from experience. Figure 2.2 represents the complex process of perception and how we interpret and respond to an external or internal stimulus. Through our senses we register the stimulus at a conscious and/or subconscious level. At a conscious level we may see or hear something; alternatively, at a subconscious level our senses are continuously scanning the environment but we are not consciously aware of external stimuli – for example, the cocktail party phenomenon. We are also consciously and subconsciously aware of internal stimuli such as feelings of hunger, cold, a migraine, a cut on our hand, etc and take steps, where possible, to resolve the discomfort.

Once we have become aware of this stimulus at a conscious and/or unconscious level it is 'filtered' and interpreted. This is dependent on a

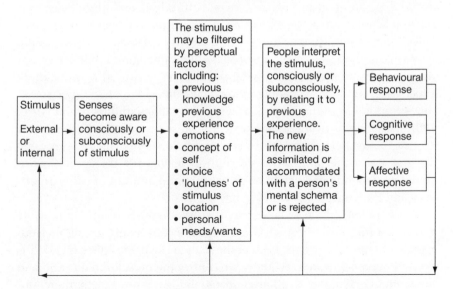

Figure 2.2 The process of perception and experiential learning

variety of factors including previous knowledge, previous experience, emotions, our concept of self, choice, the 'loudness' of the stimulus, location and personal needs.

The next stage then involves us making sense of the stimulus to assess whether it matches our existing mental constructs. If the experience happens as was generally predicted there is no change to our mental schema and we *assimilate* it. If the experience was different to our expectations we may choose to modify our mental frameworks and *accommodate* the new information and experience. Alternatively, if the experience is so alien to our expectations and ways of seeing the world we may *reject* it as being atypical, biased or incorrect (Piaget, 1950).

The final three stages involve cognitive, affective and behavioural responses to the stimulus (Bloom *et al*, 1956). For example, we may think about how we respond to what our boss or partner might say (cognitive). We may decide that we like or don't like the pressure we are being put under at work or perhaps within the outdoor training exercise (affective). And lastly, we may physically respond by stepping back on to the pavement when we notice the truck speeding towards us (behavioural).

All the time these analyses and responses are being recycled to evaluate the stimulus further. This process can happen very quickly and where we are in immediate danger, for instance from being hit by the truck, the process may be short-circuited and we instinctively leap out of the way.

It is essential, however, to recognise that although two people may receive the same stimulus they do not necessarily respond in the same way. If we find ourselves on the edge of a cliff we may be terrified or exhilarated depending on past experience and attitudes. Similarly, if faced by a bully at work we may choose to avoid the situation, aggressively challenge the bully or act assertively. Kuhn (1970) explained that two people may look at the same object and receive the same stimuli but the sensations may be very different owing to differences caused by education, experience, etc. Indeed, people who come from different societies sometimes respond in quite different ways to the same stimulus. Kuhn (1970: 198) maintained, 'In the metaphorical no less than in the literal use of "seeing", interpretation begins where perception ends. The two processes are not the same, and what perception leaves for interpretation to complete depends drastically on the nature and amount of prior experience and training.'

At a very immediate level we may perceive, in other words learn, while carrying a full mug of coffee. Our senses are continually giving us feedback about how close to the brim of the mug the swirling coffee is and thus adjust how quickly we walk, how we control the muscles in our arm and what attention we pay to other people walking nearby. Furthermore, our awareness that the colour of the mug is white represents a very temporary learning experience. We possess an understanding of what 'white' means and we thus respond to the visual stimulus of the mug. This level of learning is very fleeting but it is a response to stimuli. Bateson (2000: 293) developed a model of five levels of learning of which Level 0 represents how we develop learnt behaviour in response to stimuli.

Level 0   Learning occurs as a response to stimuli and is 'not subject to correction'.

Level 1   Learning involves 'change of specificity of response' by correction of errors of choice within a set of alternatives.

Level 2   Is a 'change in the process of Learning 1', eg a change in the set of alternatives. This learning is deutero learning (double loop learning) or learning how to learn.

Level 3   Is a change in the process of Learning 2, eg a corrective change in the system of alternatives from which choice is made.

Level 4   Involves change in Learning 3, which is probably unlikely in any human being.

The interrelationship between an experience and previous experiences and perceptions is summed up in the following quotation from Boud, Cohen and Walker (1993: 8):

> Learning always relates, in one way or another, to what has gone before. There is never a clean slate on which to begin; unless new ideas and new experience link to previous experience, they exist as abstractions, isolated and without meaning. The effects of experience influence all learning. What we are attracted towards, what we avoid and how we go about the task, is dependent on how we have responded in the past. Earlier experiences that had positive or negative effect stimulate or suppress new learning. They encourage us to take risks and enter into new territory for exploration, or alternatively, they may inhibit our range of operation or ability to respond to opportunities.

Cognition, memory and learning

The deeper one delves into the area of learning the more complex the issue becomes. As we saw in the previous section, perception may be regarded as a form of learning. And, if we continue down this line of reasoning, it can be argued that when an amoeba responds to an external stimulus it is learning in the same way as a house-plant will tend to reach towards the light from a window. To what extent our learning as humans is the same or different to that of the amoeba is partly addressed by Bateson above; but, we will leave you to answer it further since it is beyond our scope.

It would be remiss not to draw attention briefly to the areas of cognition and memory. Crowder (1976) connected both learning and memory together. Similarly, both cognition and memory may be regarded as forms of learning, and Newell (1990) attempted to unify numerous theories of cognition and described the similarities of memory, learning, cognition and perception. He discussed various forms of memory: short-term, long-term, episodic, procedural, declarative and semantic, and questioned whether they were similar or separate functions of the brain.

What research in these areas of cognition illustrates is that the distance between philosophy, sociology, education, psychology, neurology, etc is much closer than they would first appear. Whether a grand unified theory will emerge is yet to be seen. For the time being and the purposes of this book we will continue to view the world through the lens of experiential learning that integrates theory and practice.

PAINFUL LEARNING

Learning from experience has its challenges since not all the circumstances we face in life can be said to be enjoyable. Whilst many learning opportunities can be satisfying, not all learning experiences would be chosen by the individual as a route to learning. Life is often unpredictable and as a result presents many opportunities for learning – as long as our minds are open to their potential.

It is the case that many painful experiences remain with us for the rest of our lives and become reference points that we take into account before acting again in a similar manner. Indeed, these painful experiences may act as blocks to learning through preventing us from acting in a particular way. This attitude can be a valuable survival mechanism but it can also lead to our own extinction through inhibiting our behaviour.

Snell (1992) investigated experiential learning at work and asked, 'Why can't it be painless?' He concluded that hard knocks and psychological blows are inevitable in the work situation and that these shocks provide the opportunity for moral lessons and character building. Snell (1992: 15) categorized these challenges, which are detailed in Table 2.1.

Snell emphasized that for a person to learn from the hard knocks he or she had experienced meant that the person had to see them as a learning opportunity. He also drew attention to the fact that if people continued to experience a series of hard knocks then they were likely to be numbed and overloaded by their effects. In cases such as this, a person may withdraw physically and/or emotionally from whatever is causing the challenges and thus limit the potential for learning.

Table 2.1 Learning from distress

Source of Distress	Suggested Method of Coping	Means of Learning
(In general this is a psychological blow, shock or jolt.)	(In general this is to resist responding impulsively, and to find breathing space or seek counselling, if possible.)	(In general this is drawing lessons.)
A Big Mistake	Discharge anger or hurt in a private place.	Admit the mistake and look for causes.
Being Overloaded / Feeling Incompetent	Reduce the load and avoid dwelling on one's inadequacy.	Focus on specific improvement.
Being Pressurized to Violate One's Principles	Come to terms with there being no easy resolution.	Identify what one *really* wants and values.
Impasse	Discharge frustration in a private place.	Listen to the arguments from opponents.
Injustice	Avoid self-blame and resist taking impulsive revenge.	Identify the values offended and adopt them.
Losing Out	Discharge one's disappointment in a private place.	Admit that the defeat was fair and study the victor's approach.
Being Attacked	Respond assertively.	Study the mentality of one's opponents.

DETRIMENTAL EXPERIENTIAL LEARNING

So far our discussion has been to illustrate how valuable and integral experiences are to learning. On the other hand, experience also has disadvantages when it comes to influencing our attitudes to learning. First of all, think of one of your favourite teachers or trainers and how he or she encouraged you to learn in a positive and supportive environment. Next, think about your least favourite teacher or trainer and the effect he or she had on your learning of that subject and how the feeling about that subject may still be with you today. Peter Senge, author of *The Fifth Discipline* (1992), recounted the story of his young son receiving a low grade at school for a piece of art and consequently being disillusioned and demotivated. His son never again took an interest in the subject and is now an adult!

Another example of how the affective or emotional dimension of learning influences learning is provided by Macala (1986: 57), who stated:

> If you were to ask a group of adults to talk about their most interesting and exciting learning experience, chances are good that instead of describing a classroom scenario, many of them will talk about a self directed learning experience that enabled them to learn new information, a skill, theory, or process on their own. Their experiences might have included discovering how a city really works by serving on the Human Rights Commission, learning how to sail a boat by trial and error, or developing leadership or fund-raising skills through committee work. These adults learned by doing, and they probably remember well the how of the doing: They observed (what a 'luffing' sail looks like, how an alderman's body language belied his words); they asked questions, got feedback, did research, took risks, made mistakes, found mentors, informants, helpers, tried out and checked their progress, accuracy, skill; and they grew and changed as they were challenged.

The process of formal learning can negatively affect a person; fortunately, however, human capabilities can be remarkably resilient. Einstein maintained, 'It is in fact nothing short of a miracle that the modern methods of instruction have not yet entirely strangled the holy curiosity of inquiry.'

As trainers and educators, we often come across people saying that something cannot be done. On further enquiry, it is sometimes the case that the person has had a negative experience and does not wish to repeat it. A variety of factors may have a negative effect on learning, and a number have been identified by Boud and Walker (1993: 79):

- Presuppositions about what is and is not possible for us to do.
- Not being in touch with one's own assumptions and what one is able to do.
- Past negative experiences.
- Expectations of others: society, peer group, figures of authority, family.
- Threats to the self, one's own world view, or to ways of behaving.
- Lack of self-awareness of one's place in the world.
- Inadequate preparation.
- Hostile or impoverished environments.
- Lack of time.
- External pressures and demands.
- Lack of support from others.
- Lack of skills: in noticing, intervening.

- Intent that is unclear or unfocused.
- Established patterns of thought and behaviour.
- Inability to conceive of the possibility of learning from experience: 'this is not learning', 'this is not possible'.
- Obstructive feelings: lack of confidence or self-esteem, fear of failure or the response of others, unexpressed grief about lost opportunities.

If we can avoid or reduce these barriers when we are supporting our learning and that of others, then we can dramatically increase the chances of success. The dimension of attitude or emotion is a key factor in the learning process and we ignore it at our peril – not to mention its effect on our continued employment as teachers, trainers and developers of people!

LEARNING FROM MISTAKES

James Dyson is the successful industrialist and inventor of the bagless vacuum cleaner, the twin-cylinder washing machine and the Ballbarrow (a type of wheelbarrow with a ball instead of a wheel). While he was renovating his house he conceived the notion of a bagless vacuum cleaner and spent the next five years refining the concept, during which time he produced 5,127 prototypes and patented many of his ideas. The lesson that can be learnt from Dyson's experiences is that making mistakes enables us to find and identify information and knowledge that can help chart courses of action that will lead to the optimum solution. Thomas Edison, another inventor, expended a great amount of energy, and not a little frustration, in identifying a suitable filament that would last when he invented the electric light bulb.

The important thing is that we learn from our mistakes. Peter Honey and Michael Pearn at the CIPD's Human Resource Development Conference in London looked at the nature of mistakes and stated that there were three types of people:

- those who make a mistake once and learn from it so as not to make the mistake again;
- those who make a mistake once and are so traumatized that they do not venture to that territory again; and lastly
- those people who continue to make the same mistake over and over again, never learning from the previous episodes in their experience.

Only the first of the three types of people above can be said to have truly learnt. This scenario about learning was repeated by Akio Morita, head of Sony, who stated to his workers, 'It's OK to make a mistake, but don't make the same mistake twice.'

It is when we move from the familiar to the unfamiliar that we are likely to make mistakes and this causes most of us to remain within our comfort zones. However, the environment in which we normally operate also tends to diminish our awareness of other areas and methods of operating. This occurs through continual reinforcement, which suggests that the habitual ways of seeing and operating are the only, or the best, means of behaving and feeling. We thus become blind to other options and can constrain ourselves unnecessarily. Later in the book we will examine the implications of exploring beyond our comfort zones into more challenging terrains and new areas of experiential learning.

FORMAL VERSUS EXPERIENTIAL LEARNING

Before the establishment of mass state schooling the provision of education was inadequate, restricted and not serving the needs of the general population nor the nation as a whole. With the arrival of compulsory education, the process of formal or traditional education has proved to be relatively successful in educating children and ensuring that the vast majority are literate and numerate. However, while this factory system of learning achieved some successes there were still a number of reservations.

Integrating theory and practice was a preoccupation of Dewey (1938: 48–49). He drew attention to the limitations of formal education and the fact that much of what we were supposed to learn in school was no longer accessible. He considered that when learning occurred in isolation it was disconnected from the rest of the child's experience. Thus, because it was segregated and not linked through experience to the child's memory it became impossible to retrieve it.

The limited value of attempting to pour knowledge into the heads of young people without relating it to their experience was held not only by Dewey. This view was forcibly repeated some decades later by Freire (1982: 45–46) in his book *The Pedagogy of the Oppressed* where he advocated less state intervention in the learning process of children and argued:

> Education thus becomes an act of depositing, in which the students are the depositories and the teacher is the depositor. Instead of communicating, the teacher issues communiqués and makes deposits, which the students patiently receive, memorise, and repeat. This is the 'banking' concept of education, in which the scope of action allowed to the students extends only as far as receiving, filing, and storing the deposits. They do, it is true, have the opportunity to become collectors or cataloguers of the things they store. But in the last analysis, it is men themselves who are filed away through

the lack of creativity, transformation, and knowledge in this (at best) misguided system. For apart from inquiry, apart from the praxis, men cannot be truly human. Knowledge emerges only through invention and reinvention, through the restless, impatient, continuing, hopeful inquiry men pursue in the world, with the world, and with each other.

Freire is damning about the role of schools in separating learning from the world in which it is to be used. And this view is also strongly maintained by Illich (1973) in his book *De-schooling Society*. Yet even learning in schools is not in total isolation from what already exists in the brains of the pupils. Thus, the challenge for educators, trainers and developers is to find the right type of experience that is immediately appealing to the learner and also has a longer-term impact.

It is important to stress here that this book is not a diatribe against formal schooling. There is a substantial volume of schooling that combines theory and practice and also develops core skills such as the development of interpersonal skills and group working. Equally, the areas of training and development are less susceptible to criticism because they are linked to practical applications of knowledge. It is the area of traditional education in which the delivery of abstract theoretical knowledge is delivered through a teacher, lecturer, trainer or developer standing at the front and speaking or reading from a book that causes us most concern together with some restricted forms of computer-mediated learning. What we are advocating here is the case that most aspects of learning will benefit from being linked to some form of experience.

We have already discussed the difficulty of defining experiential learning. Warner Weil and McGill (1989: 27) approached the issue from the opposite perspective and stated: 'Both the experiential theorist and educational practitioner seem to agree on what experiential learning is not. It is definitely not the mere memorizing of abstract theoretical knowledge, especially if taught by traditional formal methods of instruction such as lecturing and reading from books.'

THE LINEAGE OF EXPERIENCE LEARNING

One of the most influential writers on the subject is David Kolb (1984: 3–4), who wrote *Experiential Learning*, in which he stressed its importance and stated:

Experiential learning theory offers... the foundation for an approach to education and learning as a lifelong process that is soundly based in intellectual traditions of social psychology, philosophy, and cognitive psychology. The experiential learning model pursues a framework for examining and strengthening the critical linkages among education, work, and personal development. It offers a system of competencies for describing job demands and corresponding educational objectives and emphasizes the critical linkages that can be developed between the classroom and the 'real world' with experiential learning methods. It pictures the workplace as a learning environment that can enhance and supplement formal education and can foster personal development through meaningful work and career development opportunities. And it stresses the role of formal education in lifelong learning and the development of individuals to their full potential as citizens, family members, and human beings.

The development of philosophical thought about the meaning of experience can be traced back to the Greeks, other philosophers such as John Locke (1911) and onwards to the present day. Similarly, the development of understanding about experiential learning is grounded in philosophical thought, and numerous writers draw upon this heritage, including Dewey, Lewin, Revans and Kolb. Kolb, himself, looked at the process of experiential learning and drew on the legacy of the perspectives provided by Lewin, Dewey and Piaget. Kolb (1984) asserted that Lewin's description of the learning process is relatively similar to that of Dewey, which involved observation, knowledge and judgement (see Figure 2.3).

Kolb also described how Lewin's action research and T-group training in laboratories was influenced by the concept of feedback that was used by electrical engineers. This feedback process involved concrete experience; observations and reflections; formation of abstract concepts and generalizations; and testing implications of concepts in new situations (see Figure 2.4). The similarities with Kolb's learning cycle in Figure 2.5 may be seen.

EXPERIENCE AS LEARNING STYLES

The learning styles inventory was developed by Honey and Mumford (1992) and was originally published in 1982. It is based upon Kolb's learning cycle. 'The term learning styles is used as a description of the attitudes and behaviours which determine an individual's preferred way of learning' (Honey and Mumford, 1992: 1). They argue that two people of similar intelligence and background who undergo a learning opportunity may be affected in very different ways, eg one is enthusiastic while the second person is disaffected. They maintain that the reason for this is that

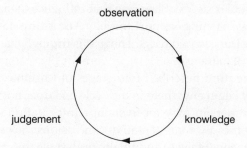

Figure 2.3 Dewey's learning process

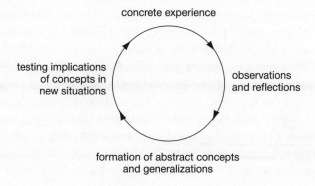

Figure 2.4 Lewin's feedback process

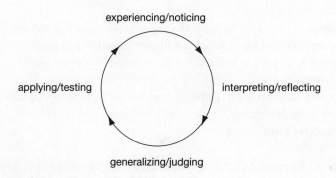

Figure 2.5 Kolb's experiential learning cycle

people have particular styles of learning that influence their attitudes and abilities towards learning opportunities. According to Honey and Mumford, people learn in two ways. The first is through teaching, and the second is through experience.

Honey and Mumford described four stages of learning and explained that a person may begin anywhere in the cycle and does not have to begin at Stage 1, eg the person may receive some information and review it (Stage 2), and then draw some tentative conclusions (Stage 3), and then plan a course of action (Stage 4) and finally undertake the course of action (Stage 1). The process is an iterative one and allows people to join the cycle at any point, the main proviso being that they complete the cycle; otherwise, the learning process is incomplete, eg they may review the experience that using a hammer to drive in a nail is a painful process to their thumb when they miss the nail, and never learn to use the hammer correctly. They need to complete the cycle by testing the theory and confirming it. Honey and Mumford (1992: 7) used the term 'experience' in each of the four stages, as can be seen in Figure 2.6.

Honey and Mumford explained that there are four types of people with preferences for each stage of the learning cycle. While it was recognized that people's learning styles can alter when they change jobs and are therefore not fixed, there is value in taking into account the preferred learning style of a person. This is not only from the point of view of the teacher or trainer but also from that of the learner who can become more aware of his or her personal process of learning. The various styles are:

- **Activists**: prefer to involve themselves in an experience and do so in an open-minded manner. They involve themselves with the activity first and then weigh up the implications of their actions afterwards.
- **Reflectors**: prefer to gather information and carefully consider it before reaching a conclusion. They are thoughtful and cautious, and tend to reserve judgement in meetings until they are reasonably sure about their conclusions.
- **Theorists**: tend to be systems people who gather information and attempt to develop a coherent theory about the experience. They are logical and prefer to analyse information and produce an encompassing theory.
- **Pragmatists**: prefer to apply theories and techniques to investigate if they work. Pragmatists are realistic people who seek out improved methods of operating.

Honey and Mumford explained that this cyclical process is a fundamental one, which is similar to the scientific method, upon which Revans also based his model. It is also similar to problem-solving and decision-making

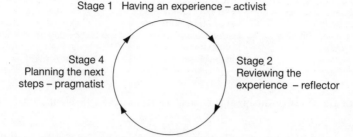

Stage 1   Having an experience – activist

Stage 4
Planning the next
steps – pragmatist

Stage 2
Reviewing the
experience – reflector

Stage 3 Concluding from the experience – theorist

Figure 2.6 Honey and Mumford's learning styles

approaches, as well as the quality cycle. W Edwards Deming was a physicist who used statistical methods to improve the quality of production in Japan after the Second World War. He was a disciple of Shewhart, a statistician at Bell Laboratories, and he developed the Deming or Shewhart cycle of continuous improvement, which involved a systematic approach to problem solving and was a cyclical process of plan, do, check, act (see Figure 2.7).

We saw in Figure 2.1 the linking of theory and practice, which has a strong similarity to the various cycles of Lewin, Kolb, Honey and Mumford, and Deming/Shewhart. While they are all interlinked and have influenced one another, there would appear to be a fundamental principle at work here in which we need to combine thinking with doing or applying in order to create an effective learning process.

A CHRONOLOGY OF EXPERIENTIAL LEARNING

It is also possible to consider the nature of experiential learning from a chronological perspective (see Figure 2.8). We can undertake this analysis

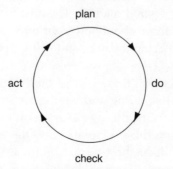

plan

act

do

check

Figure 2.7 The Shewhart/Deming cycle of continuous improvement

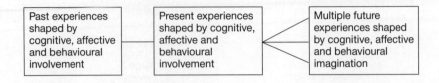

Figure 2.8 A chronological perspective of experiential learning

of experience retrospectively, concurrently or prospectively, ie with reference to the past, the present or the future.

When we undergo an event it is possible to learn from that experience at different times, ie:

- learning from an event at the time it occurs;
- learning from the past event when reflecting on it later;
- learning more about a past event when thinking about it further;
- reinterpreting the past event differently in the light of further experience(s);
- analysing future scenarios.

Concurrent learning

We discussed above in the section 'Perception is learning' that we are able to learn almost concurrently as we interact with external stimuli. So, for example, as we are driving in a car and slowing down for some traffic lights ahead we will continuously adjust the pressure on the brake pedal to ensure that we come to a halt just behind the car in front rather than crashing into it. This learning is almost instantaneous.

Many of our physical actions, as well as our mental ones, are in a continual process of assessment and change. In the classroom, training room and workplace we often learn immediately from the experience and this may involve adjusting our tone of voice or demeanour so that the person responds in the desired manner. The next time you reach for that cup of tea or coffee just think about how your movements are finely coordinated to allow you to grasp the mug and drink from it without spilling the contents.

Similarly, if we notice that there is frost on the ground we may drive more carefully to avoid skidding and having an accident. Alternatively, we may adjust the pressure that we exert with our fingers on a new computer keyboard. Both these adaptations to the external environment are a form of learning, albeit short-term; as soon as the temperature rises above freezing or we return to our old keyboard we are likely to return to our previous behaviour.

The quality of the immediate learning in formal situations may be enhanced by coaching the learner to stand back from the experience he or she is undergoing and consider what is happening. This form of activity and reflection is common in team and management development activities where the participants are encouraged not only to succeed in the task but also to consider their own and others' behaviours and interactions. This behaviour was termed by Schon (1983) as reflection-in-action, and will be discussed further in Chapter 9.

Retrospective learning

We can also learn by looking back at an event and analysing it (what Schon termed reflection-on-action). Often when we are undergoing an experience there is insufficient time and/or we are too close – physically, chronologically or emotionally – to have the ability to make sense of what is happening. These processes of thinking about a past event may be illustrated when we say, 'If only I had…' What we are doing is reflecting about the experience and making sense of it in our own mind – in effect we are attempting to fit the experience into our mental schema.

Another form of retrospective learning is to look back at an event and recollect even more closely what happened and thus learn in even greater depth. For instance, we may rewind the mental tape of a conversation we had to try and get more detailed insights into why a person behaved in a particular way.

Yet a further way of learning retrospectively is when an event can be reinterpreted in the light of subsequent experiences and there is the potential for its meaning to be considerably different to that at the time. One example is a parent rapidly lifting a child to safety before the child burns him- or herself on a stove. The child may be shocked and cry as a result of the sudden action or the frustration at not being allowed to do what he or she wants, but when the child is older the interpretation is much different, particularly so if the child has subsequently burnt him- or herself.

Not only can we learn from a new experience as we relate that experience to our existing ones, but we can also find new meanings hidden in old experiences. These old experiences may be drawn from any time in our history and although we may have incorporated them within a particular mindset we may change them as a result of our new experience.

It is possible to use learners' previous experiences to add depth, colour and a concrete reality to the more abstract environment of learning of the classroom or training room. This may involve revisiting a past experience in light of the theoretical and structured learning that has just been delivered.

Prospective learning

Whilst it is not possible to reflect on experiences that have yet to happen, it is possible to analyse and reflect on the experiences of others who have been involved with an activity that we are contemplating in the future. Through placing ourselves in the shoes of others we can have a reasonable expectation about what might happen and how we might respond. Unlike the past, which cannot be changed, only reinterpreted, it is possible to have a variety of futures. There is not, as many people subconsciously believe, only one future but there are many possible alternatives unless you are a believer in destiny.

The process of investigating possible futures involves a similar process to that of learning from past and present experience. This process is often called imagining or visualizing and we often undertake it when we make plans, perhaps for a holiday or a business project. This process is increasingly being used for athletes and other people trying to achieve high levels of performance where they positively visualize a successful outcome so that they are prepared when the event happens. Another example of this is when we rehearse what we will say to a boss or some such figure when he or she asks us to explain a specific event.

This area of visualization, imagining and mental rehearsal is growing very rapidly, and will be discussed at length in Chapter 10.

CHALLENGING THE CONCEPT OF EXPERIENTIAL LEARNING

We have argued throughout this chapter, and indeed will do so throughout this book, that from a practical and philosophical perspective the interaction of experience and reflection is probably the most encompassing, clarifying and relevant approach to learning that we have come across. However, despite its many strengths it has not been immune to criticism and in the cause of balance we will investigate three of the main criticisms below. The criticisms are based on 1) the lack of direction attributed to experiential learning; 2) the subjectivity of experiential learning; and 3) limitations that have been directed at Kolb's learning cycle.

Student-centredness leads to a lack of direction

Experiential learning has its critics who argue that there is too great an emphasis on experience to the detriment of the classical curriculum where subjects are taught in traditional and formal classrooms. Wildemeersch (1989: 61) referred to Jarvis's term 'the romantic curriculum' and stated that experiential learning 'emphasises elements like student-centredness, creativity, experience, discovery, awareness, originality and freedom'. Allowing students to determine the direction of their learning might lead to a neutering of the curriculum. Wildemeersch (1989: 62) cautioned that experiential learning 'might turn adult education into an apolitical, acurricular, reactive and consumer-orientated enterprise which casts the educator in the role of marketing expert and technician of the teaching–learning machinery' and also that 'the concept of self-direction may simultaneously lead to isolation, individualism and poor learning'.

The argument that adult learning is purely about supporting learners to grow in whatever direction they may choose is an incorrect one. While people should have the opportunity to choose and follow their own interests, how many classes in adult education have no title, no syllabus or no clear direction in which they intend to proceed? For example, most programmes have clear specifications about their syllabus content. Students sign up for the various programmes and are guided in their learning; individual areas of learning are catered for within clearly defined and negotiated projects. Students enrolled to study botanical illustration will not progress far if they then propose to the tutor that they wish to learn more about the theory of music!

Experiential learning and technology

One of the more robust arguments aligned against experiential learning is the difficulty of linking it to complex areas of technology or for example theoretical physics. Wildemeersch (1989: 62) suggested that the incorporation of experience and technological frameworks was 'puzzling'. Indeed, trying to link experience to Steven Hawking's (1988) string theory, or the development of drug treatments to counteract HIV and Aids for all but the specialist is problematical.

However, even at these advanced levels of mental activity there are elements with which we can connect. The notion of a string is used by Hawking to address much more complicated issues and the term 'string' provides a metaphor with which ordinary people can at least grasp elements of the concept. Moreover, when explanations of drug treatments are described it is often in the form of the chemical jigsaw piece attaching itself to a matching receptor.

The subjectivity of experience

One regularly repeated criticism of experiential learning is that it is very subjective since it is based on what the learner has undergone and thus does not have wider applicability. In addition, the event lacks the scientific objectivity that would otherwise accrue from an external event. Dewey (1925: 1) described the reasoning of his critics:

> On the one hand they eagerly claim an empirical method; they forswear the *a priori* and transcendent; they are sensitive to the charge that they employ data unwarranted by experience. On the other hand, they are given to deprecating the conception of experience; experience it is said, is purely subjective, and whoever takes experience for his subject-matter is logically bound to land in the most secluded of idealisms.

Dewey (1925: 1) continued:

> When the notion of experiences is introduced, who is not familiar with the query, uttered with a crushingly triumphant tone, '*Whose* experience?' The implication is that experience is not only always somebody's, but that the peculiar nature of 'somebody' infects experience so pervasively that experience is merely somebody's and hence of nobody and nothing else.

We all create our own reality and in that respect it is socially constructed (Berger and Luckmann, 1985). External events, it can be argued, are not prone to interpretation by an individual and have their own independent existence and objectivity. However, the very act of observing or measuring some phenomena and using socially constructed measures such as language and measurement creates a shared social meaning and thus, it can be maintained, does not possess pure objectivity.

Limitations of the learning cycle

The learning cycle as developed by Kolb has become strongly established and is an almost taken-for-granted theory of learning. However, it has been challenged by some writers and we will now investigate some of the criticisms to assess their relevance. Miettinen (2000) argued that philosophical studies suggest experiential learning is inadequate as a means of providing new knowledge about the world. He maintained that Kolb's interpretation of the work of Dewey, Lewin and Piaget, upon whom he based the development of his learning cycle, was selective and did not really represent the facts. Although Kolb talked about the 'Lewinian Model' of impulse, observation, knowledge and judgement, Miettinen maintained that Kolb's research is based on observations of only a small section of Lewin's work described by Lippit (1949).

Miettinen (2000: 68) compared the work of Dewey and Kolb and concluded that Kolb does not take into account Dewey's distinction between habit, 'the great flywheel of society' that enables society to function predictably when faced with recurring challenges, and the habit that tyrannically traps us into behaving in a particular way without thinking of alternatives. The use of habit is very important to our functioning, and Covey (1990: 46) in his book *The Seven Habits of Highly Effective People* states, 'Habits are powerful factors in our lives. Because they are consistent, often unconscious patterns, they constantly, daily, express our character and produce our effectiveness or ineffectiveness.' Habits, because they are often unconscious, tend to be a form of single loop activity rather than a form of double loop learning, both of which are discussed in Chapter 9.

The observation by Miettinen is that much of our lives are spent on automatic pilot, eg taking our normal route home after work and then realizing after we arrive we cannot remember anything other than the work problem we were contemplating. We just do not think, never mind reflect on many of the actions that we undertake. This is a natural process that prevents our conscious brains becoming overwhelmed with all the things that we need to think about; however, it is not included in the learning cycle. Kolb's learning cycle also does not illustrate the fact that empirical (ie experiential) thinking based on action has limitations:

- It may result in false conclusions.
- It may not help us understand and explain change and new experiences.
- It may cause mental laziness and dogmatic thinking.

Miettinen also suggests that Kolb's experience and reflection occur in isolation and that there is a necessity for the individual to interact with other humans and the environment in order to enhance the reasoning and conclusions drawn. As we will see in Chapter 9, 'Ways of learning', the dangers of drawing wrong conclusions are less likely to occur when the individual interacts with others and the environment because the hard edges of life provide a 'reality check' on weaker concepts and hypotheses.

Reynolds's (1997) article, 'Learning styles: a critique', and Holman, Pavlica and Thorpe's (1997) article, 'Rethinking Kolb's theory of experiential learning in management education', both argue that whilst the famous circle has been extremely influential, especially in management education in the USA and the UK, it is rarely seen as problematic. It locates itself in the cognitive psychology tradition, and overlooks or mechanically explains and thus divorces people from the social, historical and cultural aspects of self, thinking and action. Holman, Pavlica and Thorpe (1997) suggested that the idea of a manager reflecting like a scientist in isolation on events is like an 'intellectual Robinson Crusoe'. They argued that the social interactions of a person were very important to the development of self, thought and learning. Furthermore, they suggested that Kolb's theory was fundamentally cognitivist and had a number of limitations. The main criticism was that the four stages of the cycle – concrete experience, reflective observation, abstract conceptualization and active experimentation – were independent and represented a dualism or dialectic opposites, eg active experimentation and reflective observation.

In addition, Holman, Pavlica and Thorpe (1997: 145) disagreed with the idea of progressing sequentially through the cycle, and argued: 'Learning can be considered as a process of argumentation in which thinking, reflecting, experiencing and action are different aspects of the same process. It is practical argumentation with oneself and in collaboration with others that actually forms the basis for learning.' They also recognized, without going into detail, that emotion and individual differences play a significant role in the ability to learn. The impact of emotional considerations on experiential learning is considered in Chapters 6 and 7.

In an article titled 'Corn circles in search of a spaceship?', (Taylor, 1991: 258) aptly sums up many of the limitations of circular models used in the search for meaning:

> They first began to appear about 25 years ago. Neatly laid-out circles in the pages of training textbooks, journals and Industrial Training Board publications. They quickly came to seize the imagination of a growing band of training professionals. They must have been created by a superior intelligence, being so neat and logical and all. There were of course variations in the patterns observed, but these, it was discovered, were due to differing environmental conditions. Being a pragmatic and opportunist bunch the practitioners, although faintly curious about where they came from, what they actually meant, and who controlled them, were so much more interested in associating themselves with the phenomena so as to establish their own professional credibility and status. The mystery and novelty soon became displaced as attempts were made to elaborate and integrate the phenomenon into the known universe. Within a few short years the 'systematic training model' [or 'training cycle' to some] became the orthodoxy of the training profession.

Circles and other simplistic models do have a significant value, for both the provider and the participant in terms of accessibility and applicability. Some models, while being more accurate representations of reality, may tend to be underused and sometimes disregarded as a result of their complexity. Kolb's learning cycle can be regarded as a minimalist interpretation of the complex operations of the brain and therefore it is not surprising that this model is somewhat limited in describing the learning process. In this book we progressively draw upon a wide range of theories and dimensions in order to build the more complex learning combination lock model. This model provides an accessible structure that is both understandable and applicable, and yet possesses an immense menu upon which to design experiential activities.

By starting with these simpler models the development of the more complex learning combination lock can be more easily understood. Thus we build up the bigger picture throughout the book, one that is much more complex, using a greater range of ingredients to help to unlock human potential, accelerate learning and provide more opportunities for 'flow learning'. All the main ingredients are covered in the book. *Maximizing the power of the experience, through combining different ingredients, will maximize the learning.*

CONCLUSION

In this chapter we have begun to investigate the complex nature of learning from experience. We defined experiential learning as the insight gained through the conscious or unconscious internalization of our own or observed experiences, which build upon our past experiences or knowledge. We have seen that there is a considerable dissatisfaction with the nature of traditional education and training and that for us to learn more effectively it is desirable for us to learn from direct experience when appropriate. We also examined the influential Kolb's learning cycle and observed that it has a number of limitations. Experiential learning, of which Kolb's learning cycle is a part, has been identified and endorsed throughout history and remains the strongest and most enduring of the learning theories.

3

The Design Milieu

> *Experience is created in the transaction between the learner and the milieu in which he or she operates – it is relational. An event can influence the learner, but only if the learner is predisposed to being influenced. Similarly, the learner can create a fruitful experience from a limited event, but only if there is something with which they can work.*
>
> (Boud, Cohen and Walker, 1993: 11)

INTRODUCTION

Each learner in turn also forms part of the milieu, as he or she enriches it with his or her personal contribution, thus creating an interaction that becomes the individual as well as the shared learning experience (Boud and Walker, 1990). This continuing, complex and meaningful interaction is central to our understanding of the term experience. It is this 'milieu' that we now explore in more detail. There are many different ways in which the milieu can be created for experiential learning. Inevitably we can only present a sample of new ideas, and, as we show in the section on the facilitator's learning combination lock in Chapter 1, the number of experiential opportunities is potentially infinite and varied, depending on the sequencing and combination of people, places, objects, activities, rules and restrictions.

THE MILIEU – ACTIVITIES, METHODS, TECHNIQUES AND MATERIALS

There are many methods available for facilitators to use in order to help people to learn through experience. A training 'method' has been referred to as 'a known approach or procedure; an acknowledged practice by trainers as a way of teaching, telling or promoting learning' (Beard, 1999:

285). Beard lists and divides methods further into training tools, techniques and materials, and offers this as a simple hierarchical structure. Advice on the use and selection of methods, sequence and pacing of activities and the creative use of materials is given. Under 'methods' he lists examples of case study, buzz groups, syndicates, action maze and outdoor management development. Under design 'techniques' he lists icebreakers, energizers, dice games, attitude scales, role hats and card games. The 'use of materials' includes layered flip charts, masking-tape grids to create models or theory in action, washable cards to capture ideas, and video-cassette boxes to hold packs of group task information. Printed T-shirts with numbers or letters on can also be used. They all contribute to the milieu of creative possibilities.

In experiential learning the fundamental 'method' is the provision of the *experience*. Rodwell, in his book on *Participative Training Skills*, describes traditional outdoor approaches that use recreational or adventure activities thus: 'Outdoor training usually requires the trainee to perform a series of tasks which incorporate outdoor pursuits such as… climbing, abseiling, caving, orienteering, canoeing, sailing… and they usually involve training for management skills, team-working skills, personal development and physical challenge' (1994: 133).

Outdoor pursuits have often been the medium or activity for outdoor learning, as they are perceived as providing real activities in the sense that they are set in a real and often unpredictable outdoor environment. As we see elsewhere in this book, this notion of reality requires further exploration. Recreational adventure activities used in experiential programmes are often watered-down versions of what most outdoor professionals commonly understand these outdoor activities to be. The level of risk inherent in these 'versions' of adventure activities has necessarily to be no greater than that in any other traditional types of training activities. Whilst creating an illusion of action, excitement and danger, the reality is that they are often simply another arrow in the facilitator's quiver of experiences on offer. Badger, Sadler-Smith and Michie (1997) confirm this relatively high level of outdoor pursuit activities in their research into outdoor activities being used in management development programmes and noted that, in their sample of 100 firms, respondents said that they had participated in the following activities:

	%
Rock climbing	79
Orienteering	47
Sailing	16
Canoeing	37
Camping	31

Rafting   16
Caving   16
Others   74

The last figure of course is the interesting one, and represents the tip of the iceberg of change in the design of outdoor experiential programmes. As we shall now explore, the 74 per cent of 'other' forms of experience can represent a considerably diverse array of activities. Black Mountain, an outdoor management development company, comment (1996):

> This shift towards a wider spectrum of delivery techniques has attracted a dedicated professional team that can design and deliver indoor seminars, outdoor exercises, desktop simulations, experiential games, video projects or motivational events. Over the past five years we have moved away from the use of outdoor pursuits in response to our clients' needs which have become more focused and sophisticated. As people become more exposed to development techniques more effective and high impact solutions are required.

Whilst it is important to remember that often the activity is merely the medium for learning, this is not always the case in programmes that are of high reality, a subject we examine in detail in the next chapter. The experiential industry as a whole is now witnessing the evolution of more diversified programmes that include, for example, art, therapy, drama, poetry, dance and environmental appreciation, such as sleeping under the stars. Whilst educators and trainers increasingly recognize that the outdoors is a useful place for creating the right milieu for learning, client needs have always been sophisticated. It is the providers that have become more experienced deliverers, moving away from an overemphasis on old paradigms of outdoor pursuits provision of 'canoeing, climbing and caving' to teaching 'teamwork, communication and leadership'! As the level of sophistication of their provision has matured to embrace a deeper understanding of learning, deliverers now include, for example, more pre-activity interaction, greater emphasis on review and transfer, and more follow-up activities. In turn they have begun to meet their clients' needs more fully, enhancing client learning through new combinations of activities, embracing a milieu of adventure, fun, leisure and recreation, yet, as we shall now see, there remains still more untapped potential to be further explored.

Relatively little is known about learning in the natural environment, outside the classroom, hotel or lecture theatre. Yet the larger part of our learning takes place in such settings, and as we shall see the natural outdoor environment is not merely the place or backdrop for experiential learning; it is central and integral to the learning process. Many providers of experiential learning are beginning to look more closely at the symbolic element of the outdoor experience, and are using the outdoors in exciting, imaginative and creative ways so as to enhance learning and development. Cooper (1998) for example regards the visual arts as a powerful way of introducing people to new experiences of their natural environment, thus awakening their sense of connection to the earth. He offers a large selection of ideas and techniques in his book on visual arts and creative writing in the outdoors.

PLANNED OR UNPLANNED?

The extent to which both experiential providers and learners plan to learn from experience, or whether it just happens, is an important design consideration in experiential learning. Providers and learners both learn from programmes, but for many people life's journey, and the learning from it, is not at all planned, and life emerges and unfolds in front of them. Others are more proactive and plan many of their meaningful life journeys. Significantly, the extent to which people learn from any journey or experience depends on many factors.

Educational psychologists define learning as a change in the individual caused by 'experience'. However, people often delude themselves that they learn from experience, with comments like, 'Do you know how long I have been doing this job?', implying that doing is the same as learning. A person might bank 10 years of 'experience' and make continual use of it, gaining interest on the learning deposits, whilst others rely on one year's experience, allowing it to become a 10-year-old deposit, gaining little or no 'interest'. How people create and manage their 'experience' bank is thus crucial to the process of learning.

So how might facilitators create the ideal 'environments' for experiential learners? In order to help people to get the most from experience it is necessary to unleash curiosity so that people actively seek learning, so that they can plan to unveil something that was previously hidden. But it is equally important that learners can respond to unanticipated and unplanned experiences as they occur. To improve on the ability to learn from experience and to learn to learn more effectively, these approaches to experiential learning must be first understood. Megginson (1994) examines why people take different approaches to self-directed learning. He refers to these two basic approaches as *planned* and *emergent* learning, and created a grid, reproduced in Figure 3.1, to represent four types of learner. He researched these four different learner types, and classified people as those who have high or low pre-planning for experience, and those who are high or low in emergent, responsive learning strategies. Megginson noted that there are the two fundamental challenges that face those who help others to learn. Some people, he suggests, do not take responsibility for the direction of their own learning and some people do not learn from the experiences they have. Planned learners take this responsibility for the direction of their learning, whilst emergent learners respond to and learn from experience.

Adventurers are thus high on emergent learning and low on pre-planned learning strategies, whereas the sage is high on both. Warriors are low on emergent strategies, and so Megginson recommends activities to hold them in awareness of immediate experience. For adventurers he offers a set of goal-setting activities. The sages, he suggests, can find their own development directions. Sleepers can find any planned or emergent changes daunting and so techniques such as the use of written reflective logbooks can enhance emergent learning. The use of learning plans for the coming year or month or from a future project can develop proactive learning strategies. Gestalt verbal awareness sensitizing can help, such as the use of *stream of conscious thought* talking. Here each statement is preceded with 'I am aware of…', eg 'I am aware of my feelings of anxiety at the moment.' This can be used during an experiential event when people can express the experience they are having in their terms, and thus first acknowledge and then develop their learning from their experience. This can help access the rich reservoir of thoughts, feelings and impulses about an experience that might otherwise lie dormant. Facilitation strate-

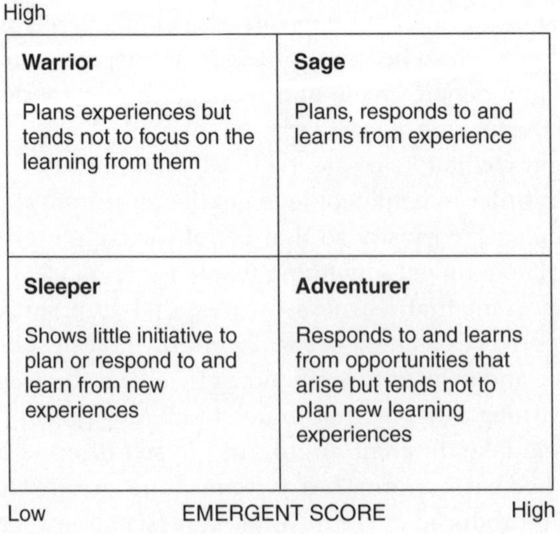

High

Warrior	Sage
Plans experiences but tends not to focus on the learning from them	Plans, responds to and learns from experience
Sleeper	**Adventurer**
Shows little initiative to plan or respond to and learn from new experiences	Responds to and learns from opportunities that arise but tends not to plan new learning experiences

Low   EMERGENT SCORE   High

Figure 3.1 Planned and emergent learning

gies require an understanding of sleepers, warriors, adventurers and sages; then different training methods can be applied so as to maximize their emergent and planned learning. Learning outcomes can be both anticipated and unanticipated.

INNOVATION, ACTIVITIES, RESOURCES AND OBJECTS – A SIMPLE EXPERIENTIAL TYPOLOGY

Recent empirical evidence suggests that creativity and originality remain very poorly catered for in our formal education system. This dearth of alternative ways of thinking and doing can so easily spill over to debilitate the enormous variety of techniques and technologies that can be brought to bear on the educational milieu.

(Baldacchino and Mayo, 1997: 85)

The purposive nature of experiential learning means that in the first instance it is necessary to determine the following: the 'wants' of the learner, ie what the learner perceives to be his or her need; and the 'needs' of the learner, ie what the facilitator perceives the learner needs.

The combination of the determined needs and wants can then be expressed in terms of learning outcomes. This requires in addition an understanding of:

- the culture of the people and the organization;
- the resources available, often a negotiated process relating to the perception of wants versus needs;
- practical considerations, such as whether the programme can be residential, and other initiatives ongoing in the organization that may be affected by or affect the training intervention.

Having determined the above, the range of traditional experiential 'activities' used in most development programmes has a common, generic set of ingredients. The learner experience is physical and mental, both intrapersonal and interpersonal, and, in addition, constantly interacting with a range of places, activities and objects and governed by rules, obstacles and restrictions. These are the basic ingredients of our experiential typology, and within each of these lies a range of innovative possibilities, which allows for an infinite and varied number of experiences. For example:

- **Places** to conduct activities might include the remote wilderness location, a hotel conference venue or an inner-city community hall.

- **Activities** can include modified adventure pursuits, drama or business simulations.
- **Objects** used vary from the rock face, juggling balls to paint and brushes.
- **Rules** can be arbitrary, legally necessary or purposive.

In each experience the choice of combination of these variables is the underpinning precept of the educative process that is experiential learning. To use a metaphor, take-away food restaurants offer a diverse menu with a great deal of choice, often having up to 150 options on the menu. This is possible because common to many of the options are the same basic ingredients, just as in many experiential development programmes the common ingredients are similar, but the outward manifestation of the experience is different. Determining issues of place, objects, activities and rules is a function of the milieu necessary to create the learning outcomes. For example, an organization whose internal culture is competitive may require competition to be reflected in the learning experience. In contrast, an organization that operates by consensus may find a competitive milieu a counter-productive experience. However, exposure to experiences outside the cultural norm of the organization may be a catalyst to stimulate creativity and innovation. It is a question of effectively determining what outcomes are required for the individuals, groups or organization, whilst recognizing that the learning is a continuous, long journey.

The need for learning often reflects a gap or imbalance, in either skills, knowledge or attitude, and the learner is coached or helped to varying degrees to move from his or her current way of operating to a preferred way of operating through the learning experience, as shown in Figure 3.2. The journey away from the norm of 'sameness' often helps people to see this gap more clearly. Sometimes however there is also a need for 'metaphorical space' to escape, to 'sense' release and feel free.

Journeying over periods of time and through metaphorical and physical space is an important ingredient in experiential learning. The journey from where the learner is to where the learner needs to be is fundamental to the experiential process. Knowing the needs determines the focus and end point. Knowing the participants determines the start point and the distance to be travelled and hence the number of steps necessary to achieve the destination. The complexity of modern life means that the end point of the learning journey is little more than a staging post that, once achieved, enables the learner to embrace the next set of challenges. The journey might also be in the form of a venture into a different world, away from the normal environment, so as to gain a different view or perspective. The notion of 'lifelong learning' is of a continuous significant life

People sometimes have to go away and come back in order to see the performance gap. This distance gives perspective. Being too close to the issues can prevent gaining a sense of perspective. But if we can't anchor learning to actual behaviour back in the home or workplace then the learning is ineffective.

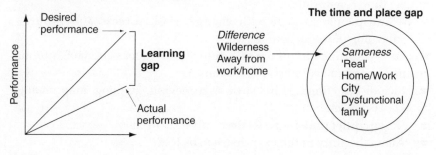

Figure 3.2 The learning gaps: altering time and place to increase learning

'journey' and, as a concept, it is gaining interest and momentum throughout the world. Creating the right medium or milieu for the learning journey is a function of a number of considerations. To assist the planning of creative experiential learning programmes we have created a typology, shown below. In this chapter we go through each of the important ingredients within the typology and explain the rationale or theory for their use. We also offer some innovative and pragmatic examples of how to translate the typology into practice.

A basic programme typology

- Create a **journey or destination** – physical movement and exercise; people and objects are moved from A to B.
- Create and sequence **social, mental and physical activities** – mind and body.
- Adjust or suspend **elements of reality**.
- Stimulate the **six main senses** / alter moods.
- **Construct or deconstruct**:
  - a physical object, eg bike, wall or raft;
  - a non-physical item, eg a clue, phrase or poem.
- Design **collaborative, competitive or co-optive strategies**.
- Create **combative and/or empathetic** approaches to the environment.
- **Create restrictions**:
  - obstacles;
  - sensory blocking, eg blindfolds;
  - rules;
  - procedures.

- Provide elements of real or perceived **challenge or risk**.
- Set a **target**, goal or objective, where goals create an underlying 'state of mind'.
- Set **time constraints**.
- Allow people to deal with **change, risk, success and failure** – stretching personal boundaries.
- Design **sorting and/or organization skills** – a mass of data, information to sort or activities to do or consider.
- Include **functional skills** such as surveying, juggling, map reading, knot tying, etc.
- Design **quiet time for reflection** – physical or mental space.
- Allow the **story of the experience** to be told.

(adapted from Beard, 1998)

Underpinning all of these ingredients is the key principle that the learner is on a journey. Its inclusion within the list reflects the fact that what the journey is needs to be considered. It is an interesting aside that most facilitators are employed by the day, following the lines of the traditional journeyman, a tradesperson who was similarly employed by the day. Some facilitators are modern-day journeymen. It is also interesting to note the frequent use of a physical journey or activity as an isomorphic representation of a wider learning journey. The physical journey can be orienteering, a short walk in the hotel grounds or distance travelled in kayaks. Many experiential programmes also design into the journey the movement or construction of physical objects, such as canisters or bikes, and non-physical objects, such as poems or cryptic clues. Physical exercise is used by experiential providers to manage the daily client energy–tension balance, and physical exercise is known to be one of the most powerful positive regulators of mood, a subject we examine in Chapters 5 and 6. Rules and restrictions, whether real or perceived, can impede or slow progress, and can require people to collaborate or compete, and to use their powers of observation in solving problems along the way, whether they be personal, group or organizational issues.

STIMULATING INTELLIGENCE

Throughout the journey other forms of intelligence need stimulation. Gardner (1983) describes seven categories of intelligence, although he accepts that the figure of seven is arbitrary and that there may be more than these seven categories. Indeed he created some 20 different varieties of intelligence at one stage in his research. The seven areas, forming the fifth tumbler in the learning combination lock, are as follows:

1. **mathematical–logical** – the ability to organize thoughts sequentially and logically;
2. **verbal–linguistic** – the ability to understand and express ideas through language;
3. **bodily–kinaesthetic** – the gaining of knowledge through feedback from physical activity;
4. **musical** – sensitivity to tone, pitch and rhythm, and the ability to reproduce them;
5. **visual–spatial** – the ability to learn directly through images and to think intuitively without the use of language;
6. **interpersonal** – the ability to notice and make discriminations regarding the moods, temperaments, motivations and intentions of others;
7. **intra-personal** – having access to one's own feeling life.

Experiential providers can plan opportunities or activities that engage these seven distinct forms of intelligence, but emotion will underpin all seven. In discussion groups it is often the *verbal ability* and *conceptual skills* that are valued above all else. In some therapy groups the expression of *feelings* is the main valid means of expression (Benson, 1987) and in outdoor-recreation-based adventure activities it is often the physical or dexterity skills, *bodily–kinaesthetic* intelligence, that is highly stimulated. However, providers continue to seek new ways to manage the emotional connections that are made with the experience by learners whether they are participants, clients or delegates.

It is important to sensitize the six senses, as they are the main conduits or entry points between the inner experience, in the mind, and the outer nature of the experience, in the environment. These senses are the *mouth, ears, eyes, nose, nerves* and, the sixth sense, *intuitive insight*. These six senses combined with the seven types of intelligence present a remarkable combination of opportunities to stimulate learning. Many of these intelligences and senses can be turned off or switched on by experiential providers during learning events, as we shall in Chapters 5 and 6.

ADVENTUROUS ACTIVITIES AND JOURNEYS – CHALLENGE AND RISK

The term adventure generally implies an educational or recreational activity that is exciting and physically challenging. The use of both outdoor and indoor 'adventure', challenge and risk offers great potential for experiential learning. As we show in Chapter 5, the indoor–outdoor relationship in experiential learning is interesting, as experiential learning providers can alter the relationship between the two and bring the outdoors indoors and vice versa. Adventure, whether indoor or outdoor, requires an element of real or perceived risk to which the participant is exposed through engagement in an activity. This risk can be physical, emotional, intellectual or material.

'Adventure' embraces many facets of people's lives and it forms the basis of the experiential milieu. The dictionary suggests that adventure is a 'remarkable incident', 'an enterprise or commercial speculation', 'an exciting experience' or 'the spirit of enterprise', and an adventurer is 'one who engages in hazardous enterprise'. 'To be an adventure an experience must have an element of uncertainty about it. Either the outcome should be unknown or the setting unfamiliar' (Priest and Ballie, 1995: 307). It is not surprising that 'adventure tourism' is one of the most rapidly expanding sectors of the tourism industry, whether it is wildlife adventure, adventure activities or expeditions into the deserts or the rainforests. A significant sector of the outdoor management development industry has grown to some extent from a form of corporate adventure hospitality, with clients wanting to try something adventurous, partly as a refreshing and light team-building reward for staff. However, these often involve the customers returning for repeat programmes, but asking for slightly more significant educative inputs or opportunities. The boundaries of education, training and development, adventure, travel, hospitality, work and leisure are all blurring. Adventure tourism is offering new experiential learning opportunities to enrich the milieu of possibilities.

The personal limits to the mental and physical zones of challenge will differ among individuals, and the location of outer limits, where people enter the panic zone, will also vary. Some challenges hold the possibility of being injured or even killed. People can of course create their own individual level of challenges, risk and adventure. By combining travel, extreme adventure and considerable self-learning, there is a very high level of experience that one can attain – literally – and that is to climb the biggest mountain, Mount Everest. The people who do it are aware of the risks. There have been many deaths on Everest. Eight fatalities in one night was the single greatest loss of life in any 24-hour period on Everest. It occurred because too many people were queuing to get to the top. Significantly the people were 'clients' who had paid sizeable sums of money to experience being guided to the top of the world's highest mountain. They were clients embarking on an extreme form of self-development, an adventure experience in the Death Zone. This zone above 7,000 metres is called this because:

> above that altitude, not only could human life not be maintained, it deteriorated with terrifying rapidity. Even using supplementary

oxygen, no one can remain in the Death Zone for long... a place where every breath signalled a deterioration in the human body, where the cells of vital organs are eliminated in their millions each hour and where no living creature belongs.

(Dickinson, 1998: 9)

In Chapter 5 we examine in more detail the many less *combative* roles that the natural environment plays in providing a diverse range of experiential learning opportunities, as well as exploring the use of artificial or simulated adventure sites. Milder elements of extreme adventure are to be found in a multi-experience package that uses a mixture of international travel, adventure, cultural exploration, novelty and sense of remoteness; such activities are increasingly in demand for experiential development purposes. Some can create very real risks; others are much less risky. The 'venture' part of the word adventure implies the element of travel, with or without a purpose. The many dictionary definitions of the term 'expedition' are that of *a journey with a definite purpose*. In expeditions there is also a target or goal, and a time constraint. An experiential learning 'journey' can thus be short, as in orienteering, or it can be longer and include major expeditions, or it can refer to a life journey.

Wilderness programmes in the USA and Australia use expeditions that last over 100 days, and these are often used as times to reappraise life. They often result in powerful life-impacting learning and, as such, expeditions are still used by many organizations to offer development opportunities for young people in growth, self-development and active citizenship. In the USA there are Family Expedition Programs to assist dysfunctional families coping, for example, with at-risk youth. The expedition thus becomes the opportunity to construct a microcosm of the family life journey so that it can be reappraised and re-navigated in real life. Other forms of adventurous journeys are also used for youth and adult development programmes. In 1978 Operation Drake was launched in the UK. With the success of Operation Drake, Operation Raleigh followed in its footsteps in 1984. Its aim was to develop leadership potential in young people through their experience of the expeditions. Operation Raleigh, renamed Raleigh International, sends 'venturers' between the ages of 17 and 25 years on a 10-week expedition. Expeditions are being increasingly used in many other ways, from management development to adventure tourism.

The UK Institute of Management suggest that:

There is growing evidence that expeditions are gaining an emerging prominence and profile within the realms of human resource development (HRD). Arising from this evidence is a suggestion that expeditions contribute to personal growth or development of desirable capabilities that are relevant to work contexts... It has been suggested that expeditions provide the sort of opportunity for personal enhancement that delivers the capabilities needed in 'crazy times' (Tom Peters) and by employers who need to differentiate outstanding employees or prospective employees.

(Surtees, 1998: 25–26)

Advertising for such expedition packages is also increasingly found in management journals, and more adults are engaging in such life-enhancing journeys; even virtual expeditions can now be found on Web sites! Surtees (1998) completed an interesting literature comparison with our typology and found that expeditions have remarkably similar ingredients. Allison (2000b), in his research on post-expedition adjustment, discusses some of the possible themes emerging from an extensive empirical study of young people returning from an expedition. He addresses the need to re-examine epistemological and ontological perspectives used for research into experiential learning. His study focuses on the now widely recognized phenomenon of post-expedition readjustment. Allison argues that this can be seen in a positive light rather than being likened to a form of post-traumatic stress disorder. Whilst this adjustment period might be due to a form of grieving, Allison suggests that the loss of expedition friends, community and the expedition environment might simply indicate the adjustment pains of positive personal growth brought about by such powerful experiential learning. Among the personal growth themes emerging were:

- increased tolerance and patience;
- increased awareness and appreciation of more basic things in life;
- a change in environmental values, eg recognizing how people use their cars to travel very short journeys that are easy to walk;
- an understanding of the intensity and nature of the new friendships and the comparison of those with friendships at home;
- better relationships with siblings;
- a greater sense of personal and spiritual perspective on life;
- a sense of service and giving;
- a change of self-concept.

(adapted from Allison, 2000b: 71–77)

Allison was able to draw out these themes that relate to the individual sense of being, where young people clearly see the world in a very different light when they return home following this powerful experiential learning event.

Journeys can also take the form of detailed micro-hikes over a few metres of the floor of a forest or the circumference of a tree. Journeys can involve an orienteering exercise, or they can involve simply getting objects or people from A to B. They can be metaphorical, in thought only. Journeys of the mind form the basis of guided fantasy work in therapy, a subject that we also cover in later chapters:

> A typical guided fantasy would engage the client in envisioning himself or herself as undertaking a hazardous journey, overcoming obstacles, meeting a wise person, and returning with a gift or message. In such a scenario, the therapist intentionally engages the client in constructing a 'self-as-hero-on-journey-of-liberation' story, as a means of empowering the client and helping him or her to celebrate his or her own powers and capabilities.
>
> (McLeod, 1997: 81)

Planning the journey and the learning from it is one of the key skills of the experiential provider, and it is of immense significance to the learner.

SEQUENCING THE CHALLENGES

Another key element of the sixteen point checklist is the sequence of primer activities, whether conducted indoors or outdoors; these often include ice-breakers and acquaintance exercises, exercises to reduce inhibitions or to create trust, empathy and teamwork (see, for example, Schoel, Prouty and Radcliffe, 1988). Experiential activities develop skill, knowledge or awareness, often starting with specific narrow skills and moving on to aggregate or 'broad' skills such as teamwork, communication, time management, emotional intelligence or leadership. This use of narrow 'activities' has to be examined in the light of their function. Broader and more complex activities provide depth to the experiential learning process, as is seen from the framework in Figure 3.3. Adapting the model of Dainty and Lucas (1992), this simple framework can be created both to classify outdoor and indoor experiential learning programmes and to show the sequencing of activities from play to intense self-development over the period of a programme.

Narrow skills such as listening or questioning can be focused on first. These might be built on later, as they are a subset of skills for teamwork or communication, which are very broad skills. Narrow skills can also be less developmental and more functional, for example knot tying, map reading or juggling skills, and they may be included to build up to complex functional skills for a journey such as orienteering. Cornell's flow learning (1989) can be combined with a model by Dainty and Lucas (1992), and we can create the following four-stage sequence:

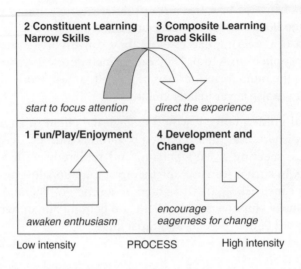

Figure 3.3 The experiential wave

1. Awaken participant enthusiasm with ice-breakers and energizers.
2. Start to focus attention with medium-sized activities and narrow skills.
3. Direct the personal experience with larger, broader skills.
4. Share participant enthusiasm using regular reviewing activities.

The framework builds on the notion of 'waves' of learning activities, a concept that we cover in more detail in Chapter 6.

MIND CHALLENGES

Experience can be a distinct advantage as people get older if learning is effectively utilized. Steve Redgrave, winner of five gold medals in consecutive Olympic games, is an exception, but there aren't many top athletes approaching the age of 40. In the world of athletics, computing and city finance, it is the young who dominate. The young are fast off the blocks. But many professions, such as psychologists, judges, prime ministers or wine tasters, seem to be dominated by older people. Why is this? When people are young they have the advantage of speed of mind and body, yet as they get older they retain a distinct advantage, and it is called 'experience'. Both young and old have a different advantage. Experienced people are simply more connected, as 'experience' is represented by more cable connections in the brain. They have 'banked' more experiences and made value or interest from them rather than simply making lots of small experiential deposits.

The brain does however shrink with old age (Robertson, 1999) and it is crucial to keep fit in the mind gym. The brain is a very powerful machine, requiring 'attentive' rather than passive stimulation. Brains need the stimulation of experience, as it is crucial for the shaping and remoulding of the electronic 'muscles' of the mind (Robertson, 1999). The mind needs to be stretched. When providing experiential learning programmes some people do not get engaged in the activities to the same extent as others. In this chapter we made reference to seven basic forms of intelligence (Gardner, 1983), and all of these will be more or less well developed in each participant; unlocking learning potential requires an understanding of and stimulation of the differing *mixed intelligence profiles* of learners. All of these seven forms of intelligence can be stimulated during experiential learning events, but two important ingredients to consider in basic programme design are bodily–physical–spatial activities and cognitive–logical activities.

Participants sometimes perceive some experiential events as having insufficient cognitive challenge. The mathematical–logical skills are not sufficiently challenged. Books on brain-teasers for trainers are now available as off-the-shelf help for mentally stimulating exercises. The left side of the brain works on logical, linear processing and is also concerned with language, reading, writing and analysis. The right side of the brain is concerned with intuition, parallel processing, images and metaphors, patterns and visual recognition. Left-brain stimulation can be created by designing appropriate elements of problem solving into the development activities, and significantly examples of daily mind stretchers are to be found in nearly all daily newspapers.

Challenging the mind: Mental Olympics – cognitive, mathematical–logical examples

1. Challenging cognitive exercises can be added to other exercises, eg the coded game:

12 M (months) in a Y (year)
365 D in a Y
4 W on a C
and so on...

Or more complex:

2. Explain the reason for the distribution of the following letters above and below the line:

55

A.........EF...HI...

...BCD......G......

(For solution see base of box)

Or:

3. This urban exercise utilizes three street bollards in the city centre, labelled as a, b and c. Tyres are numbered 1, 2, 3, 4 and 5. They are placed one on top of the other in order with 1 at the top of the pile at bollard a. The tyres must be relocated on to bollard c in the same order but the following rules apply:
   - Only one tyre may be carried at any one time and must be placed in a pile before any other tyre can be picked up.
   - A smaller number must always be placed on top of a larger number.

Some people might need to be started off, ie 1 to c, 2 to b, 1 to b, 3 to c, etc.

This session can be used with time limits with certain allocated members carrying the tyres, whilst co-ordinators, who can be restrained in any way by rules or restrictions, tell the carriers what to do. An example is that the co-ordinators might be some distance away and operate their instructions by walkie-talkie, or in a coded language. Printed T-shirts with numbers, symbols or letters are ideal for many of these exercises. T-shirts can have 1 or + or = printed on the backs for people to complete calculations.

Or:

4. Build mathematical challenges into other activities, eg physical, recreational or navigational activities. The *'bike it' exercise* involves constructing or assembling a bike – exercising the many forms of intelligence. Here participants are provided with a set of accounts, and activities to carry out for money, including the solving of cryptic clues, mathematical problems, theoretical models to create, journeys to undertake, team skills to decide, jobs to divide – all to build a bike, through earning money to buy the parts, or expertise. But the frame and the handlebars are hidden in the city or the wilderness of the National Park, and clever problem solving will find them – but that requires brainpower.

(Solution = straight and round letters!)

STIMULATING THE SENSES

Sensory stimulation or deprivation is a powerful phenomenon of both the outdoor and indoor classroom. Auditory, olfactory, visual, touch and taste are the five commonly quoted senses but there are more. Some refer to the sixth sense as an intuitive or a spiritual sense. The senses, six or more, are central to the way we perceive and receive any experience; in our learning combination lock model they represent the pivotal tumbler between the person and the place. The senses can be stimulated so as to prepare people to unlock yet more of their potential, and sensory work is a prerequisite of the more powerful forms of learning.

A cave is one of the few places where total darkness can be created, allowing people to reduce nearly all other sensations. Light is controllable in indoor environments in terms of brightness or colour and as such can be used to alter moods. Gloves can be used to reduce sensory feeling in the fingers. The combinations are endless. Fire, water, earth, mountains and rivers are just some of the many ingredients in the natural or urban environment that can be used to influence learning, a subject we cover in Chapter 5. Opposites can provide for sensory adjustments, such as light and dark, noise and silence, shelter and exposure, calm and energized, food and hunger, loneliness and gregariousness, solitude and crowded, hot and cold air, wet and dry. They can also be altered so that they flow with or against the natural rhythms of the body or of the day and night. Technology enables us increasingly to influence people's senses, with ultraviolet light, strobes, Internet and computer presentations, large screen images and quadraphonic sounds. So much can so easily be contained within a small laptop computer.

A number of other chapters in this book also contain information on sensory stimulation and deprivation. Relaxed alertness is covered in Chapter 7, as well as the use of music or smell or other forms of mood-altering methods. Sensory deprivation can also be used to create challenging obstacles, and these are discussed below.

CHANGE THE RULES AND CREATE OBSTACLES

In Chapter 8 we discuss the good practice of climate and ground rule setting. These are important functions for adults and young people alike, and require careful consideration by providers. However many other simple rules, obstacles or procedures can all influence the degree of adventure, challenge or difficulty of any experiential activity. Importantly these rules and obstacles can also allow greater flexibility in a programme design so that the experience can be altered and levels of challenge can be reduced or increased. Time constraints might for example mean that items such as bike parts can only be purchased during specific times. Two-way radios can be used on certain frequencies; battery life can be measured or curtailed. Solar panels can be used to charge batteries or equipment so that people can only carry out some tasks when the sun is shining. Items can be placed in the way of routes and the journey might only be allowed at night or through certain territory. Instructions can be given on a tape recording through earplugs so that only one person can hear them at any one time. Communication might be restricted to coded whistles or translated into another language.

Obstacles can include sensory deprivation or sensory adjustment, and might include blindfolds, earplugs, glasses to improve or remove vision, nose pegs, gloves to remove feeling or to create clumsiness or even cardboard tubes to create a form of tunnel vision. Tarpaulins can be used to separate teams and they might be allowed to pass items only through a narrow aperture.

Sorting and organization skills are also important skills to develop: a mass of data, a mass of information to sort and make sense of, or activities to decide who and when. Why? Because knowledge is one thing; organized knowledge is a million things! The range of combinations within the milieu increases the level of challenge. Whilst the milieu is endless, it does need a degree of focus, structure and reason.

The following rules and restrictions apply!

1. The time limit to complete the activities is just 220 minutes.
2. Each activity can be completed only once and will earn you money.
3. Each activity requires you to estimate your projected earnings and to submit it to the facilitator before commencing.
4. Physical activities will be paid in dollars; mental tasks will be paid in ECU.
5. The four teams will have radio contact for 10 minutes only during each half-hour.
6. One team member must be blindfolded at all times. One person must wear gloves at all times. For blindfold and glove wearing, rotation of the wearers is allowed.
7. A sum of 10 dollars will be paid for each digital picture of the team 'completing' an activity.
8. An up-to-date set of accounts must be ready for inspection at any time.
9. Teams A and B will submit a mind map plan of their proposals to the facilitators before commencing.
10. Teams C and D will not be required to produce a plan.

CONSTRUCTING AND USING PHYSICAL OBJECTS

The construction of physical objects, from bikes to rafts to dry-stone walls and bridges, has been an essential component of many experiential learning programmes. Other options include the construction of something that is non-physical, such as a diagram, a shape or a theoretical construct, by using natural objects, cards, string or masking tape. Plastic kits, for adults to play with, like giant Lego blocks, are sold in many professional training journals for providers to assemble quickly in repeat business. They can be tweaked and reused indoors or outdoors. But the kits in themselves are off-the-shelf devices used to create artificial 'tasks'. They are used to enhance the 'process' of learning. The plastic kits do not create real tasks – their reality is metaphoric. 'Training toys' are now offered on Web sites, so that trainers can buy large plastic dice and a host of ready-made 'kit'. Traditional planks and drums, used in raft building in outdoor teamwork development, are increasingly being replaced or supported by a host of new artefacts. Everything from bike assembly and marble runs to tank driving and juggling is being tried out in the search for a new form of experiential adventure.

The increasingly sophisticated and discerning audience may get bored easily if they have done it before, possibly reducing their ability to learn. Irvine and Wilson (1994) challenge some of the mystique about some outdoor experiential events, and argue that 'novelty' might form the basis of such a rationale. They also quote Long and Galagan who suggest that the outdoors is where educational and organizational norms do not exist for people to hide behind. For such 'norms' to exist, it is argued that people must have previously experienced the activity and / or environment. Ideally, therefore, the activity and / or the environment must be novel to the participants. If this deduction is correct, it is not the 'outdoors' that is important, but the need for a novel situation or environment, ie the activities do not necessarily have to take place in the outdoors.

TELLING THE STORY – USING PHYSICAL OBJECTS

In experiential learning there is also a great deal of use of objects for a different reason. They are used to enable people to project their thoughts and feelings on to inanimate, 'unreal' objects and it is this subject of reality that we also explore in more detail in the next chapter. Assagioli (1980) developed the idea of psychosynthesis, which partly uses a whole range of imaginative techniques so that people can project their inner thoughts and emotions on to images or symbols. This can resolve many of the difficulties of expression that people experience when discussing issues that lie deeper in their inner self, including emotional issues. This projection can both appear to remove the face-to-face level of embarrassment of the 'personal' and at the same time encourage open forays deeper into the 'personal'. For example, discussions or reviews can use 'natural stones', selected by participants to enable them to talk about themselves, say, in terms of why they chose that stone. By talking about the colour of the stone, its shape and size, personal meanings and values can be spoken about, and feelings and values can be *projected* on to the stone in what is a 'neutral arena' on the floor or on a table. Many people also talk about their *inner* self as being different, and that the stone only represents what people see on the outside. It is much harder to talk about these things directly face to face, person to person, or person to group. The position of the stones in relation to the others can also be significant in terms of the way groups or teams are operating. This can enable group difficulties to be broached more easily. In facilitation, this is also the basis of good feedback, ie acting as a mirror, not focusing on the 'personal', carefully describing events, what was actually seen and so on.

In the case of natural stones, the objects are the metaphor to transfer meaning. Russian dolls can be used to symbolize people, power and position of other people. Playing cards can be used indoors, where diamonds represents the hard *facts*, hearts explore *feelings*, spades dig deeper – *findings*, and clubs explore the *future* (Greenaway, 1996). One technique devised to control either excessive dominance or shyness by young people in a group is called 'having the bottle to speak'. It has a double meaning. It involves using a plastic bottle, and people wanting to speak must wait for an opportunity to take it from someone else. If a person with the bottle has finished, he or she holds it out for others to take it, and as a sign of friendship people help to create discussion by sharing the talking and taking and holding the bottle. For some it is hard to *have the bottle to try it*. The technique is effective in ensuring that some people do not dominate the proceedings. Some trainers get participants to draw objects, and after 15 minutes or so change that object or add new ones. People become interested in the issues of staying on the existing task or moving on, helping people to see and debate their own response to change.

Thus the 16-point typology has unfolded in this chapter and so creates a new tumbler in the learning combination lock (see Figure 3.4).

The 16-point typology

1. Create a journey or destination.
2. Create and sequence mental and physical activities.
3. Adjust or suspend elements of reality.
4. Stimulate the six main senses/alter moods.
5. Construct or deconstruct physical or non-physical items.
6. Design collaborative, competitive or co-optive strategies.
7. Create combative and/or empathetic approaches to the environment.
8. Create rules and restrictions.
9. Provide elements of real or perceived challenge or risk.
10. Set a target, goal or objective, to create an underlying 'state of mind'.
11. Set time constraints.
12. Allow people to deal with change, risk, success and failure – stretching personal boundaries.
13. Design sorting and/or organization skills.
14. Include functional skills.
15. Design quiet time for reflection – physical or mental space.
16. Allow the story of the experience to be told.

Basic Ingredients

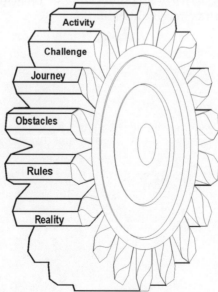

Figure 3.4 The first tumbler

CONCLUSION

Mumford (1991: 31) suggests that 'if we provide individuals with a greater capacity to learn from the widest possible variety of opportunities, we are empowering that individual to be in greater command of his or her destiny'. Creating this variety of opportunities is thus the essence of experiential learning, and this chapter has outlined the basic ingredients used in the design process. We have thus established the first tumbler in the learning combination lock that we introduced in Chapter 1. This 16-point tumbler acts as a general guide to the design process, and serves to highlight the importance of design skills in experiential learning.

Using this tumbler as the basis of the chapter, we examined a range of ideas that can be used to enhance the impact of the experience in learning. We examined the creative use of activity sequencing, planned and unplanned learning, and the use of journeys, large and small, from life journeys and expeditions to orienteering and micro-hikes. Sensory stimulation, sensory blocking, adjustment of dimensions of 'reality', and fantasy, the provision of rules and obstacles, problem solving, and the use of objects for a variety of purposes were all briefly explored so as to set the scene for detailed work in later chapters. This milieu provides a multiplicity of innovative ideas to choose from so as to enrich the learning experience, but good practice and a sound theoretical understanding must always underpin the choices made. In the next chapter we investigate in detail the effect of altering the nature of 'reality', and how it influences learning. The use of activities that include training kits, traditional outdoor recreation, circus, radio production, cartoons, theatre, drama, art, storytelling and writing receive attention.

4

Exploring Reality

> There is no separation between learning, play, work, and leisure. Life is
> all of these at once and its process is spontaneous.
>
> (Heap, 1993: 16)

INTRODUCTION

In the quest to help people to learn experientially, providers draw on
many skills and use combinations of stories, metaphors and meaningful
objects to encourage expression of thoughts and ideas about their experience, whether it be adventure, or other physical, emotional or mental
activities. Drama, sculpting, role-play and art are also used. However,
levels of reality are important ingredients within the milieu of experiential
learning provision, and the degree to which any experiential activity is
perceived as 'real' can have a profound effect on learning.

In this chapter we consider the many dimensions of reality and we
explore how it provides opportunities to unlock greater learning potential. Whilst levels of reality can be reduced or increased to influence
learning, making the right choices requires a clear understanding of the
processes involved. In this chapter we offer a range of examples of 'real'
and 'simulated' activities, and give guidance on the raising and lowering
of reality in experiential learning.

WHAT IS A REAL EXPERIENCE?

Krouwel and Goodwill (1994: 30) argue that reality is the key advantage to
using the natural outdoors: 'reality is perhaps the greatest asset of all in
management development programmes that use the outdoors. There is no
artificiality in the exercises outdoors; the problems are real, the issues are
dynamic, the constraints are felt. There is no need to act – it is the real
world.'

This statement makes the assumption that the outdoor activities are 'real activities' as opposed to artificial 'games'. This is often far from the case. Price, from his position as executive director of the Leadership Trust, says, 'It is important that it be totally real because then you get real emotions, real fear, high anxiety, high or low morale, real aggression and real learning' (Price, cited in Bank, 1994: 10). Likewise, for corporate training and development, Butcher (1991: 26) stresses the need to repro-duce the work environment during company training sessions, to make learning more 'realistic': 'It is essential that training programmes have included in their designs, components that reproduce these problems, in a more tangible and realistic form than has been employed by many training consultants in the past.'

The reasoning of all these writers could however be interpreted as being guided by rather superficial design techniques, as high levels of reality are not always the best choice in programme design. What does Butcher actually mean when he refers to 'tangible and realistic'? This is where some confusion is apparent. 'Real' does not necessarily mean work-place-like or the 'real outdoors'. As we saw in the previous chapter the notion of a journey can involve venturing from the normal, so-called real home or workplace environment in order to learn from new experiences. The ingredient of 'reality' is in fact a much more complex phenomenon than is realized, and, as we shall now argue, it requires greater exploration in terms of its impact on learners. Holman, Pavlica and Thorpe (1997) talk of the 'vague and indeterminate nature of reality' that results in the mean-ings of experiences being contested. The understanding of the impact of construction, deconstruction and orchestration of *all* the elements of 'reality' is requisite to quality experiential programme design. Reality can refer to the tasks or activities, people involved, skills, process, objects, learning outcomes or place in which the learning is undertaken.

Butcher, an ex-army training officer, suggests that 'hanging by a single rope 80 feet from the ground, controlled by a colleague whose previous knowledge of ropes was tying his shoelaces, could not under any circum-stances be described as a game' (1991: 28). Butcher avoids the nature and diversity of the subject of 'reality'. Reality, in this quoted situation, is not located with the activities, but rather in the form of the elements of *real emotions* that can emerge from such a situation, and heavily influences learning, which we investigate in Chapters 6 and 7. Butcher views reality from the influence of his own background in the armed services, where trainers 'use experience based training to prepare people for the discom-fort, depersonalisation, and emotional strain encountered in combat' (Walter and Marks, 1981: 3). These combative styles, delivered by the armed forces, often deliberately use 'in-your-face' instructing so as to push and prod people to learn. Such design techniques are also seen as combative in their relationship towards the outdoor environment. This form of 'distressed learning' is designed to increase anxiety levels so as to stimulate learning (Yerkes and Dobson, 1980). Distressed learning works for some people but such methods, which use stress imprinting and trial-and-error techniques, can be rather crude and create minds that only superficially appear to confront emotions such as fear and trepidation. Rather, such training teaches people to tame their fear, to combat and suppress it, a method originally designed for the purpose of warfare. Rightly, this approach to experiential learning is not a panacea for all learning. Adventurous experiential learning requires diversity and complexity of styles and strategies in delivery suited to the clients.

One of the criticisms of some experiential programmes is that they are located in environments that are unreal and bear no resemblance to the learner's home environment or workplace. If artificial climbing blocks can easily be installed on the walls of buildings so as to break down the teaching of fundamental climbing skills, then perhaps it is possible to take more control of aspects of a learning environment; we can create it. But this is not to suggest that experiential learning is simply a bag of tricks, to be artificially choreographed with 'set pieces'.

There are of course many facets of reality and if people cannot experience the 'real thing' they can experience something that can be perceived as real, in a physical sense or an emotional sense. This can be especially important with younger children, for example, whose conceptualization skills may not be so advanced. Steve Van Matre (1978, 1979), for example, assists children to understand how photosynthesis occurs by getting them inside a leaf-shaped tent, with ping-pong balls, where the children pretend to manufacture sugars.

Kirk (1986: 87) suggests that there are three main dimensions to reality – participant reality, theoretical reality and resource reality:

- **Participant reality** – the extent to which the design and content of the learning event relates to the learners and their jobs, organizational environments, personal abilities and expectations.
- **Theoretical reality** – the extent to which the design and content of the learning event relates to the existing body of knowledge concerning the nature of management and management learning. Here the nature of reality lies in the questions arising from the theoretical models or concepts that are being applied and whether these are seen as 'real' or 'true'.
- **Resource reality** – the extent and cost of resources that go into staging and running the learning events and whether the resource expenditure can be justified.

So why do experiential providers need to work on *real* issues and problems as vehicles for learning? If learners do not relate their 'experience' on a programme to their experience in real life, then the experience is likely to be criticized as having little relevance. Binstead and Stuart (1979) focus on three dimensions of reality and offer reasoning and guidance for adjusting the degree of reality. They elaborate on:

- the reality of the **process** of learning;
- the reality of the **tasks** that people complete;
- the reality of the **environment** in which people are learning.

By combining the work of both Binstead and Stuart, and Kirk, experiential providers can construct, raise or reduce a larger number of these elements of reality. These are important practical applications to consider in designing experiential learning that is ultimately considered as 'real' by the learners. But do high levels of reality result in more significant learning, and is the learning more readily transferable? It is debatable, and the answer to the question is, 'It depends.'

It is hard to key into past, present and potential future experiences of learners in order to create high reality. But high-reality strategies can:

- integrate learning and work role activities;
- take the learning event to the job;
- bring the job to the learning event (tutor-led);
- bring the job to the learning event (participant-led);
- provide a range of alternative activities within the learning event;
- change the work situation to match the learning event.

(Binstead and Stuart, 1979)

There are situations where lowering reality allows a different kind of learning to take place. Low-reality designs may be appropriate, for example, when more radical alternatives need to be considered, so that new horizons can be opened up. We can use fantasy to reduce inhibitions, and role-play to allow a feeling to be expressed or to create a feeling that 'This is not really me; I am just playing a part.' The learning journey here involves moving out of the reality of self in order to see something different. So high-reality events would appear to be inappropriate and often dysfunctional when: 1) there is a need for growth- rather than maintenance-orientated learning, eg to allow a learner to consider radical alternative behaviour, ideas, etc; or 2) there is sufficient threat invoked in high-reality situations for it to be a barrier to learning.

However, to ensure high transfer of learning, provision would need to be made to allow the learner to progress towards high reality at some subsequent stage. For the purposes of unlearning and new learning it can sometimes be useful to make one or more elements 'unreal' so the other issues can be highlighted and explored without some of the interference that high reality might create. So, for example, an activity that involves managers building and sailing a raft will have a low reality in terms of environment (they don't usually work outside) and of task (they don't usually build and sail rafts). There is high reality in terms of process (they do use teamwork, communication skills, etc in their work – but then, who doesn't?). The process skills practised on a mountain do not always get 'transferred' back to the office or to everyday behaviours. So, a sequence of lowering and heightening different dimensions of reality over the duration of a course is useful, but moving towards high reality at the end of the course can help transfer of learning. The case study below is a practical example.

A practical case study: Altering reality

Negotiating public access to the UK countryside: skills practice section of a three-day training course

The early part of the course uses 'narrow skills' practice. Negotiating is a 'broad skill', involving many narrow skills such as listening, questioning, diplomacy and so on. On this course we thus deconstructed 'negotiating' into its many narrow sub-skills such as influencing, persuasion, listening, tactics, entry, developing rapport, closing and so on. The latter part of the course then used broad skills practice, but with varying levels of reality or simulation. The exercises were as follows:

From: LOW CONTENT REALITY
Exercise A: Redecorating the office
The material was taken from a standard loose-leaf package on negotiating. It is a paper exercise. There is no incentive. It concerns a contract price to decorate an office suite. Content reality is low. The written case material on decorating contains a review sheet that looks at the forces in use in negotiating and the approaches that can be used by the two sides. People are asked to identify opening gambits and write their answers on paper.

Exercise B: Driving a bargain
A written exercise about cars – people are told that this is a warm-up for a real car exercise when people can pit their wits against real negotiators! This adds to the incentive to concentrate on all exercises. Here

the content reality is again low – the people involved do not negotiate car prices in their jobs.

Exercise C: Buying a new car

Real cars are used. Real logbooks are used. Real car prices are offered. Car book prices are available. Cars can be inspected and faults found, both inside and outside, as they are located in the car park. The keys are made available. One is an uncleaned four-wheel drive and the other is a nicely valeted VW Polo. The brief informs people, 'You have moved to the National Park and need a four-wheel drive for bad weather and to tow your new caravan.' False money is used but a prize is offered. The people that the participants negotiate with are real trained negotiators and they are located in an office where the deals will take place. Final agreements are written in sealed envelopes so that the winners can be decided later. Content reality is again low; process reality is high.

To: HIGH CONTENT REALITY

Exercise D: Negotiating access to UK land on behalf of the public

Here we use high content reality and high process reality. Real negotiators are again present. Real information is provided – facts and figures on sheep headage payments, ranger support offered, wall damage payments and litter arrangements. Participants are real access officers or public rights of way officers. They are observed on video by the rest of the group. The incentive is to try to do a good job in front of their peers, to try to put all the skills and knowledge acquired on the course into practice, and they try to meet their own pre-set prices and subsidy targets decided in their negotiating plans. They argue their case with real negotiators and are debriefed afterwards. The video is then replayed with self- and peer assessment taking place.

(adapted from Beard and McPherson, 1999)

Providers of experiential learning programmes hear complaints that programmes are not as real as people would like them to be, and corporate organizations increasingly request the replacement of traditional activities with something that is 'far more real, more challenging, enabling staff to get closer to the learning edge'. This can be done by individual journeys, secondments and exchanges, or by selecting real environmental or community projects for individuals or teams to work on, a subject we cover in depth in Chapter 5. Some organizations allow staff one day per month to give time to and experience charitable endeavours. We have selected whole menus for clients to choose from, using for example charitable organizations to provide a broad range of very real projects and challenges for youth development work or for corporate teams.

FANTASY

Fantasy is a form of psychic play and it is not just for children. The notion of suspending reality is frequently used to frame the mental state for an experiential event. In *101 of the Best Corporate Team-building Activities We Know!*, Priest and Rohnke (2000: 5) offer fantasy as one type of 'framing' the way an experiential activity is introduced. They make reference to the popular 'fantasy or fairy tale introductions that include such items as spiders, sharks, alligators, poison peanut butter, radioactive yoghurt, nitroglycerine, TNT, corrosive acid, floods and forest fires'. One UK company offers many innovative theatrical-based training techniques including *animating ideas* where people can 'Extend the boundaries of experience and realise your dreams and themes, through your own fantastic animated creations. You select the style, develop the characters, devise the stories and provide the voices... Hours of endeavour. Seconds of footage. Years of satisfaction' (Experience Creative Development, 2000).

Other training resource companies offer outdoor fantasy adventure 'kits' for use in the indoors. You can choose from being stranded on an island, capsizing on a lake or being stuck in a jungle. The brochure suggests that you can enhance realism 'with a set of 20 slides that will make your participants glad they are warm and dry. Tropical Rain Forest audio-cassette helps set the mood for the exercise' (http://www.users.globalnet.co.uk/ -rogg/activities/outdoor_indoor.htm). Participants are even given 'I survived the rainforest badges' after completion of the programme! During experiential activities the deliberate movement from fantasy to reality can be carefully constructed, as can the journey from fantasy to reality. For the latter a simple example is to *make dreams come true*.

Fantasy can create a sense of atmosphere, excitement and adventure, involving suspending disbelief, and the use of magic and mystery. Such experiences involve careful preparation of the emotional state of the mind. Some adventures tend to be completely set in a fantasy world or they might involve moving from the real world to the fantasy world and back again. This often requires some form of trigger between the fantasy world and the real world, for example in *The Lion, The Witch and The Wardrobe* by C S Lewis (1980), people walk into the wardrobe and into the land of Narnia. A cave can be a place to hide the secret combination to the lock.

There can be some form of 'quest'. On a deeper level a lot of the characters involved in children's fantasy go through rites of passage, with helpers guiding them into maturity. Some learn to believe in themselves, their lives are enriched from the experience and the quest is what does it for them.

Guided fantasy is a mental journey involving images with a deep symbolic meaning. Fantasy and guided imagery can be used to develop more awareness of thoughts and emotions, leading to the creation of greater self-awareness and personal growth.

Practical example

Relaxation techniques also use guided fantasy to take people on a mental journal to favourite places and imaginary environments that lower the heart rate and stimulate positive feelings. We recently experimented with a guided fantasy session with adults in an indoor workshop, using a variation of the Temple of Silence (Ferrucci, 1982). Set in an imaginary world, the story we tell concerns a journey up a cold mountain in the snow, where in a cave there is a fire. Sitting by the fire in the warmth is a wise old man – the sage. But in real life we had opened the door of the room we were in to let in some fresh air. As we lay on the floor in the dark the wind got up and it started to snow heavily and the snow actually came into the room. The atmosphere was beginning to get special as, quite by chance, we had let the real outdoors in through the door and into our fantasy world of snowy mountains. Inside the building it was hard to know which was fantasy and which was reality! Two people from Outward Bound Singapore, for example, had never seen snow before! The workshop participants were then asked to go out into the surrounding fields and woods and find somewhere to be alone with their thoughts, somewhere they could not be seen and where they could not see anyone else. This was to let their imagination develop further.

PLAY AS EXPERIENTIAL LEARNING

Play may be observed in a variety of mammals as well as humans; for example, kittens may be seen playing together, stalking and pouncing. It would appear that play serves to *rehearse and exercise skills* in a safer environment. Games and similar activities have been played for thousands of years and there is clear evidence from the Egyptians of 'acrobatics, gymnastic games, tug-of-war, hoop and kicking games, ball and stick games, juggling, knife throwing, club throwing, wrestling, swimming, guessing games, games of chance, and board games' (Booth and Moss, 1994: 5).

It is very clear from general observation how successful children are with learning, and it is also clear that play forms a key role. By the time they are three they have learnt to walk, speak, handle a variety of objects, control their limbs and bodily functions, and operate in social environments. They learn in a 'natural' way and, it would appear, often carry out an activity just for fun. Probably the most important thing about play is that children appear to enjoy themselves. It is normally non-threatening and usually conducted in a safe environment for themselves and for other children. Significantly, 'their involvement with the learning process is total. There is no separation between learning, play, work, and leisure. Life is all of these at once and its process is spontaneous' (Heap, 1993: 16).

These might be lessons perhaps for adults to relearn, ie it is OK to play. Innovators are said to regard their work as play. Generally, however, many adults have difficulty in learning to play, because of much attention being focused on 'ought to be' or 'could be' doing. These worries, concerns, regrets and mistakes, about things in the future and of the past, can present a continuous inner turmoil (Carlson, 1998; Mallinger and De Wyze, 1993), preventing deep relaxation and the ability to relax and play. Relaxation and play are both means of accessing superior learning.

Adult–child relationship difficulties are described for example in studies on workaholics: 'A workaholic parent may be physically present but non-existent as a nurturing parent... Each stage of [child] development lasts for only a very brief time, and once completed, will never be repeated. Miss out on enough such experiences, and you will end up with only a pale, vitiated sense of ever having had children' (Mallinger and De Wyze, 1993: 171).

In contrast children are busy experiencing 'being', naturally living 'the moment', the 'here and now'. This tendency to be workaholic occurs when the work–leisure or getting–being balance is out of sync. It is said that you have achieved success in your field when you don't know whether what you are doing is work or play. Handy (1989) offers a fascinating analysis of Western working life in *The Age of Unreason*, and comments that work used to consume 100,000 hours of our life, but in the space of two generations it has been potentially contractually reduced to 50,000 hours. Importantly the work hours are no longer experienced as one continuous sequence, and the 'job for life' is fast disappearing. More people are taking time out to *experience* many other things, to learn about life in more interesting ways, so that work is no longer the epicentre of their experience of life, and work does not plough a continuous straight path to retirement and death. Many people are changing work-life patterns, to experience more 'being', rather than 'getting'. Many people are choosing to live what Handy (1989: 145) calls 'portfolio lifestyles', the structure of which consists of the main categories of work: 'wage work and fee work, which are both forms of paid work; homework, gift work and study work which are all free work'. 'Homework' consists of the things we do at home, with children, partners and the home itself. 'Gift work' is free work and can include community, charitable or service work. Handy (1989) argues that it is the *balance* of these important aspects of people's lives that is crucial, and generates a healthy emotional make-up in any individual. These forms of work also present ways to learn. Adventure and 'play' in its broadest sense can thus be a very successful means of unlocking greater learning potential for both young and adult alike. Indeed, it can be much more effective than formal learning.

Children play considerably with the use of words and it is not uncommon for young children to enjoy asking and challenging others with riddles and puns that explore the various meanings and usage of words. Rogers (1983: 19) referred to an example by Marshall McLuhan:

> if a child is moved to a foreign country and allowed to play freely for hours with her new companions, with no language instruction at all, she will learn the new language in a few months and will acquire the proper accent too. She is learning in a way which has significance and meaning for her, and such learning proceeds at an exceedingly rapid rate. But let someone try to instruct her in the new language, basing the instruction on the elements that have meaning for the teacher, and learning is tremendously slowed, or even stopped.

Piaget (1927), who studied his own three children and other children, identified three types of play:

- **sensorimotor play** – involves the practice of behaviours and exploratory learning often seen in young infants;
- **pretend or symbolic play** – found in children from two to six years;
- **games with rules** – played from the ages of six or seven years upwards.

Children often seem to enjoy free play with materials such as sand, paints, water and clay. They frequently become totally absorbed in this creative process and the materials provide an opportunity for learning about the nature of materials, conservation of material, spatial, textural and other dimensions.

Recognition of the value of play is not a recent phenomenon. Plato (1953) advised that 'the future builder must play at building... and those who have the care of their education should provide them when young with mimic tools'. An illustration of a parent actively applying this principle was the mother of Frank Lloyd Wright who bought him wooden blocks called Froebel Gifts to play with. She had decided before he was born that he would be an architect (Gura, 1992).

In the years 1890–1920, $100 million was used to build playgrounds in the USA (Cohen, 1987). These playgrounds were formed in order to minimize delinquency and improve morals and health. The first adventure playground was built in Copenhagen in 1943, and its director Bertelson stated, 'There can be no doubt that in the case of so called difficult children, free play presents a solution to their problem' (Cohen, 1987: 32). This innovation was successful and led to the establishment of the International Playground Association. Bertelson defined an adventure playground 'as a place where children are free to do many things that they cannot do elsewhere in our crowded urban society' (Cohen, 1987: 32). In many respects the assault courses that are used by adults in management training exercises are a sophisticated form of playground.

Unfortunately not all children play. The economist John Stuart Mill was not allowed to play by his father, who wanted his son educated from birth. Similarly, Froebel, born in Thuringia, Germany in 1782, had an unhappy childhood and, influenced by the writings of Rousseau, developed a kindergarten (garden of children) where children could, like flowers, 'blossom'. This was a reaction to the drilling methods used in schools, and in the kindergarten children were allowed to play and were encouraged by adults.

On the whole play is viewed by children as an enjoyable activity. However, play in children is not always undertaken in a light-hearted and pretend manner, as can be seen in Golding's *Lord of the Flies*. Play has the potential to have a negative influence. Cohen (1987: 1), while doubting that play is always fun, stated, 'Play is a learning experience.'

So how do we experience play as adults? If we reflect on our childhood we may be able to recall playing with building blocks and how enjoyable it was. Parents will be only too aware after spending money on presents that sometimes the present is discarded by the child in favour of playing with the packaging and using imagination. It is difficult to draw boundaries that clearly define play from other forms of activity, and Smith *et al* (1986) described how it is also difficult to categorize the various types of play. However, they identified five main characteristics of play:

- **intrinsic motivation** – the child plays for the sake of play and not for other external reasons;

- **positive effect** – the child enjoys and finds satisfaction in the play;
- **non-literal** – play is pretend and is not taken seriously;
- **means/ends** – the child is more focused on the process and behaviour rather than the actual outcome;
- **flexibility** – there can be a variation in the context or form of behaviour.

Play for adults includes not just sporting activities and board games at Christmas but, according to Cohen (1987: 15), psychological games in which he included 'encounter groups, growth movements, self-help groups of some sorts, following the guru, self therapies, and all kinds of ego-fests. Obviously, many people take these activities very seriously and some need help. But for many people, going to groups has become a form of "deep" play.' Furthermore, the playing of games would appear to be an activity that is conducted by children of all ages. Berne's (1973) *Games People Play* proposes that we all possess within us the ability to play the role of parent, adult and child in our interactions with others.

In *The Handbook of Management Games*, Elgood (1984) discussed the nature and value of games (he is not entirely satisfied with the term 'game' because its use may detract from the seriousness of purpose), simulations and exercises. He argued that even with well-prepared lectures the content is of no value to the learner unless he or she understands and integrates the knowledge with what is already possessed. In contrast, he asserted that while the game contains less quantity than a lecture it is personal to the learner and allows him or her to personalize and make use of the information. He (1984: 14–15) continued:

> There is a world of difference between knowing that something is true because one is told it by someone in authority and knowing that it is true because one has experienced it (albeit in a simulated situation) for oneself… The depth of learning is increased, then, because one is not just learning from what somebody else has done, but also from what one has experienced.

Elgood (1984: 8) identified four criteria that a game or device should satisfy:

1. It has a sufficiently clear framework to ensure that it is recognizably the same exercise whenever it is used.
2. It confronts the players with a changing situation, the changes being wholly or in part a consequence of their own actions.
3. It allows the identification beforehand (if desired) of some criterion by which it can be won or lost.

4. It requires for its operation a certain level of documentation, physical material, computation or administrative/behavioural skill.

Three models of games were identified by Elgood. The first are *definitive models* in which there is a clear answer and desired result to the game. This reflects the creator's view of the world in which, if certain behaviour occurs, there will be a specific result. The second type of game involves *probabilistic models*. This type of game is not as rigid and predictable, and allows for individual behaviour. It helps to create awareness of alternatives and the fact that people are prone to misunderstand what are thought to be common concepts, eg workers negotiating a wage structure with managers. The third type of game is concerned with *individual models*. These involve exploring and comparing the individual solutions to the game in a non-judgemental way that recognizes the value of differences. Elgood (1984: 12–13) categorized games as follows:

-   games based on a definitive model:
    -   traditional model-based games;
    -   puzzles;
    -   in-basket exercises;
    -   mazes;
    -   programmed simulations;
    -   enquiry studies;
    -   encounter games;
    -   adult role-playing games;
-   games based on a probabilistic model:
    -   structured experiences;
    -   organization games;
    -   organizational simulations;
    -   practical simulations;
-   games based on individual models:
    -   in-basket exercises;
    -   exploratory games.

What is all too apparent in this discussion about games is that they are an essential learning process for young people to develop the skills necessary to survive in later life. Games develop cognitive, affective and behavioural skills that can be used in both personal and work lives. For adults, involving oneself with certain types of play activity, with the exception of formalized games, is often frowned upon. It is assumed that as adults we are mature and have passed through the stage of playing games. However, as we have seen, we play games much of the time. As Elgood stated, the use of the word 'games' to some extent trivializes their value, and therefore, perhaps, they should be renamed 'experiential exercises'.

SUSPENDING REALITY: DRAMA AND ROLE-PLAYING

Trainers and facilitators are thus often looking for new experiential methods to alter the degree of reality, stimulate the imagination and stir the senses in order to engage people in learning. Pollock (2000) refers to the term 'infotainment' and reports that 'companies are turning to music, storytelling, visual art and even comedy in order to develop their people, engender creativity in the workplace and enhance the corporate image'. The following quotation creates an interesting, if perhaps cynical, juxtaposition of amusement and learning, but suspending reality has potentially many more benefits to explore in the milieu of experiential learning: 'generally, there is felt to be a very sharp distinction between learning and amusing oneself. The first may be useful, but only the second is pleasant' (Brecht, quoted in Baldacchino and Mayo, 1997: 216). Drama and theatre, and other art forms, can be used to alter 'reality'.

Drama is defined as: 'The enactment of real and imagined events through roles and situations. Drama enables both individuals and groups to explore, shape and symbolically represent ideas and feelings and their consequences. Drama stimulates and shapes aesthetic development and enjoyment through valuing both affective and cognitive responses to the world' (Curriculum Corporation, 1994: 16, in Attard, 2001).

From a social psychology perspective, the range of role-playing techniques has been roughly classified as:

- performed or imagined (passive or active) (Hamilton, 1976);
- scripted or improvised (Hamilton, 1976);
- involving one individual or many;
- participants required to play themselves or somebody else;
- participants required to play themselves under a familiar or unfamiliar set of circumstances;
- stooges may or may not be used in role plays – and sometimes are used as *agent provocateurs*;
- subject may be pre-briefed and deceived, or pre-briefed and not deceived, or not pre-briefed at all;
- scenario inductions can involve one-line prompts or several;
- participants may be constrained into a highly structured-response format or, alternatively, be given a free-response format.

(adapted from Yardley-Matwiejczuk, 1999: 36)

The list provides innovative ideas for facilitating such events, as role-play as a training tool has common usage. It can increase participation, facilitate problem solving and enable people to enhance their awareness and understanding. It can have a degree of spontaneity. However:

In reports of such role-play activities there is an overwhelming assumption that we all know what we are talking about when we mention role-play. Occasionally hints emerge, about aspects of induction or technique, that suggest the authors might know a thing or two about good practice, but these are rarely articulated fully or made explicit. Moreover, there is no evidence of a critical stance towards the question of whether role-play is being appropriately or inappropriately utilised.

(Yardley-Matwiejczuk, 1999: 34)

Playwrights from Sophocles to Brecht have used their 'plays' to teach, and convey facts and political attitudes to their audiences, but variations from the traditional play now exist. The term 'spect-actors' is used to describe a technique that involves people moving from observation as 'watchers' to being involved as 'actors'. *Invisible theatre*, for example, might involve two people walking into a shop where they start to argue about something. The real people eventually take sides and then join in! But there are ethical issues here that we examine later, in Chapter 8.

Drama has many applications that can be used by facilitators. Drama is also attractive to many adult learners, especially because so many people watch plays, films or soap operas and become affected by the experience. There is a distinction between using dramatic techniques as a teaching method and teaching theatre. Theatre is an art form, which focuses on a product: a play or production for an audience. Drama used in experiential learning is more informal and focuses on the process of dramatic enactment for the sake of the learner, not an audience. This teaching technique is referred to as 'creative dramatics' in order to distinguish it from theatre arts. Classroom drama is not learning about drama, but learning through drama. Drama's goals are based in pedagogical, developmental and learning theory as much as or more than being arts-based. Significantly, the focus is on the growth and development of the learner rather than the entertainment or stimulation of the observer.

By means of dramatic activities students use and examine their present knowledge in order to induce new knowledge. Bolton (1985) argues that while school learning is an accruing of facts, drama can help students reframe their knowledge into new perspectives. Therefore, this teaching technique places the learner at the centre of the programme design and encourages reflection and the development of greater understanding of self and others. Facilitators too can utilize the reflective dimension of drama in training programmes. This will help participants to make a personal commitment to training and develop greater knowledge about themselves and others and their role in the workplace. Drama works on the theory of raising a dilemma. A facilitator stops the action, and the learners offer possible methods of resolving the situation. The actors play out the various suggestions in context, and debate can follow concerning the outcomes.

According to van Ments (1994) the idea of role-play, in its simplest form, is that of asking people to imagine that they are either themselves or another person in a particular situation. Learners are asked to behave exactly as they feel that the other person would and, as a result, they and/or the rest of the class will learn something about the person and/or situation. Role-play then is a form of imaginization and communication that can be used for different purposes. Different types of role-plays demand different approaches – the way in which the role-play is introduced, the description of roles, the facilitation and the post-play analysis will vary according to the type of role-play that is being used. It can be used for example to describe or demonstrate events, to practise skills, to give feedback or to sensitize people to reflect upon events.

Any simulation is a technique that aims to provide the student with a highly simplified reproduction of part of a real or imaginary world. Gilley (1991) states that simulation fosters experiential exercises and learning. Drama can thus be used to explore a variety of concepts or themes. Participants can develop new insights and awareness as well as utilize those past and present experiences that will affect future learning. This method calls for active learner involvement and provides a unique type of 'learner ownership'. Organizations offering drama based training can address people skills required to deal with difficult issues such as diversity, sexual harassment prevention, and conflict and violence reduction. The following case studies illustrate the potential range of other real or acted experiential activities.

Case studies: Alternative activities – the circus and the radio

OLS Unique Solutions is a small business based in the UK, and prides itself on its creative approach to finding training solutions for the commercial sector.

Case study 1

OLS was asked to help energize and motivate an HR department after they had been through a major organizational change. The client requested that the end result could only be achieved through team co-operation and, secondly, that there needed to be scope to see colleagues 'in a new light'. OLS designed a workshop where the dele-

---

gates had 48 hours to devise, rehearse, resource and perform a circus show lasting 45 minutes for an audience of 300 schoolchildren. Specific skills varied from erecting the big top and learning clowning performance and trapeze to top-quality sound production. After the workshop, the HR manager described the event as 'the most effective team build I've ever been involved in'.

Case study 2

OLS was asked by a business consultancy to devise a training programme that would provide a mindset shift in the areas of problem solving and project management from the delegates. The programme also needed to benefit the local community. The project chosen was at a scout camp. The task was to deliver a challenge course with exacting requirements. Over a four-day period there were both theoretical and practical planning, action and evaluation phases. On day four, the scout camp took control of a newly completed challenge course. The client said that all the objectives were not only met but also exceeded by the project.

Case study 3

OLS was involved in a key strategy meeting for a national public service provider. The senior team was facing a major piece of strategy development work that required a positive mindset to ensure success. OLS set the team the challenge of producing a professional-quality 30-minute radio play. This involved designing, scripting, recording and the post-production of the piece. The initial reaction of the team was of disbelief, as they did not feel they could accomplish such a task in the time-frame. However, by the end of the day, all the individuals were amazed and felt enormous pride at what they were able to achieve. As a result of this new-found confidence, the business meeting the following day was highly positive and effective.

On completion of any delivery, the evaluation phase focuses on the outcomes. Feedback is vital.

The case studies above may explain why many leading-edge outdoor experiential providers, like Brathay in the UK, now possess drama studies and art labs alongside their kayaks and climbing gear.

METAPHORS AND STORYTELLING

There is a traditional saying, in 'metaphorical speak', which is, 'Let the mountain (the experience) speak for itself.' This refers to non-intervention strategies, but there is a school of thought that suggests that experiences, in the form of stories, need to be told:

> I believe that an awful lot of learning is possible through stories, so this approach could be very powerful. We at BP are all very good at corporate-speak, but, as a global organisation with ten percent of our revenue coming from Africa, how does that help someone refuelling a plane in Mozambique? We're trying to appreciate diversity, and storytelling could help us to do that.
>
> (Pollock, 2000: 21)

Pollock, in an article aptly titled 'That's infotainment' (2000), describes the diverse use of storytellers in the business world. The story is one of the basic tools invented by human beings for the purpose of gaining understanding. Indeed stories solidify our memories, and everyone looks for opportunities to tell their stories in one way or another (Schank, 1992). Collison and Mackenzie (1999) assert that there have been great societies that have not used the wheel, but none that have not used stories to generate ideas, morality and values. The earliest stories were probably chants or songs and contained epics, myths, parables, fables, fairy tales and folk tales:

> Asked to name the most powerful communication tools, few business people would be likely to list storytelling amongst them. That, however, may be changing, as organisations are re-awakening to the potential of one of the oldest forms known to man of passing on knowledge. In the UK, the organisations ranging from large retailing firms to government agencies are finding that working with story is a highly effective way to facilitate internal and external communication, develop teams and leadership skills, and to engage the attention of clients and customers.
>
> (Collison and Mackenzie, 1999: 38)

Some of the uses of stories in organizations include the communication of corporate values and ideals; adapting to change; defining and better adapting to organizational culture; communicating the essence of a complex message; exploring and developing leadership styles; developing communication and presentation skills; developing employees' relationship to a product or the organization. Parkin (1998), in *Tales for*

Trainers, describes the use of stories and metaphors to facilitate learning. She refers to the use of sets of cards that ask people to describe themselves as birthday presents or cartoon characters, or smells, or drinks. People might respond, she illustrates, by saying they are teddy bears because they are soft and cuddly, or that they are like water because it is pure, it flows and it supports life. In personal development, facilitators can create fantasy metaphors, and Parkin describes how the inexpressible can be explored by speaking in a non-prosaic language. The tale of the 'ugly duckling', for example, is a classic story relating to self-esteem. Parkin offers examples of stories aimed at personal development, business development and a wider world context. They can help people to 'analyse and maybe change their views about themselves and their levels of self-esteem' (Parkin, 1998: 18).

Storytelling and conversation analysis have also been used extensively in social science research and in conference work where management development issues and concerns need to brought to the forefront (Gold, 1996; Gabriel, 1998; Samra-Fredericks, 1998). The core of all psychotherapy is also based on storytelling, as clients tell and retell their stories as individual life-story or personal narrative. McLeod (1997: back cover) argues that 'all therapies are, therefore, narrative therapies, and that the counselling experience can be understood in terms of telling and re-telling stories. If the story is not heard, then the therapist and the client are deprived of the most effective and mutually involving mode of discourse open to them.'

The *survival note* is an example of the use of story to help surface and explore organizational culture. Teams are asked to agree and write a basic survival story of the key things that a replacement team would need to know about working in the organization. They are asked to focus on and describe to the newcomers the key to maintaining their existing 'way of doing things' to minimize the impact on existing customers or clients. Facilitators can also use stories to lessen participant anxiety, by creating stories that contain elements of self-disclosure, as seen below.

A short self-disclosure story

Learning from mistakes: interviews – an unfortunate incident on a Scilly island

The Scillies are known as the Fortunate Islands. Colin Beard tells a true short story of one unfortunate experience on the way to this island for an interview. He caught the wrong train, got off the train, tried to get a taxi to catch up with the right train – an intercity

---

express, but... no money, he went to the bank, oh no... queues, eventually in the taxi he was back on track, arrival at the heliport... oh no... he was booked on the helicopter the previous day... funny... he thought it was today... it was the wrong day for the interview... what a silly mistake... met the local vicar waiting in the queue... he was supposed to be on the interview panel! Was delayed by fog the previous day... he invited him to stay... then more fog and delays, arrive eventually on the Scillies... oh no... they gave the job to someone else the previous day...! Back home to lots of 'How did you get on?'

A note left by father-in-law (the moral of the story): 'S/he who never makes a mistake never makes anything!'

Having examined the many uses of humour in storytelling, and given practical suggestions, we now examine a specific case study on the use of images and stories, through the use of cartoons.

Case study: Adjusting reality – art and images

The use of cartoon images as a reflective tool embraces a mixture of art, humour and storytelling and, as Janni of the Royal Academy of Arts comments, 'arts-based learning is all about using different parts of your brain' (in Pollock, 2000: 19–23). Artists can be employed to create such images. Back in the early 80s Colin Beard used an artist to assist in a training programme for Shell executives in their prestigious Lensbury Club on the Thames. The delegates were people who were close to retirement, and to help them to move into semi-retirement they were asked to work with a Shell initiative, designed to help environmental projects. It was called the Shell Better Britain Campaign. Coming to terms with some of the difficulties of facing retirement, as well as working with environmentalists and environmental charities, was difficult for the people concerned. The culture of the organizations that they were likely to meet was probably going to be very different from their own. In their new role as officers for the Shell Better Britain Campaign, their job was to help advise groups and offer grants. By the end of each day the artist had many of their fears and concerns sketched on to huge sheets of paper in the form of cartoon images. It was cathartic to smile and laugh together at the images of Shell executives in Batman capes, abseiling down the Shell HQ in London, armed with rucksacks of information on the environment! Bulges of cheques filled the side pockets, and some were falling out, slowly floating down to the ground. The drawings also showed Inland Revenue letters about their tax, pensions, expenses and other issues hanging out of their back pockets, reflecting some of the other more personal concerns! The cartoons were great fun and they helped in the 'seeing' and 'airing' of difficult subjects. The funny, depersonalized neutrality is a strength in cartoon work. The 80s were the time when adult comics boomed (Mallia, 1997: 93), and our inspiration to use this medium came from more established superhero characters like Bob Kane's Batman in Gotham City and from *Peanuts*, created by the great Charles Schulz.

MANAGEMENT DEVELOPMENT AND CARTOONS

We regularly use powerful cartoon strips of learners on experiential learning programmes to convey important messages in both adult work and youth work. Sometimes we incorporate these into our own pre-prepared 'corporate newspapers'. Youth 'comics' or newspapers can take a different form and these might mimic the amusement arcade photo-booth approach where two people sit together to have their picture taken. The resultant photo is in the form of a printed page of a pretend newspaper, the *Daily Inquisitor*, reporting that 'two aliens have landed'.

In emotional intelligence work, we include a stereotypical picture of a woman sitting knitting on the sofa and a man reading the paper, ignoring the comment from his wife, 'It's not what you say, but what you don't say... and the way you don't say it!' The message is in the analysis of the humour of the dialogue or script, and the events and actions, as well as the physical character or expressions of the people portrayed.

One interesting account of the use of comic strips we came across, by Mallia (1997), refers to pioneering experiments with an ongoing soap-opera-style comic to aid the development of total quality management programmes (*Kaizen*) in a Maltese microelectronics industry. Comics, Mallia suggests, are capable of inducing interest in young and old alike, and yet have the potential to be a powerful reflective tool.

One of the earliest definitions of the genre is by Waugh, who suggested in 1947 that a comic is a form that must include these following elements: 'A narrative told by way of a sequence of pictures, a continuing cast of characters from one sequence to the next, and the inclusion of dialogue and/or text within the pictures' (Mallia, 1997: 96).

Here then we see the close link between cartoons and the art of story-telling and journeying. Parkin (1998: 3) comments that storytellers would typically be travellers or minstrels, passing on important information from town to town:

> Storytelling was seen as a vocation requiring many skills such as powerful communication, appropriate use of language, insight, sensitivity and accuracy, and in order to do the job well, the story-tellers had to develop their own minds in ways that other people at that time did not. They had to develop their memory and visualisa-tion skills, and using these skills, be able to trigger memorable pictures in the minds of their listeners, for it was in this way that the information would be best understood and remembered.

Parkin suggests that the ingredients for a good story are characters, a good plot, some sort of conflict and a resolution! Experiential providers might also consider becoming adept at storytelling, as 'scenarios' often form the backcloth to experiential activities. Consalvo (1995) suggests that scenarios that are fantasy or patently artificial require the internal consis-tency of a 'good story' to facilitate the suspension of disbelief, 'buy-in' and active engagement of the trainees.

Harrison, quoted in Mallia (1997), comments that 'essentially, the cartoon is a drawing which (a) simplifies, and/or (b) exaggerates'. Such simplification does not however exclude some cartoons from being intrin-sically complex. Comics, Mallia suggests, are next in line for acceptance within the world of experiential education and, as a unique form of enter-tainment, 'comic strips have become a social phenomenon. Their ability to capture contemporary economic and social events with remarkable accu-racy and finesse means they are preferred areas of study for... education-alists, who, at one time were apt to moralise about comic strips, [and] now use them as a teaching aid' (Schetter, 1992: 35).

Mallia suggests that the use of comics for instructional purposes is infi-nite. For example, he suggests that they can be used to act as ice-breakers at strategic points in the lessons. They can also be used to create interest in a subject being discussed, aesthetically elevate traditional instructional text, inspire emulation, generate tools for a new channel of communica-tion for the learners and project an atmosphere of informality.

In a cognitive capacity, comics can:

- communicate information;
- simplify instructions;

- be used to illustrate a point being made;
- be a tool in linguistic instruction;
- stimulate discussions;
- be a source of visual culture;
- be a mnemonic tool of cognitive retention.

(Mallia, 1997: 103)

CREATING COMIC STRIPS – SUGGESTIONS FOR GOOD PRACTICE

Cartoons can be used to tell a key outcome of an event, compare different perspectives of the same event, reflect upon the emotions, reflect upon learning or tell something about the characters involved. There is a tendency to think that jokes and humour must pervade all that is portrayed but learners should be discouraged from feeling a need to compete with professional cartoonists who do it for a living. Humour and jokes often have a deeper meaning. What really went on might be entered into speech bubbles or thought bubbles and captions (see Figure 4.1). Warm-up exercises are important, and drawers must not be too ambitious too early on. It is easier to fit story lines and dialogue to pictures than to create new pictures (and words) to fit a given story. Cartoons can allow difficult issues to surface in a non-threatening way.

Drawing hints and tips can be provided to include the need to use simple warm-up techniques for facial expressions, movement, characters and story creation. The sequence of pictures and speech bubbles go from left to right, ie whoever speaks first should be on the left of the picture, and it is necessary to start drawing any sequence from front to back, ie first draw whatever is nearest to you.

The speech and thought bubbles are easy to create in MS Word and MS PowerPoint, and can be found in AutoShapes/Callouts on the Drawing toolbar. Write the speech or thought before wrapping it with the bubble in case it doesn't fit. Simple lines and puffs of dust can be used to show movement.

USING PHOTOGRAPHIC IMAGES AND COMPUTER SOFTWARE

Digital images can be created using a digital camera, by scanning or by importing clip art, and these images can be simply brought together and reduced into a cartoon strip by importing them into presentation or drawing packages (such as MS PowerPoint).

Figure 4.1 Simple line drawing practice and reflection bubbles.

The method is unlike that of drawing techniques, in that empty speech and thought bubbles can be inserted beforehand and they can always be stretched or deleted later (see Figure 4.2). A computer database can be built up of own scanned images or digital photos.

Some images lend themselves to thought bubbles ('Hmmm…'), speech bubbles or captions, others to adding clip art to help explanation and understanding. Consider the selection and sequencing of images, ie who does this selection and when, as there are issues of power and control here. Similar results can be achieved without using high-tech equipment: an instamatic camera can be used to record images, and the photos can be sequenced (and rearranged) on a flip chart, allowing captions and speech bubbles to be added by hand on to the flip chart paper.

Cartoons and comic strips can be a powerful reflective tool. Combining art, dialogue, situations and outcomes, they can tell the story succinctly and humorously.

Cartoons offer a way of expressing feelings, anxieties or other emotions that may not surface via more traditional techniques. By capturing the essence of what is going on, rather than attempting to be an exact record, cartoons can help us dig a little deeper. However, using cartoons as a reflective tool is more difficult than it might at first seem. It is much easier to add speech or a script to pictures that are created or pre-prepared, or to photographs, than to try to create one's own pictures and words. Warm-up exercises can be used to build up a 'library' of picture elements, which can then be used to create the cartoon images. Alternatively, instamatic or digital cameras can be used to create real-life images and these can then be

Figure 4.2 Reflective tools – digital camera images and speech and thought bubbles.

sequenced, either manually or digitally, to form a cartoon strip. There are many other variations of cartoon and camera image work.

Cartoon sets of cards are now available for trainers to purchase (see Terrell, 2000). Each has statements and images about characteristics of people in teams. Then there are *photo snapshots*, a photo-mind method that can be used through pretending the person is a camera, creating snapshot images in his or her mind between blindfolded periods. This can be used in urban and wilderness settings, to create flashbacks, for recognition skills, to share special places and to create images that can have a lasting effect if carefully chosen. It can also be used to revisit places, physically or through imagination, or to capture special moments in activities that can be described by the 'camera' person.

READING AND WRITING – REFLECTIONS ON REALITY

Finally we consider the use of reading and writing as a powerful reflective tool in experiential learning, as 'biographical' work. Writing techniques are recognized and valued as important in facilitating experiential learning, and there are many techniques and formats that can be used. The techniques include *lifelines* and one method involves people using rope or cord to create a sequence of waves representing a linear picture of highs and lows in their life. A knot is tied along the line to delineate the point in life where people are now and so reflective thoughts and discussion can then focus on 'What next?' It is a powerful method of examining life and its joys. *Life periods* involves writing about events in life as if they were chapters of a book. McLeod (1997: 62), for example, describes work on psychodynamic narrative and structured life story interviews. He begins by asking people to think about their life as if it were an unfinished book, with chapters representing major parts of a person's life. It is suggested that there should be between three and eight chapters, and each chapter requires a name and an overall content description. The links between each chapter are also discussed in his work.

Others techniques might include:

- **writing lists and mind maps** – clusters of ideas on the topic;
- **guided imagery** – involves free writing stimulated by an image such as 'being on a journey';
- **stepping stones** – reviewing formative life experiences from the vantage point of the present;
- **the daily log** – to record the day's events;
- **the period log** – to record a current period in the writer's life;
- **dialogue** – creating a dialogue with a person, event or object from the writer's life;
- **altered point of view** – writing about oneself in the third person, or about someone else in the first person.

(from Lukinsky, 1990, in McLeod, 1997: 77)

We have used the writing of one's own obituary or that of a colleague through the process of interviewing. We use a newspaper page, with a column blanked out for the insertion of a new obituary. Alternatively an imaginary newsworthy story of something that someone has done can also be a powerful reflective tool to encourage people to review significant life events and focus on new aspirations and life plans. *Critical incident techniques, good practice audits* and *journal keeping* are all explored by Hunt (1999) in an excellent chapter on reflective practice.

Reading is something that many development trainers might incorporate more in learner programmes. Reading clearly provides opportunities for adventures in the mind, although it is perhaps seen as an academic thing to do, associated with school, university or college. This infrequent use of reading reduces opportunities to create indigenous or natural learning and conceptual thinking, a subject we explore in Chapter 8 on good practice and ethics. We also provide details of a reading experiment in Chapter 7 in a section on relaxed alertness. In the experiment we create a relaxed ambience and use a 'coffee and newspaper' approach to reading, exploring and encouraging indigenous thinking and modelling without any pressure.

Tony Buzan (2000), in his book on speed reading, refers to Vanda North, his book editor, who is ranked as one of the world's fastest readers. After speed reading training, she realized that: 'For 21 years she could have been reading twice the amount, with better comprehension, or she could have read exactly the same amount and had nearly a year extra to be with friends, to travel, to explore and to have even more fun!'

This is a good investment strategy under anyone's terms.

CONCLUSION

In this chapter we explored the nature of reality. The degree to which reality is perceived as real and the extent to which reality is manipulated is a key consideration in the design and delivery of experiential learning. Perceptions of reality apply to many dimensions of experiential learning, including the learning process itself, the activities provided and the location that they take place in. So-called 'real' projects or activities might include environmental or community work, a subject explored in detail in Chapter 5. Activities using plastic training kits, outdoor recreational pursuits, circus and radio production, newspaper editing and comic design, theatrical activities, drama, art, storytelling and writing might be perceived as simulated. However, providing activities that are perceived as either real or not real isn't the only way to influence the learning processes. The extent to which the learning environment is real, whether it be natural or simulated, outdoor or indoor, hotel rooms, urban jungle or wilderness landscapes, also influences learning potential, as we shall explore more in Chapter 5. Levels of reality can thus be lowered or raised to induce more effective learning, but making the right choices requires practice as well as a clear understanding of the processes involved. The degree to which activities, processes or the external learning environment itself are seen as real is also a significant factor to use to enhance learning. In this chapter we considered many facets of 'reality' and we explored how altering these levels provides opportunities to unlock greater potential to learn from experience.

5

Places And Elements

> ...*a salty breeze, burning leaves, the squish of mud, the sting of hot sand and the cold of snow are just a few among the plethora of sensory images we experience while outdoors.*
>
> (Consalvo, 1995: 2)

INTRODUCTION

More research will eventually lead to a greater understanding of the facets of the key tumblers in the learning combination lock and their relationship to one another. A limiting factor in the design and delivery of experiential learning programmes is the overemphasis on the design of 'activities', and this can result in less effective programmes. A lack of understanding as to the value, role and function of the location can have a similar consequence. Whilst there are numerous places to conduct experiential programmes, the learning environment will inevitably be much more than a classroom, an advanced kind of playground or a battlefield of unpredictable elements in the wilderness. There is more to its role than just the place or location; it is an essential integrated component of experiential learning interactions. A central debate connected with the nature of experiential learning revolves around the use of learning interventions by other people, and the extent to which the learning is indigenous. But the whole transactive process must also consider the learner's interaction with the place or the elements in the learning environment. The extent to which that too is contrived, natural or artificially constructed might alter the process of indigenous learning by participants, and as such is worthy of further exploration (see also Chapters 6 and 7). A four-way relationship can be seen in Figure 5.1.

The 'outdoors' for example conjures up words such as 'natural', 'earth' and the 'environment', all of which are used interchangeably in the literature, and it is here that many new opportunities for learning are to be found. In Chapter 3, we explored the role of journeys in the typology of

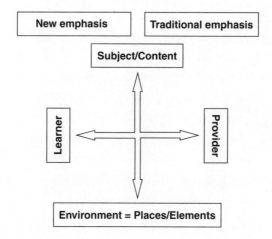

Figure 5.1 The four-way transactive process

provision, but the journey people experience will lose much of its mystery and richness if there is no time to pause to smell the flowers or to savour the breaking dawn. The natural surroundings of mountains, lakes and 'fresh air' energize and revitalize people, and beckon them back to their primitive roots. Consalvo (1995: 2) introduced her book of ready-made games for trainers with the following comment, which illustrates the immense sensory richness of the natural environment. Let the imagination flow and recall the sensations:

> Blue sky, red sunsets, white puffy clouds, green fields speckled with flowers, pine covered paths, moonlit meadows, crickets chirping, birds singing, snow crunching under foot, the smell of the spring thaw, summer sweetness, autumn decay, a salty breeze, burning leaves, the squish of mud, the sting of hot sand and the cold of snow are just a few among the plethora of sensory images we experience while outdoors. These sensations often tap emotionally and spiritually uplifting memories.

This quotation conjures up so many essential facets of the experience, which some providers cherish whilst others take them for granted. The environment is essential to creating pleasurable sensations and positive moods. The environment gives us natural ecstasy, and there are many elements or ingredients that can be used to increase sensitivity to learning:

- the changing seasons;
- heat and cold;

- wet, humid and dry;
- ebb and flow of tides;
- differences in day and night;
- natural rhythms of life;
- unpredictability of the elements;
- topography;
- dramatic landscapes;
- flora and fauna;
- natural art;
- spiritual awareness;
- remoteness;
- wild sounds.

The natural world is immensely variable, and includes many unpredictable sensations that can be used in the design of experiential learning opportunities.

These elements can be further divided into their sub-components. 'Remoteness' for example could include solitude, space, quietness and mental 'sorting-out time'. A cave is a good place to sit alone and listen, to experience total darkness, solitude or sensory deprivation for a short period. It is also a place to pick up new cues for developing communication skills for the phone or videoconference work, by talking in the dark with other colleagues so that no visual clues are present. Whilst some of these ingredients can also be simulated indoors, especially using virtual reality and computers, these techniques require more research in programme design. The future is exciting for experiential providers, as the outdoor learning arena gives rise to an endless array of experiences for people to interact with the terrain, the natural elements and the spirituality associated with the outdoors.

INDOOR–OUTDOOR, NATURAL–ARTIFICIAL

Indoor and outdoor places have much in common; they both have the word 'door' in them! To experience learning people can stay indoors or be taken outside. The opening of doors, metaphorically speaking, presents people with new opportunities, to go through doors in order to arrive somewhere else. When we use the term 'outdoor learning' we tend to think of a place, outside of the house, the space where the learning can occur; it is the so-called natural environment in which many experiential activities are conducted. The provision of experiential programmes is predominantly concentrated in two types of setting or environment: indoors, in rooms, and outdoors, usually but not exclusively in places of scenic beauty. The two differ greatly, but the boundaries are not always clear. Opportunities exist for experiential providers to diversify the use of the outdoor and indoor milieu too. A traditional classroom has ceilings, walls, floors, desks, books, computers and many other objects, all of which can be used in creative ways to enhance the learner experience. The floor is ideal to create models and concepts with large groups of people, using masking tape, large pieces of coloured card and other training aids. The walls are places to create 'graffiti walls' using decorating lining paper, so that people might contribute thoughts or reactions to events through drawing or scribbling words or phrases. Walls can also be used to place and move stick-it labels, or to project colours or images to influence mood.

The indoor location can take many forms and can be a drama studio, stage, art lab, greenhouse, hotel training room or climbing wall; and it might have ramps, underground caves or tunnels, or other features like artificial ice-climbing walls; and it can be real, virtual or imaginary. The indoor learning environment could be considered as a very 'artificial' or unnatural place to be, yet a cave is considered to be 'outdoors' and natural, even though it has a roof and walls and is 'inside' in a sense. A building without a roof, or walls on two sides might be regarded as both outdoors and indoors!

The outdoors can be brought indoors through simulation, when people create the outdoors through fantasy. Saunders (1988) describes a number of examples of indoor 'simulation gaming' under the umbrella of experiential learning. He includes an example of a game called Island Escape, where participants are stuck on a volcanic island that is about to explode, and comments that 'whilst this is a fantasy game, participants rapidly introduce themselves to other people, and reveal their backgrounds, interests and skills' (1988: 136). Saunders argues that simulation gaming combines the features of games (rules, players, competition, co-operation) with those of simulation (incorporation of critical features of reality). He suggests that it can be used most effectively for encouraging communication, and as a diagnostic and prognostic instrument. 'Diagnostics' involves detective work to identify issues for people to work on, with case studies that replicate the essential features of a real-life situation, whilst the 'prognosis' involves predicting future performances of people. The simulation takes place indoors, in a classroom or hotel for example, and uses a fantasy island for participants to escape from.

Greenaway (1999) offers an interesting insightful view of the terms outdoors and indoors. On his Web site, he refers to 'indoor–outdoor management development'. Common examples he describes are the well-known team decision-making exercises such as the NASA Moon Game and Desert Survival. One training organization is now apparently offering a whole range of resources of outdoor scenarios (for using indoors) from which to choose: stranded on an island, stuck in the jungle or marooned in the Arctic Circle, for example. Their brochure describes how trainers can enhance realism with a set of 20 slides that will make participants glad they are warm and dry. Greenaway describes this as being in direct contrast to the outdoors, where metaphorical associations with work are provided by mountains becoming cashpoints, canoes becoming taxis and ropes becoming telephone cables. This presents an interesting contrast. Whilst indoor trainers liven up sessions by bringing in the excitement of the 'simulated outdoors', outdoor trainers seemingly take for granted the outdoors, concerned with making metaphoric links to the indoor world of work, ensuring transfer and justifying being outdoors. Greenaway then goes on to look further at the similarities, not the differences, noting that the outdoors and the indoors have much in common:

- **Powerful images**. Both real and simulated outdoors evoke powerful images.
- **Neutral settings**. Real and simulated outdoors provide a neutral setting where participants will be equally disadvantaged.
- **Back to basics**. Without sophisticated technology to assist or blame, the demands and issues tend to be simple, basic and inescapable. Excuses and pretensions tend not to survive for long in 'survival' situations (whether real or imagined).
- **Novice learners**. The novelty of an outdoor scenario (real or simulated) instantly places managers in the role of the learner. This willingness to appear before peers as a 'learner' seems more likely in an outdoor setting than in a setting that more obviously resembles work and in which a manager is already supposed to be reasonably competent.
- **Span of relevance**. To bridge the gap between outdoor and work settings generally requires a wider span of relevance than bridging the gap between two work settings. Practice in making connections across wide gaps increases the range of experiences that managers can bring to bear on any one problem.
- **Depth of learning**. Where learners do succeed in making connections between two very different settings, they tend to be more at profound levels. It is important to distinguish here between the relatively superficial connections that are designed into exercises, and the more profound connections made by individual managers when flashes of insight jump across the gap between 'outdoors' and 'work'.
- **Versatility**. Managers can more readily test, discover and demonstrate their potential and versatility (an important asset for managers facing change) in settings or simulations that are most different from their everyday work.

- **Enhanced realism**. Both approaches claim to make the training experience more realistic, but what could be further from reality than imagining that a neatly trimmed lawn is an alligator swamp or that a mountain top is a cashpoint (both outdoor training exercises), or imagining that an air-conditioned training room is a jungle or an Arctic wilderness (both indoor training exercises)? These would all be triumphs of the imagination over reality! What is surely meant by 'realism' in these contexts is more intense involvement – whatever the balance of fact and fiction, and however similar or different to work the experience may be.

In the latter point Greenaway explores the nature of reality and its relationship to the degree of engagement or involvement of the participants, a subject explored at length in Chapter 4.

Numerous outdoor locations are available to define and enhance experiential learning further. The parameters of the term 'outdoors' are limited not just to land-based activities. Some providers, such as High Performance in Hampshire, UK, use their 70-foot boats to do much of their experiential management development work. Is this outdoors or indoors? Why use water, and why boats? It could be that for many people the experience is novel, for some there might be a fear of water to overcome or a special journey to be undertaken, or it might represent power and status for an elite group. Understanding why is crucial to design of the learning environment. Outdoor experiential development can of course take place on boats, outdoors or indoors, in the air, on water, in underground caves or on land. But all these locations can be still further divided. Land can include habitats or terrain such as jungle, forests, desert or mountains. Figure 5.2 illustrates the range of environments.

The urban, built environment is attracting more interest from experiential providers for a number of reasons. The urban environment can be accessible, cheaper on travel and time costs, a very challenging and rich social environment for experiential learning for people of all ages. Sometimes referred to as the 'concrete jungle', it can be exhilarating and exciting, and Proudman (1999) suggests that there is a need to 're-mystify' the urban environment. The powerful 'solo' experience or meditative sorting time, crucial to our inner reflective processing, might be taken in an urban cathedral or church, for example. The quiet hotel overspill car park can also be a good place for outdoor activities, where marked parking bays offer grids for the imaginative provider to use. The urban environment can be closer to home or work for many people, and it is rich in cultural ingredients that provide learning opportunities for the observation of social phenomena. It can also be frightening and intimidating, and can be seen in a negative light. The authors' international outdoor

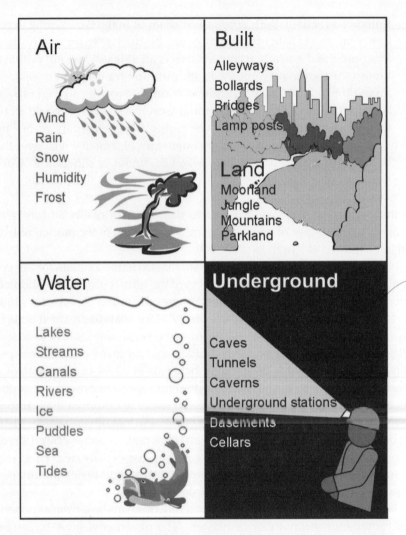

Figure 5.2 The environment grid

management development work in places such as Kenya and Beirut has highlighted to us the real and very different risks associated with venturing outdoors to work in a city environment, as opposed to the comfort of the hotel or National Park. High levels of anxiety about venturing out into the city were expressed by many African and Arab participants on one development programme. Urban safety management, maps and careful briefing can help, but the risks should be taken seriously, and challenge by choice, addressed in Chapter 8, is an important rule.

Urban adventure programmes can provide similar development opportunities to wilderness programmes, and the resemblance can be remarkable. The recognition of the value of urban socio-ecology underpinned the development of the 'urban wildlife movement', emerging originally in the UK from the heart of Birmingham in 1979. There is a fantasy connection here too, as J R R Tolkien's *The Lord of the Rings* was based on a wet woodland known locally as Moseley Bog, and it was the protection of this site that became the inspirational force that gelled the early pioneers of the urban wildlife movement. Urban wildlife projects can make ideal activities for people to undertake as the activities for experiential learning, a subject that we explore later in this chapter. Urban parks, woodlands and waterways can serve as places for adventure experiences. The urban canal system offers opportunities to journey on land and water, and the physical environment of buildings and walls provides ideal abseil and climbing opportunities. In the USA, the term 'buildering' has been coined to describe this activity (Proudman, 1999: 331). The urban environment includes bollards, kerbs, lamp-posts, pavements, trees, gutters and benches for innovative use in experiential programmes. Urban spoil heaps can provide for scrambling and biking. In the UK, one outdoor activity centre has benefited from funding from the Lottery and built a 'rock park'. The first of its kind in the UK, it consists of huge boulders lined by bridges, allowing climbers to cross from one to the next in continuous sequences. This leads us to consider the nature of artificially constructed learning environments, and where the boundaries of 'real' environments and 'artificial' environments interface, a subject of much debate. Many so-called natural landscapes are indeed created by human activity.

ARTIFICIAL URBAN ENVIRONMENTS

Throughout the world a diverse array of artificial environments is being constructed for the purposes of adventure and play, often emerging out of industrial dereliction. A climbing 'wall', for example, can be located on the outside or inside of a building, or in an alleyway at home within an urban or rural environment. Attarian (1999: 345) defines such an environment as a 'man made structure, device, or environment that simulates a natural setting, which can be used specifically for teaching or participating in outdoor activities'. Such structures can take many forms, from complex aircraft flight simulators for pilot training to indoor ramps, caves and tunnels. Their use for experiential teaching and learning is of greater significance than has hitherto been realized. In the USA in Arizona in 1970, the first major artificial surfing environment called the 'Big Surf' was created on an island lagoon:

the United States is a land of technological extremes, where simulations are a cultural norm. For example, respondents pointed out that they perceived the United States as the world leader in simulation training for aircraft pilots, automobile drivers, and the militia. Americans, in some parts of their nation, cannot get easy access to adventure environments and hence, have developed such artificial challenges as ropes courses to simulate 'real' adventure experience. Americans are more accepting and more promoting of simulation than the British for these reasons. The British prefer to do the 'real thing – what it's really all about' as several related in their comments.

(Priest, 1995)

The urban environment lends itself well to working with interesting urban community initiatives, with inner-city schools and other urban groups, and it is the environment where many of the 'at-risk' youth are growing up. Working with urban projects can provide opportunities for youth development and management development alike. It is also in the urban environment that many young people are using initiative, in a very entrepreneurial way, turning their experience of urban play into business ventures (Beard, Rhodes and Waller, in press). In the UK, in Sheffield, many artificial recreational sites, developing in an ad hoc cluster, transform urban decay and dereliction. Europe's largest dry-ski resort with ski-slopes, snowboarding, tobogganing and ski water-jumping is built on old spoil heaps. Nearby, converted out of semi-derelict buildings, 'the Foundry' was a first for Britain in that it was the start of a new breed of fully commercial indoor climbing walls, attracting 60,000 people at its peak in 1996. It was host to the first European indoor climbing championships. But it was young students who transformed their undergraduate dissertation ideas into a real experience, creating the Foundry. Located opposite are the offices of a company that offers the ultimate in adventure tourism. The company, called Jagged Globe, formed by experienced mountaineers, offers people a chance to pay to reach the summit of Everest.

Nearby a skating and rollerblading building called 'the House' is located. It was created by unemployed young teenagers by transforming an old abandoned warehouse. They were initially just enthusiasts, wanting somewhere to stunt-play and have fun, and they seized upon an opportunity to rent a derelict warehouse. These young people now operate a successful business, providing skateboarding and rollerblading for many other young people. Their experience of 'business' is exciting and natural for them, and it has grown from their own indigenous experience and sense of adventure. They naturally shifted from play to entrepreneurial activity, following their natural instincts. This illustrates experiential learning at its best. Their business brings with it a whole subculture of clothing, music and language, and the House appears to be a replacement of the 'youth club' for some of their customers.

Unofficial motorbike scrambling also occurs on the nearby slopes, and mountain bikers are attempting to gain European funding to enter the adventure zone and create a commercial artificial mountain bike site. A few miles away at Sheffield's Rother Valley Country Park, a recreational site developed on old coal spoil heaps, the British championships of a new type of board sport called 'all-terrain boarding' were held in 1998. This boarding is just like snowboarding, but with pneumatic tyres and suspension, so you can ride all the year round on grass, through trees, on dirt tracks, even on track and on road. At nearby Doncaster, the world's first environmental theme park – the Earth Centre – mixes tourism and adventure with visitors' education and experiential learning about the environment. It too has been developed on the site of an old coal mine.

In 1994 a company called Rockface in Birmingham created a much broader leisure experiential environment, again from a derelict warehouse in the city. Whilst the climbing walls form the foundation of the centre experience, there are also bars and restaurants. The centre offers a range of experiences for different visitor groups, including programmes for people with disabilities, training for executives, children's activities, and family fun and adventure. The climbing walls are adorned with a range of artefacts, such as artificial drainpipes and toilets, which amuses many of the teenagers. The walls and ceilings house abseiling platforms, rope bridges, a Jacob's ladder, a tower game and an artificial cave. The cave has been created using wooden panels to form a box structure around the rear of the climbing walls. Painted black to create almost total darkness, the caves also house climbing holds, chimney breasts, ramps and circular tunnels of various dimensions, and the routes change levels using trapdoors in the floors or ceiling. In darkness people experience many sensations, some 'natural' and some artificially stimulated. Masses of thin rope dangle down from the ceiling in places on to people's backs, and some floor areas are crunchy natural gravel. Small bells tinkle to give delicate sounds, which the designers have built in especially for people with various levels of sensory disability. The site is continually evolving and it is difficult to classify it as a teaching classroom, a recreational site, a funfair or a leisure centre. It is this multiple perception that underlies its unique success as a place to experience. Nearby is the Snowdome, where the artificial snow is created to supplement artificial surface technology. Quite by chance some cities are developing their 'adventure zones', replacing old industries and the world of production and traditional 'work' with rejuvenating businesses involved in the world of leisure, tourism, training, coaching, play, learning and adventure (Beard, Rhodes and Waller, in press):

places of work	to	places of adventure, coaching, leisure and learning;
workers	to	business owners and managers;
mines/mechanical production	to	places for recreation and play;
derelict	to	regenerative in nature;
environmentally damaging	to	reducing recreational pressure on the natural;
old industries	to	new ones.

And in time some will become institutionalized, moving from:

inventive fun	to	recreation;
recognized recreation	to	competitive sports;
sports	to	Olympic sports.

PEDAGOGY AND PERSONAL DEVELOPMENT

Whilst the overt goal might be to add to the dynamic of stunts, fun, recreation or play, pedagogy and personal development clearly underpin such initiatives. In the urban factories and surrounding streets, young people invent new stunts, developing their own adventure, creating their own challenges and rewriting the rules of education. They learn through fun and recreation. Their skills eventually become institutionalized as qualifications embrace the skills of their 'stunts'. Whilst qualifications exist for sailing, swimming and gymnastics and are already well established, new skills are emerging for skateboarding, stunt-biking and indoor climbing. The young climbers' Spider Club in the UK has developed its own star ratings for its young climbers to progress systematically through stages of learning. This development of the Spider Club grading was partly in recognition of the unsuitability of the adult international route classification system based on the 'degree of difficulty' (Arran, 1998). The young climbers start at a grade associated with recreational fun climbing, but opportunities are provided for the development of more serious competitive climbing if children want to.

Experiential learning: Urban climbing and young people

Levels of UK Spider Club awards – the Foundry, Sheffield

Five indoor levels of competence – leading to two outdoor levels:

- **White Spider.** I can climb to the top of the basic vertical wall; I can belay using a stitch plate under close supervision; I can tie a figure-of-eight knot with help; etc.

- **Yellow.** I can safely put on a safety harness; I can describe the differences between top roping, leading, bouldering, traversing and soloing; etc.
- **Orange.** I can tie a bowline knot with a fisherman's knot as a stopper; I can belay a lead climber with close supervision; etc.
- **Green.** I know how to tie off a stitch plate; I can tie a clove hitch knot; etc.
- **Blue.** I can 'down-climb' a route of grade 15 on any Foundry walls; I can traverse both sides of the corridor using only features for feet, and red/blue handholds; etc.
- **Purple Outdoor Spider.** I can climb a top-roped grade severe on limestone; I can climb a top-roped grade severe on gritstone; etc.
- **Gold Outdoor Spider.** I can demonstrate how to protect a climb by placing cramming devices, wires and hexes as running belays; I can name and describe the characteristics of three types of rock; etc.

(Arran, 1998)

These urban adventure sites allow for competitions with carefully simulated routes being designed for coaching, training and development programmes. But the young climbers are also forming a new breed; some have not tasted so-called 'real' natural outdoor climbing at all. Artificial climbing walls are now used by 82 per cent of UK climbers, 42 per cent of them on a weekly basis.

Recent advances in technology have also given rise to a new breed of artificial ice walls that have the consistency of toffee and so return to their original shape ready for the next climber. All these artificial environments offer the advantage that they can easily be manipulated or altered. Reconfiguration creates a new set of challenges, and new climbs or skate stunts are being sought by many young people as they search for their own adventure learning on the doorstep, after school and particularly in the winter months. Surface technology and route design are key to this thriving new business area of simulated indoor activity-based learning and play, and there are clear technical, social, environmental and commercial advantages. These sites also create new opportunities for providers of experiential learning, for corporate training or youth development programmes.

The advantages of simulated recreation environments

- **Social**:
  - can take part regularly; high levels of accessibility, by walking or public transport; for the urban and rural population;
  - potential for greater social interaction: crowds, spectators, cafés, clothing, music, youth culture, etc;
  - reduced trespass, eg mountain bikers;
  - reduced conflict with other users: public on streets, as in skate-boarding, and in National Parks, as in mountain biking;
  - located off the streets.
- **Commercial**:
  - potential to increase the number of participants and beginners;
  - all-season participation possible;
  - suitability for experienced and beginners;
  - creates a new market of participants;
  - suited to experiential development programmes for managers, youth, children, etc;
  - equipment and clothing sale/provision at location;
  - café/bar and tourism functions;
  - time and space zoning.
- **Environmental**:
  - controlled environment: 'conditions';
  - less susceptibility to the unpredictable elements of the natural environment;
  - less travel: people and equipment;
  - potentially less environmental impact;
  - less direct physical environmental damage;
  - less pollution;
  - less ecological damage;
  - less environmental unpredictability;
  - less risk.
- **Technical**:
  - mimic the 'best bits': features and obstacles;
  - local natural environment may not contain the necessary features in one place;
  - a valuable training resource;
  - creating new champions, in sport and recreation;
  - added safety for schoolchildren/youth, managers, etc;
  - artificial lighting provides winter opportunities in UK: floodlit;

> - controllable conditions;
> - can create unique/unnatural challenges: totally new and *not* found in natural conditions – beyond the natural.
>
> (Beard, Rhodes and Waller, in press)

Further significance of these artificial environments also lies in the fact that they offer more locations for the four-step approach that we discuss in Chapter 8 on ethical practice. Barrett and Greenaway (1995) offer ways to overcome the negative effects of returning from a significant wilderness experience, and here we create a four-stage process that uses urban locations for entry and exit to residential programmes in wilderness locations, such as National Parks, or overseas. The notion of a journey through time and space so that the learning gap or need can be 'seen' is covered in the model in Figure 3.2. Here the 'support wave' (see Figure 5.3) provides a step process for people to realign themselves, and so avoid the negative shock and consequence of a sudden dramatic return to start-point environments.

THE SENSORY POWER OF NATURE

…an exceptional creation – a corner of the world that is immensely old, full of surprises, lovingly and sometimes miraculously well maintained, and nearly always pleasing to look at. It is one of the busiest, most picked over, most meticulously groomed, most conspicuously used, most sumptuously and relentlessly improved landscapes on the planet.

(Bryson, 2000: 1–2)

1. **Close-to-home introduction** – indoor, urban, artificial or work location
2. **Outward Bound experience** – natural environment/wilderness experience
3. **City-bound** – for working on preparation for the last stage
4. **Homeward: family- or work-bound** – for supported transfer of learning

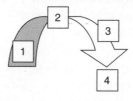

Figure 5.3 The four-stage support wave

The landscape in most countries is mostly artificial and created by human intervention. Outside the classroom lies the urban environment, then the urban fringe, then artificial landscapes and finally remote and largely unaltered wilderness. All such environments provide unpredictable extremes of stimulation. In Chapter 2 we commented on the fact that many people experience an avalanche of hundreds or thousands of consumptive advertising stimuli every day from television, radio, notices, street hoardings and so on. This creates a blinding over-stimulation and habituation to the stimuli. Away from all this, in the more 'natural outdoors' this sensory dulling and habituation is removed and replaced with completely new, unfamiliar stimuli and signals. Certain activities can increase the stimulation of the senses as the conduits for learning. This is vital to the enhancement of the experience.

In a widening range of learning environments we can increase our ability to heighten sensations in order to take our learning into the realm of an exciting adventure. Although wilderness can provide the environmental stimulation, the routes to learning are through key sensors, ie the mouth, ears, eyes, nose, nerves and, the sixth sense, intuitive insights. There is a view that there are many other senses, including awareness of air pressure, and other extra-sensory sources. These sensory 'entry points' are key routes, and they all offer exciting new opportunities to be more effective in experiential learning. They can be tuned in, as we shall explore in Chapter 7, by music or other impulses. The senses are often in tune with the natural rhythms in the natural environment, and so sensory channels can be pre-sensitized prior to an experiential activity or event. Such sensitizing is a vital part of our ability to create a good experiential learning climate that enables the doors of our mind, body or spirit to be opened up.

The senses offer at least six different routes. In the outdoors these evolutionary attuned sensory entry points can be more intensely stimulated. The rainforests for example are the extremes of such natural sensory bombardment, as it is here that people can listen attentively to thousands of animals that continuously send out signals, such as those associated with encroaching animals or humans. The senses can be alerted to read the changes in light, humidity, wind, colour and shadows. People can feel a storm coming although they cannot see it. Experiential learning is as much about observing and reflecting as doing, and the outdoors is a good place to sharpen observational and sensing skills. One such sensory technique is the 1,000-centimetre micro-hike, to focus on minute detail!

Understanding the availability of natural resources and maximizing their use without damage is an essential skill. Outward Bound Singapore (OBS) is located on the beautiful island of Pulau Ubin. It is also known as the Adventure Island. The location was specially selected for such activities and from here many of their development activities use the local rainforests, mangrove swamps, a quarry and the surrounding seas and offshore islands. Outward Bound Singapore also have a swimming pool in the tropical jungle, and a gymnasium and climbing wall that is not really inside or outside. The climate in Singapore is humid and warm, and so some 'classrooms' are covered but not completely walled, so as to create a cool breeze. These rooms are neither indoors nor outdoors.

In the UK the majority of outdoor development providers are clustered in the places that are designated as Areas of Outstanding Natural Beauty or National Parks. Indeed it is said that in the Lake District National Park in the UK there exists the largest cluster of development training organizations in the world.

Nature and Culture

Native American people, and their beliefs, are discussed in an article called 'Spirit of the Earth' by Georgina Peard. Peard (1999) offers an analysis of a speech by a Native American chief. The useful summary analysis shows the perspectives on nature taken by Western civilization and by Native Americans:

Native American	Western civilization
at home in nature	fear
belonging	ownership
community	individualism
spiritual	capital
sustainable	exploitation
freedom	domination

This dichotomy is oversimplistic; the Norwegians for example have an important concept of *friluftsliv*, or feeling at home with nature (Barnes, 2000). The natural elements can help us to be in tune with the environment and move us towards empathetic strategies, thus removing basic fears about nature. Mohawk (1996) describes how Western fairy tales paint pictures of nature as foreboding and dark. 'Natural' places are where Hansel and Gretel got lost, and where Sleeping Beauty was surrounded by thorn bushes and immense forests. Natural places possessed 'wild' animals and 'savage' people, and both had to be tamed. The psychological origins of modern negative mindsets are not only rooted in folklore. They are found in modern law, the negative nature of corporate environmental policy, and environmental taxation (Beard, 2000). Experiential learning in the natural outdoors can provide ways of re-framing our thinking about the natural environment, by altering our inner scripts, changing the 'metaphors', 'images', 'labels' and 'functions'. Using the natural environment would be very powerful in corporate environmental awareness training, yet this form of training rarely uses the natural environment as a teaching medium (Beard, 2000). People often refer to being exposed to the elements, but what are these elements we find outdoors? Five important basic ingredients of the earth interact with people in different ways according to Reed (1999). These are earth, air, fire, water and spirit. Reed suggests that they are important symbols. Fire, he suggests, is a symbol of action and creativity, and of destruction and new life. Fire can send people into simple, meditative, reflective states simply by being watched. Water can symbolize feelings, emotion and dark undercurrents. Air symbolizes ideas and intellectual pursuits but also insubstantial dreaming and lofty idealism. The fifth element, spirit, pervaded all that Reed's group did over a weekend but he noted that 'the ether is invisible, insubstantial but ubiquitous'. Higgins (1996, 1997), in his writing on outdoor education, refers to nine elements:

- earth;
- fire;
- water;
- air;
- weather;
- shelter;
- food;
- darkness;
- silence.

Colours cause changes in our emotions, and the faster the impulse or wavelength frequency the warmer the colour. Room colours can easily be altered by projection through coloured glass or plastic, or coloured light bulbs or overhead transparencies or electronic software to influence or alter moods. Red helps to stimulate blood and is good for activity areas. Violet is good for sleep, calms the body and balances the mind. Blue lowers blood pressure and reduces stress, whereas green balances the body and is a spirit colour. Negative ions are known to produce good moods and these negative ion concentrations are found after rainstorms and around bodies of circulating water such as waterfalls, seashores and rivers. They may even be associated with shower water. Positive ion concentrations produce bad moods and are associated with smog or warm, dry winds (Thayer, 1996). Watching fire, listening to the flowing water and noticing the silence are powerful experiences. Breathing the clean morning air, savouring and appreciating basic shelter and food, and experiencing darkness are less common everyday experiences for increasing numbers of people. For stressed people these can be very welcome experiences. However, they must be treated like the volume control when listening to your favourite music: too loud and the stimulus can be painful, too low and it has little impact. The ideal stimulus solutions for learning lie somewhere in between, but they can vary according to our needs and moods.

Examples of places (environment) and elements are (see also Figure 5.4):

Places (Environment)	Elements	Places (Environment)	Elements
hotel grounds	earth	mountains	heat and cold
urban city	fire	moorland	wet, humid and dry
underground stations	water	cliffs	ebb and flow of tides
caves	air	scree	day and night
cellars	weather	bog	natural rhythms of life
alleyways	shelter	classrooms	spiritual
pavements	food	carpets	topography
basements	darkness	walls	dramatic landscapes
lakes	silence	ceilings	flora and fauna
rivers	changing seasons	parkland	natural art

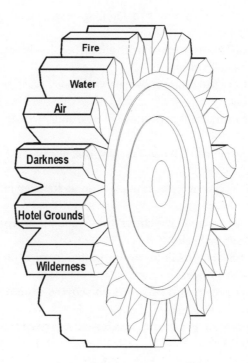

Figure 5.4 Tumbler two: place and elements

Physical activity is not the only way to achieve an energy boost or emotional 'high', and this is where a greater understanding of the role of the natural environment in creating moods and sensations is essential. In 'Fire in the sky', Walker (1999) explores the three dimensions of 'self, others and nature', as used by Colin Mortlock. He proposes some activities that he suggests can improve participants' interconnectedness to the earth (see below).

Activities to awaken the senses

Activities to awaken the senses include:

- **self-introductions** (respect for diversity of individual stories, how you got there);
- **sitting on the ground** or natural materials (simple contact with the earth);
- **sitting to talk in circles** not lines (cyclic nature of life processes and natural things);
- **sitting silently observing** together (sharing different perceptions of the world);
- **being inactive and alone** (quietening down, going inwards, inviting nature in);
- **walking differently from in the city** (eg slowly, silently, blind-folded – unfamiliarity);
- **walking barefoot** (direct contact with dewy grass, rock, wood, earth, leaves);
- **walking in unfamiliar places** (gorges, undergrowth, logs, snow);
- **leading**, giving help (risking, reaching out, human care and contact);
- **being led**, receiving help (expecting, understanding human care and contact);
- **focusing on natural rhythms** (tide, wind, sunset/rise, stars, moonrise/set, night sky);
- **focusing where possible on wood fire** (natural processes, history of life, universe);
- **telling, inventing and listening to stories, legends of the earth** (images of other ways of life);
- **sleeping on the ground**, if possible outside (expanding awareness, dreaming).

(Walker, 1999)

Figure 5.5 shows the senses tumbler of the learning combination lock.

Senses

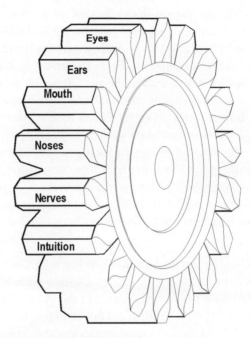

Figure 5.5 The third tumbler: the senses

EMPATHETIC STRATEGIES AND THE OUTDOOR 'CURE'

A deep interest in the environment can develop at any time, but for some people, the time when the pace of life slows down will have a significant effect in this respect. More time becomes available to be interested in other things such as phenomena in the natural environment...

(Ogilvie, 1993: 18)

Many writers are concerned about the overusage of the wilderness by an ever-growing population escaping to the outdoors seeking a 'fresh air fix' (Ogilvie, 1993; Cooper, 1998). Ogilvie suggests that this degradation is now on a scale such that lip service to environmental issues is no longer enough. He notes that the UK Sports Council, in a report called *A Countryside For Sport*, published in 1992, calls for sustainable participation and the need to maintain the natural resource in the long term:

The traditional attitude of many outdoor users to the environment in regarding it mainly as a playground or testing place for the self... can place them in the uncaring category. In adventure or survival courses and even in some types of personal development courses based purely on challenge, the outdoors is seen as an antagonist to be conquered and overcome because the priority is the benefit that is derived for the individual. Much lower down the list of priorities is the effect on the environment. Such exploitative rationale will encourage attitudes which induce the participant to see the environment as a rival or a competitor, as something to be dominated, subjugated to the human will… Leaders need to instigate a process to change attitudes by incorporating in their aims and practices, values that embrace the ideas of reverence for, protectiveness towards and harmony with the natural environment. The competitive, exploitative approach too often entails violation and desecration. A desirable shift in aims would be to replace it with the gentler, more respectful, co-operative ethic which would be conducive to reduced wear and tear.

(Ogilvie, 1993: 25)

Ogilvie also embraces the environment in his adapted version of John Adair's action-centred leadership model. Ogilvie adds a fourth dimension, the earth, arguing that in the context of the 90s it would make sense to construct this model with a fourth circle (see Figure 5.6).

With the pressure to provide novelty (Irvine and Wilson, 1994) some providers feel that adrenalin-raising activities or confrontational-type experiences will excite and motivate some people (see, for example, Vanreusel, 1995). The requirement of challenge and risk can also create adversarial, aggressive approaches to the natural world, where some elements of nature are seen as providing a powerful negative force to be overcome. Many organizations continue to fail to respect the fact that they make direct profit out of the natural environment, and regard it as a free resource. Mortlock (1984) warns against professional insensitivity towards the environment and suggests that there should be an awareness of, respect for and love of *self*, balanced against an awareness of, respect for and love of *others*, balanced against an awareness of, respect for and love of the *environment*.

Encouraging people not to take the environment for granted, to take positive action and give something back to the environment can be promoted in so many different ways, and such behaviour can help to avoid environmental alienation and exploitation. The earth is the bank upon which we draw all our cheques.

The economic value of the environment is underestimated. The environment has an important role in any enterprise. The environment provides a place to dump our waste, the arena for recreation and adventure and places to go on holiday. But there are difficulties associated with

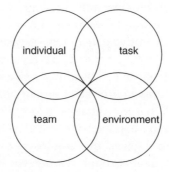

Figure 5.6 The team, the task, the individual and... the environment

applying traditional economic models to any monetary value of nature. The environment for example is the ultimate provider of all our resources. If we harvest too many natural resources then the environment becomes degraded, and education, leisure and recreation are all adversely affected.

We have already explored how the environment affects our moods, how the environmental rhythms link into people rhythms and how some elements of the environment can inspire and uplift us. Charlton (1992) in a chapter about the development of leaders using the outdoors, comments that the use of the outdoors as an educational 'resource' has a long history in Western culture. He notes that there have been many protagonists of the view that there is not a single social ill or physical problem that would not respond to a course of treatment in the outdoors. Charlton noted the prevalent dichotomy of approaches towards the outdoors, and uses terms such as 'combative' (conquering) towards the natural elements, or 'empathetic' (affinity). Paradoxically the Western world does tend to see the environment both as a cure and as something to be used and exploited, creating some degree of personal alienation to and disconnection with natural forces. The historical perspective of the outdoors as a therapeutic environment is reflected upon by Charlton. He noted that as long ago as 1762 Rousseau (in *Emile*) was urging parents to send their children into the countryside 'so that they may regain, amid fields, the vigour they have lost in the unwholesome air of places too thickly populated' (quoted in Charlton, 1992: 454.). In scouting, it was long ago regarded that exposure to wilderness was a suggested cure for everything from flat-footedness to 'bad citizenship'!

The environment has long been regarded as an important place for healing, repair and personal development. Miles (1995) offers a US view on wilderness as a healing place, a place for programmes helping people 'at risk', renowned for its rehabilitating power, for recuperation, for developing management skills, for personal spiritual well-being and for youth work. Significant epistemological and ontological challenges face such research. 'Biophilia', for example, concerns the environmental effects on people such as the post-operative patient recovery rates when subjected to stimulation in the natural environment; the results are promising. The person–environment relationship is of course a two-way process, and the subtle impact of the natural environment on our health is now receiving more attention. Research that was carried out long ago by Ulrich (1974) set out to measure the attractive and aversive human physiological responses to natural phenomena. It suggests that combative strategies may operate against natural stimuli that are produced when we are in natural outdoor environments. Some early research was carried out on post-operative patients in hospital and early indications were that patients who overlooked natural green space had shorter post-operative stays and fewer post-surgery complications, and required less medication and analgesics.

More recently, Kellert (1993) suggests that spending time in green space has the following physiological responses:

- reduced heart rate;
- reduced blood pressure;
- decrease in circulating stress hormones;
- increase in cognitive functioning, performance and creativity;
- alterations in brain activity in the alpha frequency range;
- relaxation of stress-induced muscle tension.

These responses are said to come from a number of stimuli:

- colours;
- textures;
- natural smells;
- decreased noise pollution or more interesting sounds, such as running water;
- exposure to the elements (wind, rain, heat, cold, etc).

Some doctors now advise 'countryside walks' as an alternative option to drug or medicine prescriptions. The natural environment is a place for learning about self-healing, although many people remain sceptical about the claims made, doubting the power the natural environment has. The sceptics rely on others to prove it to them, yet the overwhelming evidence suggests that it is the very spiritual and emotional nature of the outdoor environment that underpins the reason for its power; perhaps it cannot be measured. This leads us towards a realization that indeed there might be something very, very magical 'out there'. The truth about nature and the nature of truth are elusively intertwined.

The earth, particularly the outdoor natural environment, still has much to offer both as the 'location' for the delivery of experiential learning programmes and as an integral part of experiential product ingredients. This is significant in terms of the design and delivery of experiential programmes. A skill that is increasingly required of providers is the ability to alter, in a positive and beneficial way, many of the environmental ingredients that make up an effective experience for learning.

RAFTS OR WILDLIFE PROJECTS?

We discuss some of these issues in more detail in Chapter 8, which explores good practice. Programme designers and providers use the outdoors, increasingly introducing new and innovative methods that have resulted from the deconstruction of the ingredients found in the more traditional outdoor recreational-based activities. Many are now substituting environmental activities or community-based activities in place of recreation pursuits such as climbing or abseiling (Beard, 1996). These programmes are much more empathetic to the natural environment, and many designers are working closely with the National Parks officials, NGOs and other organizations to plan environmental projects for experiential events. In this way experiential programmes can have a real purpose, a productive end, rather than being simple pack-away simulated activities that await reconstruction by the next client. More significantly, real projects seem to have a positive motivational impact on client learning, affecting the way participants engage in learning from experience. Corporate facilitators have become interested by the high levels of energy towards such projects, which are 'perceived' as doing good work, of a charitable nature, giving a 'service' focus. Our belief is that the high emotional response to such an experience leads to high-quality learning experiences. This phenomenon still requires more research, but the reconnection with the community and the earth appears to be of value. This speculative benefit of using natural environments to create natural thinking has a lot more development potential for the future of working practices (Beard, 1996).

Environmental and community projects are not only real learning environments; they have an altruistic appeal. This is likely to be increasingly important in holistic experiential learning. Popular community projects include the building of playgrounds for children, and delivering hospital radio programmes or theatre performances. The options are indeed endless and with creativity the benefits can be considerable to all parties concerned. Charities such as the Royal Society for the Protection of Birds (RSPB) and the National Trust in the UK offer 'team challenges' in their volunteer work brochures, and have specialist staff to help to coordinate such projects. These are tasks that require completion for the management of many of their land holdings or nature reserves, and the charities say that such projects are suitable for corporate management development projects. This ties in with the increased corporate interest in social accountability, social auditing and the notion of business as a positive social force. In the UK the Institute of Social and Ethical Accountability was formed in 1996. Such activities are also witnessing an influx of people willing to travel from overseas destinations to help with the work.

ECO-ADVENTURE AND MULTIPLE LEARNING

Paradoxically, whilst there is an increased interest in artificial urban adventure environments for use in experiential learning, especially owing to their nearness to populations, there is at the same time a renewed interest in 'travel as education'. A plethora of activities are on offer in many locations around the world. Eco-adventure travel is an area that has increased rapidly over the last decade to become one of the leading areas of income for the tourism industry today (Swarbrooke *et al*, in press). Greenforce, Frontier and Earthwatch are three such organizations that offer an unusual and new combination of learning journeys. Such journeys offer a mix of experiential ingredients to encourage people to improve themselves, and to travel, whilst at the same time helping to repair the environment or conduct scientific wildlife monitoring. These organizations are also charities, recruiting paying volunteers to support wildlife projects around the world, by combining community development, travel and adventure with education and conservation to construct a new form of multi-learning experience for young people. Greenforce was inspired by the commitments made at the Earth Summit in Rio in 1992 to identify and protect the biodiversity of the planet. One brochure is titled 'Work on the wild side! Conservation expeditions'. Volunteers are offered an 'experience of a lifetime'. But more significantly there was, in Europe as a whole, a growing interest in environmental courses in the 1990s. Many graduates were keen to carve out a career – but the opportunities to do so were few and far between, and often required extensive experience before a candidate could be considered for a post. These and many other practical environmental organizations grew out of the great demand for 'experience'. Frontier is a non-profit organization promoted by the Society for Environmental Exploration, and has the following in its 2000 brochure:

> Taking part in a Frontier expedition is a once-in-a-lifetime experience... Future employers will be impressed with your achievements both in getting there and in succeeding in your project. Many former

volunteers have used their expeditions as the basis for project and dissertation work for Bachelor's Degrees and Master's Degrees. Frontier is also a 'Sponsoring Establishment' for Research Degrees through the Open University, the ONLY volunteer conservation organisation to have achieved the status of a field university. If you want a career in conservation and overseas development work, Frontier is the only option. With all volunteers eligible for a level 3 BTEC qualification in Tropical Habitat Conservation just on the strength of ten weeks of training and work on a Frontier expedition, becoming a volunteer gives you a chance to kick start a career in this highly competitive field. A recent survey found that 62% of ex-Frontier volunteers have achieved such careers thanks to their experience with Frontier.

Operation Raleigh, as we have mentioned, is a charity that develops young people by taking them on major expeditions around the world, and they too offer such projects in the international dimension of their development programmes:

Challenges in the outdoors, and involvement in community or environmental projects, are well established as a successful means of developing staff. Combining these with intensive international work in remote areas, Raleigh creates a framework within which learning can be transferred to the workplace. Working and living with people from different backgrounds for an extended period helps equip employees for today's fast-changing and demanding business environment. Working in real time, generating solutions to real problems, the experience proves sustainable and effective at developing the following qualities: team-working, leadership, interpersonal skills, confidence, motivation and assertiveness, initiative, flexibility and resilience, adaptability, maturity, awareness of self and others.

These experiential projects however remain almost exclusively for those who have, or are able to raise, the necessary funds.

SUSTAINABLE DEVELOPMENT

Caring for and valuing the natural environment is more than just the design of low-impact activities. For many businesses going 'green', being empathetic towards the environment or being 'environmentally friendly' can unfortunately be perceived as a trade-off between profit and corporate citizenship. As a result some organizations remain distanced from sustain-

able development, a process that meets the needs of the present generation without compromising the needs of future generations to meet their
own needs (WCED, in Beard, 1997). Some outdoor educational institutions regard themselves as environmentally friendly and as a result divest
themselves of 'experiential' responsibility through action. Ultimately
some form of action is required to repair the environment. The earth's
'bank account' of natural resources available for our life experience for the
present generation and for future generations to use is diminishing.
Previous generations and present generations have taken considerable
amounts of earth resources to provide for their needs and wants, dumping
the same resources back into the earth to be absorbed as 'waste'. This
traditional consumer–business cycle of 'take and dump' produces two
environmental negatives (E-). Who then is going to reinvest in the natural
capital and produce the elusive E+ products and services that contribute
to the environment? The answer is that both individuals and organizations can do a great deal. Beard examines the design of equipment and
clothing that have environmental benefits. Making reference to Patagonia,
the USA-based outdoor clothing company that developed the manufacture of fleeces from recycled plastic bottles, he notes their concern to
develop a business that will 'contribute to the formation of an economy
which restores the ecological health of the planet' (Beard, 1998: 20).
Patagonia also use the Natural Step Model:

- Do not take anything from the Earth's crust that you cannot put back.
- Maintain the integrity of the natural ecosystems.
- Do not spread long-lived human-made materials around the environ-
  ment.
- Leave enough for others.

Our view is that business will indeed produce more products and services
in the future that actually generate an environmental benefit or credit, or
an E+ effect, and more products will have what Beard calls bio-functions
(1996). This biological function might be in the form of living building
materials, washing machines that produce exit water that is cleaner than
entry water, and cars that are mobile air-cleaners: these may be the next
generation of products that support a concerted effort towards environmental regeneration (see Figure 5.7).
We continually try to encourage many outdoor management development providers to buy such environmentally friendly equipment and
clothing, and so support market trends in this direction. We also
encourage providers to increase the levels of environmental awareness in
clients by generally acknowledging the beauty of the environment they
are working in, and by making their own personal contribution. They can
do this by, for example, planting trees or rebuilding farm walls. If they are

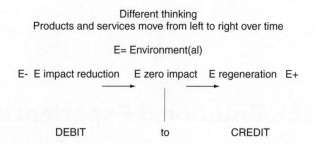

Figure 5.7 Environmental regeneration

unable to do the practical work as part of the outdoor programme, they could make a donation to an organization that might do it for them, ie conservation volunteer organizations.

6

The Emotional Experience

> *Emotions and feelings are the key pointers both to possibilities for, and barriers to, learning.*
>
> (Miller and Boud, 1996: 10)

INTRODUCTION

Managing the emotional climate, accessing emotions, mapping or altering the basic emotional make-up of learners is a difficult yet often-required skill of experiential providers. Being able to sense and steer the emotional basis of client behaviour is important, and here we explore ways to harness the great power of experiencing positive emotional change. In this chapter we focus on discovering people's emotional needs, and the development of positive benefits brought about by changing people's emotional response to their experience. In the learning combination lock, the emotional response is the foremost tumbler of the internal state, a tumbler linked closely to forms of intelligence and the processes of learning.

Expressing emotion has been associated with weakness and irrationality, and frowned upon in many institutions, yet emotion is inextricably linked to learning. Experiencing waves of emotion is crucial to a stimulating and satisfying experience, and a satisfying life. Not all people experience the right waves at the right time or place, or size, or frequency. Few learners can find sufficient time to step back to look at life, to find calm periods to reflect upon exciting waves and to learn from what has gone before. On a personal level emotional intelligence can help learners to access and surface unconscious feelings, to control negative thoughts and anger, and to reduce conflict. This will enable learners to take greater control of their feelings and emotions so as to progress towards more productive behaviours that they wish to develop, such as increased calm, the ability to challenge a belief set, or the development of increased sensitivity to self and others. The benefits of emotional intelligence for managers at work might be a contribution to improved team morale, more collaborative working, less energy waste on politicking and game play, and reduced loss of client goodwill through poor attitudes or indifference. Understanding and managing emotional intelligence, emotional effectiveness, motivation, enjoyment and satisfaction is a good investment.

In this chapter we explore the emotional underpinnings of experience, and examine some of the sub-components of 'emotion', for example the nature of learning states, smiling and humour, fears, pain, identity and anxiety. We take a brief look at a range of new and old ideas that enhance positive change in people, such as mind fitness, imagination, sculpturing, rewiring, mapping, sensory awareness, emotional catharsis and release, the use of rituals, and spiritual feelings and sacred places.

EMOTION AND EXPERIENTIAL LEARNING

We find ourselves in continual transaction with the physical, psychological, mental, spiritual world, and philosophy should be a systematic investigation into the nature of this experience.

(Crosby, 1995: 11)

It is frequently the case with traditional education and training that emphasis is placed upon cognitive and intellectual considerations. Boud, Cohen and Walker (1993: 14) emphasized this perspective and stated, 'Of all the features that we have mentioned, emotions and feelings are the ones which are most neglected in our society: there is almost a taboo about them intruding into our education institutions, particularly at higher levels.'

In order for any experience to be interpreted positively it is important that learners possess a number of constructive attributes, including:

- **confidence** in their abilities;
- **self-esteem** – in order to recognize the validity of their own views and those of others;
- **support** – from others whom we work with and bounce ideas off;
- **trust** – we must have confidence in the validity of the views of others and be able to incorporate them with our own where necessary.

It would therefore appear clear that, for learning to occur and an opportunity for learning not to be rejected, there has to be an attitudinal disposition towards the event. In essence, the affective domain can be seen to provide the underlying foundation for all learning. Postle (1993: 34), in support of this perspective, quotes Heron thus: 'Valid knowledge –

knowledge that is well grounded – depends upon its emergence out of openness to feeling.' He continues by drawing on the work of Langer: 'the entire psychological field, including conception, responsible action, rationality and knowledge is a vast and branching development of feeling'. Notions of feeling similarly underpin the philosophical foundations of experiential education. John Dewey wrestled with the nature of 'experience' and 'experiential learning', and he expressed concern that the emphasis on the intellectual or cognitive side of people alienated them from their immediate environment, and thus from their emotional, affective self (Crosby, 1995).

Emotional intelligence is defined by Bagshaw (2000) as 'the ability to use your understanding of emotions, in yourself and others, to deal effectively with people and problems in a way which reduces anger and hostility, develops collaborative effort, enhances life balance and produces creative energy'. The notion of emotional intelligence as 'EQ' was popularized by Goleman (1996). He argued that having a high EQ was a different way of being smart, and his focus was on the emotional competence required to be a star performer. Some authors, such as Woodruffe (2001: 26), are more sceptical about such claims, arguing that it is not new territory. Whilst emotional intelligence (EQ) has emerged from older research on *social intelligence*, it does now have a niche of its own, set apart from the other three intelligences – intellectual, physical and social intelligence. Other writers have expanded this simplistic three way classification. Woodruffe refers to emotional intelligence, in an article titled 'Promotional intelligence', as simply a new brand name for a set of long-established competencies. Woodruffe quotes one company making great claims that emotional intelligence can 'identify and develop better internal leaders, maximise productivity, create more effective teams, improve the selection process, reduce turnover, boost sales, improve organisational culture and morale, stimulate creativity and co-operation, and outperform the competition'. If only success in business were that easy to achieve.

Goleman based much of his thinking on research by Salovey, who classified emotional intelligence into five main categories: 'handling one's emotions, managing emotions, motivating oneself, recognising emotions in others, handling relationships' (Goleman, 1996: 46). To be able to understand this as an emotional basis to learning is of primary significance to experiential providers, who are increasingly called on to understand, manage and contain the emotional climate of their learners or clients. Fineman (1997) lists the work of many influential writers on the subject of the debilitating nature that anxiety, fear and stress have in interfering with learning, but notes that emotions are seen as 'unwanted' and 'undesirable' in the rational, logical workplace. The rules of emotional expression are corporately defined, and there can be significant differences as between individuals' privately held feelings and the emotion they display at work. These are some of the emotional issues addressed in high-ropes courses. The 'leap of faith' involves climbing to the top of a telegraph pole, releasing one handhold then another and standing upright, and then building up courage to leap towards a trapeze. Inability to reach the trapeze results in the safety harness kicking in; grabbing the trapeze results in an emotional high. Success, however, is about sensing and handling the fear and later transferring the learning to other life situations; these are key learning outcomes.

Managers learn to survive, learn how to avoid blame, learn how to operate in their organization and learn when to be deferential. These, according to Salaman and Butler (1990), are emotional behaviours that can help to avoid the painful experience of being singled out or blamed, and because we need allies. It is suggested that such fear-based management strategies in the workplace are likely to be ineffective and undesirable (Applebaum, Bregman and Moroz, 1998). Also emerging is popular literature on the negative aspects of fear-based parenting, citing evidence that young people, in these climates, are likely to self-destruct (Gray, 1999). Fineman (1997: 21) also comments that, in virtual working, networking and teleworking scenarios, 'managers will need to learn new ways of defining and expressing their feelings, status and identities, while developing alternative approaches to managing others' emotional lives under these working conditions'.

In our lives we experience a whole array of both emotions and moods. Researchers continue to debate which emotions might be considered as primary types. Goleman (1996) reports the main candidates as anger, fear, shame, sadness, enjoyment, surprise, love and disgust. Some of these primary emotions such as fear have an important impact on learning, and are further explored later in this chapter. An A–Z list of some of the common emotions, which form a central tumbler in our learning combination lock (see Figure 6.1), include the following:

- aggression;
- anger;
- anxiety;
- boredom;
- depression;
- disgust;
- enjoyment;
- envy;
- fear;
- grief;

- guilt;
- happiness;
- hate;
- loneliness;
- love;
- pride;
- rejection;
- sadness;
- shame;
- spiritual feelings.

Moods can be regarded as a subset of emotions, but they are said to be different from emotion in that:

> We can think of mood as a background of feeling that persists over time. Usually our moods are subtle, but sometimes they can be intense and overwhelm us. Moods are not the same as emotions, but they do have a great deal in common with them. Moods are sometimes defined as less intense and longer lasting than emotions, although this lower intensity isn't true in the case of serious depression. Unlike most emotions, moods don't seem to have an identifiable cause. That is, there usually isn't an obvious cause-and-effect relationship between our moods and events. This isn't true of emotions.
>
> (Thayer, 1996: 5)

Thayer regards the central dimensions of mood as a balance of energy and tension, and he says that mood indicates a greater tendency to do certain things. A person often says 'I am in the mood to…' What is important here is that the experiential provider is expected to manage both the mood and emotional climate of people to varying degrees. It is the balance of the energy–tension dichotomy that is of significance to the experiential learning provider, as a reduction in tension, for example, can increase energy levels. But moods are heavily influenced by rhythms, and chronobiologists call these 'endogenous' biological rhythms, as they are governed by our internal biological clock. This internal clock becomes more apparent to us when we fly across time zones and the disrupted internal clock then makes us feel less alert or more energized in time with the old time zone, a phenomenon known as jet lag.

Thayer notes that energy levels rise to their highest levels in the first third of the day, around noon. They then drop in the mid- to late afternoon, reach a sub-peak in the early evening and decline until sleep, thus creating the rhythmical wave of daily energy. Larger waves are created by

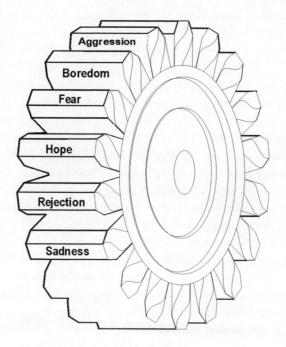

Figure 6.1 Tumbler four: the primary emotions

seasonal variations such as the reduction of light in winter, and these too are of significance to mood. Moods can also be influenced by levels of exercise, food, drink and the fresh outdoor air, and it is this daily energy wave that underpins many of the basic strategies for the active management of moods, as it influences the sequence of daily events in training and development work. 'Positive, optimistic thoughts accompany positive moods. In other words moods and thoughts are congruent' (Thayer, 1996: 35).

Thayer also discusses *state dependency*, a phenomenon whereby, if we learn something in a particular mood state, we remember it better when we are in that same mood state, and Thayer, using a banking metaphor, suggests that there are separate mood memory banks for particular positive and negative moods.

THE EMOTIONAL NERVE CENTRE

Many emotions can be perceived as either positive or negative depending upon long-established nerve connections in the mind. In the lower rear section of the brain, the amygdala is located, and it is responsible for fast-response behaviour. When people see, hear, smell or feel something, the information is doubled up. One set of information is speedily conveyed down a short circuit to the amygdala, giving a split-second response. The other set of information is logically analysed and reflected upon elsewhere, sent down by the slower route to the area known as the neocortex. If a stimulus has been linked to danger in the past, then the amygdala will spring into action. This amygdala is in fact the storehouse for emotional memories, and so is a major source of instant reactions and gut reactions, which are hard to ignore (Robertson, 1999). This quick response represents a survival kit, helping people to avoid anything from snakebites or bumping into people to car crashes. However, some fast responses are not always up to date and can be inappropriate in the fluid social world we humans now inhabit (Goleman, 1996). The sight of a dentist or the words 'merger' or 'corporate change' can instil fear and panic in some people, giving a strong irrational reaction in them. Rewiring or reprogramming some of these instant emotional responses to overcome negative feelings and create more positive feelings is a challenge many experiential providers face when providing appropriate training and development. We believe all facilitation requires a sound understanding of emotional intelligence:

> The affective experience of learners is probably the most powerful determinant of learning of all kinds... Feelings and emotions provide the best guides we have as to where we need to devote our attention. This may be uncomfortable for animators, especially if they are not reconciled with their own emotional agendas, and they may be set aside because of immediate circumstances, but we cannot learn if they are continually denied.
>
> (Boud and Miller, 1996a: 17)

THE POWER OF THE EMOTIONAL STATE

People's lives undergo permanent transition, changing in many different directions during the course of a lifetime. Helping people to learn from experience can help them to survive and adapt to the continuous change that they face. Having a vision, a focus or sense of direction in life can help people to cope with change, not least because it gives the change a purpose. Chisholm (2000: 5) develops the idea of a 'life success strategy' and offers simple advice to people who want to be high achievers: 'keep changing what you do until you get what you want'. Megginson (1994), a professor in human resource development, does this by writing down 10 goals each year. These are goals that he wants to achieve to create balance in four main areas of his life: his mind, his body, his emotions and his spirit. To ensure a consistent focus each day he sets specific 'SPICE' goals: spiritual, physical, intellectual, career and emotional. These help him either to stay on course or to change direction.

People can be asked to review their life by taking a piece of string. One end represents birth, and death lies at the other end. A knot is tied at the place that represents their current age in life. People then shape the string to create waves up to the point of the knot, and these represent emotional highs and lows in their life. Interpreting and sharing these can be a powerful experience, and the thought of consciously creating the future set of waves can be uplifting or emotionally daunting. A key factor to consider in the underlying emotional response is how people receive or perceive an experience. A simple prescription of positive affirmations or positive thoughts, whilst helpful, is unlikely to change the deeper feelings that underlie their interpretation. Emotional reactions to the same experience are due to one critical difference: how the experience is perceived.

The film *Papillon*, for example, has an interesting end to it. Two very different people are prisoners on Devil's Island, a place where there is no escape and where the two people were left to see their days out and die. But Papillon chose to do what apparently was impossible: to escape by making a coconut raft, jumping off the cliffs and risking his life among crashing waves and dangerous sharks. His very close friend did not want to go with him. He chose to stay on the island and tend his plants; he chose to play safe and enjoy what he had on the island. He chose not to jump over the cliff edge, but to stay put. His decision is dependent on a personal cost–benefit analysis largely based on the accumulation of all his experiences to that point in life, adopted either consciously or subconsciously. Papillon was engaging in a struggle to escape for a reason, and there were benefits to him that outweighed the risks. He did not want to give up trying to escape. What Morris (1969: 158) suggests is that the object of any struggle is to experience 'optimum stimulation':

When a man is reaching retirement age he often dreams of sitting quietly in the sun. By relaxing and 'taking it easy' he hopes to stretch out an enjoyable old age. If he manages to fulfil his 'sun-sit' dream, one thing is certain; he will not lengthen his life, he will shorten it. The reason is simple – he will give up the Stimulus Struggle.

Whilst this 'struggle' for balance in life, for optimum experience, is largely an emotional one, it can take on many dimensions. Alder (2000: 6) in offering a 'Life Content Model' suggests that:

'Being' is the ultimate goal type. To be 'happy, 'content', or 'fulfilled' is as near as we get to understanding human desire… Quite simply doing, knowing and getting is with a view to being happy rather than sad. Some people, however, are 'being' people even on a day-to-day basis. They experience the 'now' rather than putting off being to some future time, which may never be. They take time to stop and smell the roses.

Deferment is a common way of reducing the value of experience. The 'being' is delayed until later: 'When I get this, then I will…' This presents a basic underlying life tension, a dichotomy of 'being' and 'getting' as an emotional balance (see Figure 6.2).

The phenomenon of 'being' emerges in many forms in the literature on experiential learning, psychology, adventure and sport. Yaffey (1993: 10) describes this emotional phenomenon of 'pure perception, uncontaminated thought and freedom to Be' as the key ingredients in the state of mind known as 'peak experience', a term originally coined by Maslow (1971). We now examine more closely the nature of 'being', and we look at experiential opportunities that can significantly determine *what*, *where*, *when* and *how* learning takes place, so enabling providers to create optimum stimulation for the optimum learning wave of experience (see Figures 6.3 and 6.4).

EMOTIONAL WAVES

The idea that people's life experience is a continuous stimulus struggle was a topic examined in *New Scientist* in an article called 'Thrill or chill' (Schueller, 2000), with photographs of white-water rafting, surfing, paragliding and other extreme sports. The article describes how some people will do anything for high levels of stimulation, to get an adrenalin rush, while others prefer the quiet life. People can of course get an adrenalin surge without jumping off a building or hang-gliding. Farley, a former president of the American Psychological Association, described how those who push the frontiers of the mind rather than the body could get an adrenalin rush through other means. He said, 'Einstein was way beyond the handrails. He was literally creating his own vision of the Universe.

Figure 6.2 The dichotomy of 'getting' and 'being'.

What sustained his mental life was the thrill of it' (Schueller, 2000: 23). Significantly this adrenalin rush can also come during mentally demanding learning. As with any adventure, the pleasure comes once you have landed safely and the relaxing opiates called endorphins gush through the body; the natural ecstasy is produced from the learning, creating strong positive emotions.

The sensation of experiencing a high can be exhilarating, a form of peak experience, and it can come in many guises. But providing learners with repeated high-energy activity may produce low returns for the learners if their optimal stimulation levels are exceeded (see Figures 6.3 and 6.4). High-energy seeking can also be overplayed. The troughs shown in Figure 6.3 represent emotional relaxation – calm waters, the lulls between the waves, the time to smell the flowers – and they are as important as the high-energy waves. Balancing the energy and the emotional waves is significant to the experiential provider's role.

EXPERIENCING EMOTIONAL CALM – SORTING TIME

Finding emotional calm is essential sorting time. It is also time just to 'be', and involves stepping back and finding mental and physical space to think. A practical exercise in experiencing calm is given in Chapter 7; it is an example of getting inner calm and stimulating the senses. Experience has to be reflected upon so as to make sense of it, by making connections to other experiences. So-called 'mindless' activities appear to have a clear function in that they allow the everyday sensory bombardment to cease for a while, allowing the mind to sort things out and take stock.

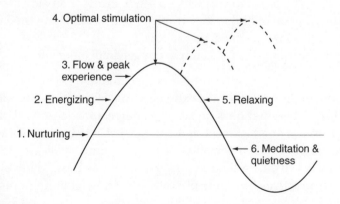

Figure 6.3 Catching waves and finding calm

The same sort of spontaneous sorting through of existing information occurs during certain mindless, rhythmic physical activities like jogging, swimming laps or mowing the lawn; or during habitual routines that no longer need the conscious brain's full attention, such as showering or commuting on the same route each day. Just as it does during sleep, this spontaneous process of reflection allows one to momentarily suspend the intense flow of new information to the brain. This enhances the processing of existing information, thereby preparing the person to handle the demands of the rapidly changing environment.

(Daudelin, 1996: 39)

Daudelin (1996) offers some fascinating thinking on the process of reflection, and refers to the work of J Allen Hobson, professor of psychiatry at Harvard. His book, simply called *Sleep*, explains how sleep reduces the level of incoming sensory data and allows for the reorganization and storage of information already in the brain, thus better preparing people to handle the demands of the working day. This same sorting and filing also occurs during waking time, through activities that appear to be of a mindless nature. This is often what is happening in some adventure programmes when people plod the mountains, walk the hills or drift over water in Canadian canoes. Such activity can also include meditation, prayer or journal writing. Similarly, the garden shed or greenhouse is a place for people to potter in, to find space to be alone or to plan the day; there are classic everyday thinking alone times. Performing a 'solo' is a regular Outward Bound approach to this phenomenon in that it involves people being alone for 24 hours in the wilderness. Voluntary castaways left alone on islands have provided unique television footage of personal interactions and relationships, and are now a form of live soap opera. Significantly such programmes often contain interviews of people describing their unique and special place to be alone, whether it be a hilltop, a rock outcrop, a sandy beach or an old barn. They are personal places to think and sort things out, and the provision of this space is essential in experiential programmes.

Meditative experiences for example can generate more intense states of mind:

There are many words for the extreme forms of joy. In the Buddhist tradition, it is called bliss and is considered to be a natural state arising from non-attachment and compassion. Meditation is a way of attaining it. When a person is no longer bound by his desires or emotional needs, then life can be experienced as bliss. Many other religious practices bring about ecstasy, literally standing outside oneself. In ecstasy we transcend time and space.

(Wilkes, 1999: 256–57)

It is useful to explore these emotional states prior to, during and after experiential activities (for example, see the practical case study on flow learning through relaxed alertness later in this chapter). Fox (1999) offers three ingredients at the top of a list of 32 recommendations to experiential providers to encourage spiritual experiences: 1) allow time for relaxation; 2) allow time for solitude and personal reflection time; 3) allow time to explore and interrelate with nature alone.

By combining the 'adventure waves' (Mortlock, 1984) with flow learning from Cornell (1989) and the work of Dainty and Lucas (1992) we can create a six-stage emotional wave (see Figure 6.4):

1. **Create conditions for pre-contemplation** – reading, thinking, imagining.
2. **Awaken participant enthusiasm** – ice-breakers and energizers.
3. **Start to focus attention and concentration** – medium-sized activities, narrow skills.
4. **Direct and challenge the personal experience** – larger, broader skills.
5. **Share participant enthusiasm** – using reviewing activities.
6. **Encourage quiet personal reflection**.

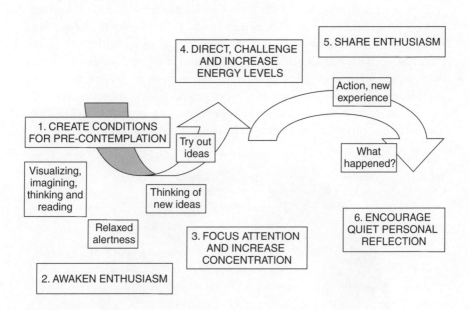

Providers encourage six stages (upper case)
Learners complete six stages (lower case)

Figure 6.4 Learning waves

Energy waves are implicit in many other development models, such as the four stages of *nurturing, energizing, peak activity* and *relaxing* developed by Randall and Southgate (1980) and the gestalt cycle (see Figure 6.5). A six-stage programme developed by Porter (1999) can also represent a wave of change, and consists of *entry, pre-contemplation, preparation, action, mainte-nance* and *relapse or integrated change*.

Throughout this book we focus on the nature of the rises and falls of the waves that form the learning 'experience'. Ice-breakers stimulate the first wave, and energizers add stimulation to subsequent waves. Pre-sensi-tizing exercises can increase the awareness of sensory systems and hence the experience itself, prior to a wave. The pacing of energy waves, and the sequencing of physical or mental activity is equally important; rising waves can be full of adrenalin, whilst the subsiding wave can induce endorphins and cause calm and relaxation, important to reflection time. Too many waves of any one kind may result in habituation and reduced responsiveness and so monitoring energy levels is important.

Learning is more effective if people are in the right frame of mind. A state of mind can be created that is one of relaxed alertness, an optimum inner atmosphere for learning. Heron (1999: 233) refers to the ability of experiential providers to influence these energy and mood levels. Mood and energy can be influenced for example by the use of two basic types of speech: *clock time* and *charismatic time*. Clock time is used in most conver-sations by experiential providers and tends to 'be verbally dense, fast, loaded with information, somewhat urgent and in a subtle way over-tense'. Speech in charismatic time is warm and slow, and tends to contain pauses and silent moments. The voice mode here is deeper, has clear, rhythmic inflections and sounds almost poetic. Clock speech waves are staccato in form, whereas charismatic speech waves are gentle and rolling. The voice is a powerful tool that can be used to create a range of effects.

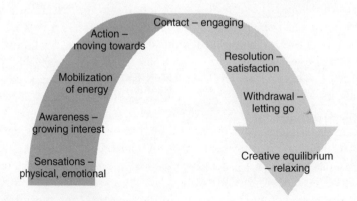

Figure 6.5 The gestalt wave

ECSTASY AND ACCELERATED LEARNING

The notion of a form of *enhanced learning* is an interesting one. Macaloon and Csikszentmihalyi (Boniface, 2000: 66) refer to the creation of a 'flow experience', and suggest that providers should create activities that 'must be finely calibrated to a person's skills – including his physical, intellectual, emotional and social abilities'. The idea of matching activities to these four criteria within learners is clearly an important skill for learning providers in the design of effective programmes.

Getting people to focus and concentrate on a specific task, or to focus on an object in an almost meditative way, reduces or removes many other external stimuli, and removes attention from self-centred emotional needs; it is the basis of a powerfully positive experiential state of mind. It is a state of mind that leaves behind boredom and worry. In much of the literature relating to this subject, reference is made to these and other special and spiritual environments in the emotional, intellectual, physiological or physical sense. In literature on adventure, for example, Miles and Priest (1990) say that personal transcendence is also experienced when risk is courted and met, when we invite adventure into our lives.

Boniface (2000) presents an excellent analysis of these and other positive experiences, and refers to the work of Csikszentmihalyi, who suggests that people who are deemed 'beginners' do not experience the much-sought-after socio-psychological condition of *flow*. Beginners find the activity demanding, and conscious thought and/or anxiety are present in high levels – there is a level of conscious incompetence. In order to attain flow states, certain levels of experience, skill and conditioning appropriate to the level of challenge must first be attained, moving through levels of conscious (deliberate/clumsy) competence to unconscious (automatic/without thought) competence (Strangaard, 1981).

Opportunities for flow experience lie somewhere between tasks that are too simple and those that are too challenging. The relationship between perceived risk, level of challenge and personal competence thus appears to be a central factor in the flow state experience. Such powerful experiences have also been referred to as 'peak experience' or 'peak performance'. These terms are used interchangeably, but there are some essential differences. Wilkes (1999) suggests that the flow state is a form of extreme joy. Flow states, she says, are characterized by extreme concentration, a loss of self-consciousness and an altered perception of the passage of time. Athletes and artists experience them; indeed, she suggests that all activities that are perceived as highly meaningful can yield flow states. In competitive swimming some people are able to swim fast in a focused state yet see their own hands in slow motion flowing along the glistening water, and enjoy the experience with an almost out-of-body sensation. In intense creative artwork some people almost enter the picture and lose track of time. It is suggested that jazz musicians, comedians, and teams and trainers all report achieving these flow states (Hopfl and Linstead, 1997). Csikszentmihalyi made specific reference to artists, and concluded that painters must want to paint, and that it was the students who were able to savour the emotional 'sheer joy of it' who went on to succeed as serious painters (Goleman, 1996: 107).

The flow state can thus be acquired through mastery of one or more of the seven categories of intelligence; and it lies in a channel somewhere between boredom and anxiety. Boniface refers to Ravizza, who reports nine common characteristics of peak experience in sport, some of which are:

- loss of fear and no fear of failure;
- a sensation of being totally absorbed in the activity with a narrow focus of attention;
- a sensation of complete control;
- a time–space disorientation (time usually seems to slow down);
- a perception of the universe being integrated and unified, as if in some moment of special insight;
- a perception of the experience being unique, temporary and involuntary.

To create these characteristics in learners would be ideal, as peak perform-ance is associated with superior functioning, often described in athletes as having an underlying state of clear mental focus, combined with a highly energized state, relaxed yet adrenalin-ready, and in control and confident. Of significance to experiential programmes, Wilkes (1999: 250) argues about the design of programmes: 'we cannot make flow and joy happen, but we can provide the interior situations where they are most likely'. Below is a very simple yet natural and practical example of how to encourage a form of relaxed alertness through reading, develop a playful approach to intellect and create powerful productive learning. Deep reading and deep thinking can be powerful parts of an experiential programme, and can give rise to original, indigenous learning.

Practical case study: Flow learning through relaxed alertness

Simple techniques: play and fun – coffee, music and the Sunday papers (academic literature)

At a number of residential programmes over the last few years many mature students studying for Master's degrees in training and devel-

---

opment, and outdoor management development have taken part in a very simple experiment on states of mind and learning. I decided to offer a session that was designed to allow students quiet personal space, to be relaxed and to allow them to learn to 'play' with ideas and concepts following a period of silent reading (and a later sharing of thoughts) over early-morning coffee and croissants. The setting was carefully selected with music and smells for relaxed alertness, and there was no underlying pressure; it was designed to be just for exploration and fun!

We used the mood-setting frame of lounging about reading the Sunday newspapers, but instead of newspapers we used journal articles from a range of well-known sources. The participants soon had their shoes off, sitting or lying on comfortable sofas, sometimes with cats sleeping next to them, and with soft rainforest music playing. Coffee percolators bubbled away, Earl Grey tea was on offer and lemon scented the air. The articles were from *People Management*, *Management Learning*, *Management Education and Development* (*MEAD*), *People and Organizations*, *Training and Development*, *Industrial and Commercial Training*, *Sloan Management Review*, *Harvard Business Review* and many others. Hardly Sunday morning reading! Subtly included in the reading material were articles that encouraged students to be aware of themselves, to be critical of these articles. We were encouraging students to become more relaxed about the 'literature' associated with their subject, to encourage them to share, become fascinated, get copies of lots of material because they wanted to take it home, and to learn to communicate and explore their findings with one another.

Following the reading I acted merely as a scribe and facilitator, letting go of my concerns about my expertise, and as a result the sessions produced much debate. The subsequent evaluation of the session showed that students wanted more time in future to repeat these explorations of the literature and to play with concepts and ideas in this relaxed way. One student said:

> One of the more effective learning community development exercises, in my view, followed the coffee and papers sessions each morning. During these sessions, differing views concerning the same articles were discussed and new insights developed based on individual experience outside the articles. This led to a spin of ideas that spurred more new ideas, and reshaped some of my initial thoughts of the articles. It appeared that many of the participants shared this experience regarding the coffee and papers sessions.

> The use of this style of experience of reading and indigenous learning through exploration is undervalued in many programmes.
>
> (adapted from Beard and McPherson, 1999)

EXPERIENCE, LEARNING AND 'IDENTITY'

All learning is grounded in the work–life balance and prior experience. The past consists of banked emotional 'experiences', and these can both drive forward and restrict new learning from experience. The element of the change, the unknown, can cause concerns about future likely experiences, and the comfort zones of the mind can easily become overstretched. But why is it that people can enter more mentally challenging experiences with ease sometimes, yet at other times it is more difficult for them? The risk might be perceived as high, but it is often fear that underpins our deeper feelings of reluctance, worry and concern. These fears become strong barriers for some people but, for others, fear can act as a powerful drive towards new learning adventures.

Postle (1993: 34) addresses barriers on a more personal level:

> as I see it, we often cling, with the intensity of addiction, to the comfort that comes from staying with our preferred mode and keeping away from the other modes. I remain convinced that this is usually because at some point in our history, one or another, – or all – of the four modes of learning may have become debilitated or ruined. If this debilitation or damage was severe, whether locally or generally, then staying with the preferred mode may also successfully defend us against the feelings associated with that early hurt. If so, then our interest in action, or dreaming up futures, or caring, or arguing, whichever most keeps quiet our painful history, can indeed come to have the intensity of addiction.

Attributing an experience with a positive or negative emotional interpretation may influence the degree and type of learning. Postle (1993: 37) describes three kinds of learning that inhibit us:

- **omitted learning** – lack of love in an upbringing, which results in a person being unable to receive or give love;
- **distorted learning** – can occur when a person is told that he or she is hopeless, not talented, etc;
- **distressed learning** – learning that occurs with distress in the form of forced learning and compliance.

These are significant issues to learning providers. Negative learning experiences significantly influence our outlook on life, how we interact with others and with our experiences, and even the extent to which we are prepared to venture into new learning experiences. Postle (1993: 38) emphasized the vast importance of previous experiences in the shaping or avoiding of future experiences:

> Distorted, omitted and distressed learning have vast power. They can drive us on and out into the most bizarre forms of 'I have to' or 'I can't' behaviour. They compel us to devise and install incredible institutions both of personal and social behaviour with the purpose of keeping us safely in our familiar 'comfort zone'. We may then go too often to the same parts of life's landscape and rarely or never to other districts.

People do not always choose to undergo distressed learning, for instance climbing a cold mountain. Some people may enjoy the experience of climbing in the 'death zone' of Everest (where lack of oxygen can cause severe trauma or death) while most others will fear it and not go anywhere near it. The same experience can be affected by a personal attitude that interprets the mountain as positive or negative. If the right climate is created for the experience, people will for example climb up steep cliffs and leap off into the raging swell of the sea if it is perceived as a leisure activity such as 'coasteering'. Some people experience fear when they return to education, or have to make a presentation. However, the presence of a small element of fear can also enable people to perform at their best; again it is the balance that is important.

The above discussion serves to illustrate how negative emotions and feelings can inhibit present and future learning. This may lead to the conclusion that a negative experience will also lead to negative interpretations about the experience. This need not be the case, and many of life's most powerful learning opportunities occur as a result of painful experience. People hate work when there is too much to do, and often dream of not having to work at all. Yet people fear being unemployed and celebrate finding employment. More significantly, what we do at work is often a significant element of the description of our identity, 'what we do for a living'. This point is also illustrated by Parr (2000). In her book on education and identity, she describes her research with mature women returning to education and how, on the face of it, their reason for entering education later in life is the wish to gain the qualifications they did not gain at the 'conventional age'. Digging below the surface, however, she uncovers more complex reasons. She declares that the reason to return to education was:

as much about identity as it was about paper qualifications. It could have been described as a 'life-raft' for some students – as one of them said 'it's saved my sanity'. What emerged very clearly from what they said, was the desire to redefine at least part of their identity, to see themselves in a different way and exert a degree of control over some aspects of their lives.

(Parr, 2000: 1)

Parr goes on to describe how, when people are questioned about their education and learning, superficial responses can be misleading. Many women, later, under a more trusting climate, talked readily of trauma in their lives. Some questioned the way in which they had been defined by others, and talked of the social pressures on women to conform to a particular identity. Some told of psychological, physical or sexual abuse, overbearing parents, alcoholism or the death of a child or other family member. For many there was an inner drive that steered their return to education, and it was associated with power and control, confidence building, independence, self-image or a desire to prove their ability. Despite the fact that a number of women had experienced their early school educational experience as largely negative, many saw their return to (adult) education as positive and therapeutic, as a form of cathartic leisure activity, by doing something for themselves for enjoyment. This presents an interesting juxtaposition of leisure and learning. Perceiving their learning as a 'leisure experience' and paying to learn made it more enjoyable and increased their motivation.

SPIRITUAL FEELINGS

Man discovers his deepest self and reveals his greatest creative powers at times when his psychic processes are most free from immediate involvement with the environment and most under the control of his indwelling balancing or homeostatic power. The freest type of psychic play occurs in sleep and the social acceptance of the dream world, therefore, constitutes the deepest possible acceptance of the individual.

(Stewart, in Walter and Marks, 1981)

Returning to the subject of peak experience, Cooper (1998) makes reference to peak experiences in connection with spirituality and the environment. In this context he refers to these experiences as a form of connectedness to the earth, and a heightened sense of being alive. These experiences, he suggests, can be very spiritual and very powerful for some people, and may present a turning point in life. Cooper goes on to recall the experience of a professor of education, J Gary Knowles, when leading a night-time kayaking session. The experience changed his life. He was out with a group of 15-year-old kids from the city as they set off into the night under a myriad of stars. They were then faced with an amazing sight of thousands of glow-worms:

> They were breathtaking. Each tiny glow came from a single phosphorescent light-emitting creature. Suspended like delicate jewels, the larvae of the fungus gnat had emerged to feed, their diffused glow reflecting on the faces of the exuberant students... we listened intently to the night and to each other. I was silent, allowing nature to speak... many students marvelled at the power of beauty and the place's serenity... In my mind, and in the minds of several students, a sacred place was established. It was the site of a special event, a place, if you will, at which individuals united with the powers of nature.
>
> (Cooper, 1998: 65)

Gary Knowles returned to the same lake later with other groups but the experience wasn't the same. Leaders cannot predict such events, but they can set the scene, pre-sensitize people and make use of opportunities as they arise – if they themselves are sensitized to such things. Such experiences can be very inspirational and lead to a 'oneness' with the earth. Few people actually experience real darkness in the outdoors, such as being away from the lights of a built-up area or down a cave. Few people experience a dawn chorus of birds awakening in the forests. Few people experience the strange silence when surfing waves. As well as describing the emotions and feelings associated with spiritual experiences, Fox (1999: 58–59) in 'Enhancing spiritual experience in adventure programs' offers an analysis of anecdotal accounts of spirituality, and clusters the accounts under the following headings:

- spirituality as a fundamental aspect of human nature;
- spirituality as a sense of mystery;
- spirituality as a sense of awe and wonderment;
- spirituality as a belief in the connectedness or sense of oneness towards people, self and all things;
- spirituality as aesthetic beauty;
- spirituality as transcendent;
- spirituality as peak experience;
- spirituality as creating a sense of inner peace, oneness and strength;
- wilderness as a spiritual attraction.

Maslow described the need for food, for shelter, for physical health, for family, for education, for social integration and for intellectual, social and material accomplishments. But it is only when these things are met that people reach their ultimate stage of human development: self-actualization, a state of spiritual feeling. Here people pour out playfulness, creativity, joyousness, a sense of purpose, with a mission to help others and with great tolerance, and these are accomplished in an environment of love and compassion. Maslow was describing spiritual intelligence. There is connection here with Chapter 8 on codes of practice and ethical behaviour for experiential learning providers and educators.

Tony Buzan (2001) refers to commonly held spiritual values as:

- truth;
- compassion;
- love;
- tolerance;
- unity;
- patience;
- honesty;
- co-operation;
- understanding;
- integrity;
- gratitude;
- justice;
- courage;
- freedom;
- charity;
- trust;
- humour;
- equality;
- simplicity;
- peace;
- responsibility;
- purity;
- persistence;
- harmony.

Spiritual intelligence is less well explored in training and development work, but some experiential providers explicitly refer to spirituality in their promotional literature. The Findhorn Foundation, for example, is an organization that was started in 1962 in a caravan park in Scotland, and now this highly successful organization seeks to demonstrate the links between the spiritual, social, economic and environmental aspects of life.

Over the years the community has grown into a major centre of training and adult education with more than 4,000 residential visitors a year. It is also the centre of a developing eco-village. Co-operation and co-creation with nature are major aspects of the Foundation's work, and they declare that they are 'at the heart of the UK's largest international community based on spiritual values'.

The Earth Centre in Doncaster in the UK is said to be the world's first environmental theme park. The Findhorn Foundation sent staff to help them in the training of a newly appointed workforce. The Earth Centre won a national tourism award owing to the help that visitors received from on-site staff, who came from the ranks of the unemployed. The staff's special training lasted six weeks, by which time they had to be ready to launch. Some were unable to read or write very well. Most knew little about the environment. Whilst one of the group had a Master's degree in an environmentally related subject, the group as a whole had few educational qualifications. What is significant about the training of the local people, however, is that the first stage of a three-part programme was delivered by the trainers of the Findhorn Foundation. They developed the group, working first with feelings and needs, and developing a sense of belonging. Using many of the spiritual principles offered by Deepak Chopra (see below), they examined and explored the important spiritual values associated with this mining community and their 'special place', a site that, like themselves, was undergoing a new and significant transformation. The local environment was shifting from being a coal-mining area to an internationally known green 'theme park'. The men and women were a close community, and hardship had beset them at the time of the closure of the coal mine. Their experiences in the dying last days of industry had been negative, and there was a sense of mistrust.

The people all sat, arms folded, looking in disbelief at the strange trainers from Scotland when they first arrived. There was strong initial resistance, mixed with a strange fascination. Eventually this fascination got the better of them; they succumbed to the charm of the whole experience, and many ended their training by participating in quite challenging events. Many created and read out their own poetry. Many unexpectedly shed tears with other local people as they unearthed some of their deeper feelings about their community and their sense of loss. Their emotional bedrock was not only exposed at times but was strengthened in preparation for the next phase of environmental training. Whilst the local people might have been seen as having low levels of formal education for their role as environmental guides, they eventually proved to be highly capable and well trained. The prestigious tourism award given to them derived largely from the spiritual experiential base that formed a central part of their training (Hartmann and Beard, 2000).

Seven spiritual laws

1. Experience higher, spiritual self; list unique talents and three ways of expressing them; ask daily, how may I help serve humanity? *Law of dharma*
2. Experience silence; commune with nature; practise non-judgement. *Law of pure potentiality*
3. Offer a gift for everyone; receive gifts from life; wish everyone happiness, joy and laughter. *Law of giving*
4. Witness choices in the moment; ask, will it bring fulfilment and happiness to me and others?; ask heart for spontaneous right action. *Law of karma*
5. Accept people and situations as they are; take responsibility for my situation without blame; defencelessness – no need to convince or persuade. *Law of least effort*
6. Make a list of desires and release the list to the universe; remain established in self-referral. *Law of intention and desire*
7. Allow self and others to be as they are; factor uncertainty into my experience; step into the field of all possibilities. *Law of detachment*

(Chopra, 1996)

The emotions associated with such spiritual experiences are very difficult to describe. This is further illustrated by two very interesting stories in Greg Child's book about mountain explorers, *Mixed Emotions* (1993). The two stories focus on the spirit world, death, superstition and unexplainable phenomena. One story is called 'The other presence' and is about a person's mysterious feelings of being accompanied by a ghostly companion who comforts and guides him to safety when faced with extreme situations. It starts off with a reference to a climber at 28,000 feet above sea level on the north ridge of Everest pausing and offering a piece of mint cake to his companion who had been with him all day. But he found himself offering the snack to the thin air of the Himalayas: there was no friend; he was alone. Another story is about Roger Marshall on Kanchenjunga. He was stumbling down the mountainside with his strength slipping away. He was perilously close to falling down precipitous slopes when he heard a Japanese voice; he moved toward the voice, found a rope left by a previous Japanese expedition and descended to safety. But there were no Japanese people present on the slopes that day.

Science leads us to seek rational, logical explanations for this: a physiological phenomenon, oxygen deprivation or distorted perceptions maybe?

But science and myth are one and the same. 'Even when all the possible scientific questions have been answered, the problems of life remain completely untouched' (Handy, 1994).

CONCLUSION

Learning is enhanced when people discover things for themselves, through their own emotional engagement. This requires a commitment to discovery, experimentation and reviewing of personal emotional goals and visions. Whilst experience is all around people every day, many people do not make the most of experiential opportunities, and it is the emotional state that prevents maximum return on experience. Such emotional underpinnings will often be signposted, and experiential learning providers will have to use these to read and use the underlying feelings that might restrict or enhance learning and change. Emotional intelligence underpins learning as a basic building block. Yet many experiential learning providers, educators and trainers cannot give full attention to emotional issues for many reasons, despite emotional competency being at the core of success in learning.

All experience, all adventures are essentially an emotional experience; they are experienced in the mind. In this chapter we have offered ideas as to the role and function of emotion in experiential learning. In the next chapter we give insight into ways of reading the signs and working with emotions as part of the experience, and we offer ways of accessing the roots of emotion in experiential learning.

7

Working With Emotions

> ...use allegories, figures, wondrous speech or other hidden, round
> about ways, to convey meaning and resolve difficult situations.
> (Benson, 1987: 203)

INTRODUCTION

In this chapter we offer more ways to read emotional signs and to work with emotions as part of experiential learning. We offer more methods to access the roots of emotion and ways to surface feelings and challenge emotions, and we further explore how humour, metaphors, trilogies and storytelling can be used to access and influence the emotional connection to learning.

This sensing, surfacing and expressing of both positive and negative feelings requires great skill and care. Difficult feelings do not go away by being denied or censored. It is good practice to enable the colour and richness of the feelings of learners to be expressed and considered in a controlled way so as to maximize their understanding of the learning processes. As we have already stated, to deny feelings is to deny learning. Yet to access the deeper emotions of learners can be difficult, and with it comes an associated sense of risk; it is often perceived as unknown territory.

In Chapter 1 we created the learning combination lock to show how the senses form the basic conduit for an external experience to be translated into an internal stimulation. The stimulation of the senses creates an affective response, one that is a powerful determinant of subsequent learning. Helping people to be conscious of the emotional experience can allow them to manage and intensify their own learning.

THE EMOTIONAL CLIMATE – MOOD SETTING
AND RELAXED ALERTNESS

Learning is more effective if people are in the right frame of mind. A psychological state known as 'relaxed alertness' is an optimum inner mental atmosphere for learning, and can be created. This requires the careful stimulation of certain senses of the learners. New tools are continually entering the marketplace, designed to stimulate the senses and so affect mood. These include 'relaxation glasses' and 'mind-lab' audiotapes, and there are adverts for 'progressive accelerated learning', using state-of-the-art sound technology to create and encourage particular types of brainwave patterns. These enable people to experience a focused state of consciousness and, because the brain gives messages to the body, sounds and light pulses can influence our physical condition. Music, stories or other stimulating material can create special moods or states of mind. Police even advise pubs to play music from children's programmes to reduce aggression on the streets at closing time. Music affects the rate of breathing, blood pressure, pulse rate and muscle activity, and specific types of music can be played to correspond to brainwave activity. The associated mind waves can correspond to welcoming and introductions, raising energy levels, inducing a reflective mood or preparing for departure. Pulses of flashing light and sound vibrations are known to influence brainwaves and therefore mental and emotional states. Many writers comment on the powers of music in facilitation and, in particular, in the importance of setting the atmosphere or learning climate (Benson, 1987; Robertson, 1999; Heron, 1999). Four main types of brainwaves can be stimulated: alpha waves indicate alert relaxation, when the brain is open to new information and thought processes are clear and calm; beta waves are present in the state when we are most able to use critical faculties, solve problems and make decisions; theta waves are slower still and support creative thinking; delta waves indicate deep sleep.

Olfactory sensations are also important (Wilson, 1997: 282):

- Orange improves communication.
- Basil and lemon increase mental clarity.
- Pine is refreshing and inspirational.
- Ylang-ylang relieves anger.
- Bergamot is calming, and found in Earl Grey tea.

Many of these smells are now available as canned products, and they allow for experimentation with sensory stimulation to influence mood, providing yet more simple tools for the experiential provider to influence the emotional side of the learning climate.

A practical exercise: Experiencing calm

Use before sorting time or solo time:

- Make yourself comfortable: find your own place to lie or sit relaxed with your hands down by your side or clasped on your lap.
- Read these instructions once and then proceed.
- Concentrate on the large circle below.
- First take three minutes to listen to your own breathing.
- Now concentrate on the exact middle of this circle O; use only your peripheral vision, and *slowly* stimulate the senses:
  - see three objects around you;
  - hear three sounds;
  - smell three things;
  - feel three things.

(You might have a slight feeling of an out-of-body experience.)

Robertson (1999: 240) describes how volunteers were easily tipped from sadness to elation by simple techniques. He describes some simple experiments he conducted, such as how simply pulling eyebrows together for a few seconds can change people's mood. Moment by moment the brain is changed by experience: by what people think, see, hear or remember. By using a variety of relaxation exercises and brain gymnastics, Robertson suggests that people can make their experience more effective.

OVERCOMING EMOTION – FEAR

Emotions have a powerful effect on learners. Emotions influence everyday behaviour and they can have a distorting effect on learning. Understanding learner emotions is therefore of primary importance in facilitating change. Johnson (1996: 185) describes in detail a case study where he changed powerful, fear-based blockages in a person in a maximum security prison, a rich context in which to explore ideas about working with experience on such emotional issues. Johnson reports that he 'tapped into his emotions... unblocked an emotional dam, unfroze his major emotional plumbing and facilitated his renaissance'. Some of the basic issues addressed in this and the previous chapter are that anger and aggression are often based on fear, and that trust is a strong antidote to fear.

Fear is one of the strongest primary emotions, which can be both conducive to improved learning and toxic to learning. Fear is the result of powerful emotional circuitry embedded in the brain (Goleman, 1996), resulting in a conditioned response. Mallinger and De Wyze (1993) describe these fears as being present in many people. For example, some clients pride themselves on being reliable, hard-working and self-disciplined; they are perfectionists. Their offices and homes are neat and organized, and they are always in control. They are successful and financially secure. But there is a downside. They may be confident and poised on the outside, but they might be hurting inside. The standards they set themselves are so high they are constantly setting themselves up for disappointment, and their rigidity may be preventing them from enjoying life and forming relationships. An uneven life–work balance, which we discuss in our chapter on good practice and ethics, can often be due to fear. Such fears need managing so as to create a new balance, for being too much in control can result in being out of control. Learners with signs of being 'too perfect' might have:

- a fear of making errors;
- a fear of making the wrong decision or choice;
- a strong devotion to work;
- a need for order and a firm routine;
- frugality;
- emotional guardedness;
- a tendency to be stubborn or oppositional;
- a heightened sensitivity to being pressured or controlled by others;
- a need to know and follow the rules;
- an inclination to worry, ruminate or doubt;
- a tendency to be stubborn;
- cautiousness;
- a need to be above criticism – moral, professional or personal;
- a chronic inner pressure to use every minute productively.

(adapted from Mallinger and De Wyze, 1993)

The research that produced Mallinger and De Wyze's book, *Too Perfect*, was initially conducted on neurosis, but many of the doctors and researchers professionally associated with the authors commented that the findings were close to many of their own feelings and behaviours. The book describes how being overly in control can get completely out of control, and encourages people to look at their own mental scars produced as a result of their fears. The suppression of fear, a fear of the truth, of how it actually is, is a reason for much misguided behaviours, especially managerial actions at work. There is reluctance about being honest with other people and one's self. Worse still, people often fail to see that there is something fundamentally wrong. Harvard professor Chris Argyris describes this phenomenon within communication at work. His article, 'Good communication that blocks learning' (1994: 77), comments:

> What I have observed is that the methods these executives use to tackle relatively simple problems actually prevents them from getting the kind of deep information, insightful behavior, and productive change they need to cope with the much more complex problem of organizational renewal... and they do not surface the kinds of deep and potentially threatening or embarrassing information that can motivate learning and produce real change.

The communication blockage can be further illustrated by reference to the communication model in Figure 7.1. People are experts at rituals and cliché, gossip, fact, solutions and judgements at work. It is the 'functional communication' of work, for some managers. The communication triangle has significance for experiential learning providers, in reviewing and reflection skills. If learners are not in touch with their own fears,

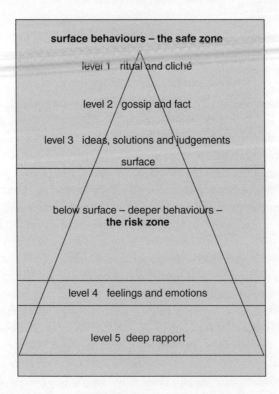

Figure 7.1 The communication iceberg

emotions and feelings, then a priority need is to help them to access the right levels of inner communication through deeper levels of rapport, to move beyond the superficial haze of rituals and cliché, facts and solutions.

Argyris (1994) suggests that logical, robust, solutions-focused behaviour is not always appropriate and that in the name of positive thinking managers often suppress what everyone needs to say or hear. In a self-protective haze of defence, single loop responses provide single loop solutions. The fix-it hat is donned and the same old hat gets the same old responses. Trusting others is part of the process of letting them learn. Managers who have been coached to put to one side their fix-it hat describe feelings similar to having cigarettes taken off them. They pace up and down, not knowing what to do with redundant hands, not being able to fix:

> It is not difficult for people to identify with the notion that work life is 'emotional'. Fear, worry, contempt, envy, anger, infatuation, loneliness, pride, joy, guilt, tedium and so forth are embedded in working experiences – to a greater or lesser degree. The extent to which they are overtly expressed, or publicly admitted, depends on the nature of the individual and the openness of the organisation's culture. Emotions can be seen to shape, and be shaped by, myriad work actions, such as decision-making, training, selling, persuading, hiring. Learning – creating, retaining and reproducing new knowledge or behaviour – can be regarded as implicit or explicit to these activities.
>
> (Fineman, 1997: 13–14)

Learners do tend to talk more easily about any emotional elements of experience in the past tense rather than the 'here and now'. Experiential providers often encourage learners to speak about their experience in 'here and now' as a continuous dialogue. Sometimes a range of questions such as 'How are you feeling right now?' when a person is on a high-ropes course can be the simple trigger required to surface the inner feelings. Similarly the question, 'Has anyone else had these feelings?', can encourage other members of the group to become aware of and express their feelings. Observation of body language by providers, especially facial expressions, and carefully and gently feeding back what is seen can also be a trigger for learners to express feelings.

MAPPING FEARS: ACCESSING THE INNER FAMILY

Maps are used for many things. They help people to get where they want to, even though in reality they sometimes do not represent the 'truth'. Take the London Underground map. The rail lines do not travel in the straight lines that the map would have us believe, yet if the map showed reality it would be far harder to use. We have used mind mapping software such as Mind Manager to help people to use visual images to increase productivity, organize tasks quickly and communicate ideas easily. Experiential learning providers can also use maps to help participants map out their fears. By visiting the bank account of experience we can take a look at some of the information held in there and maybe with practice change some of the unwanted circuitry in the brain. We can do this for example by creating 'fear maps' and then rewriting them. Asking people when they have been sad, bad or glad in their life can be a very productive start to this process. In a critique of Kolb's theory of experiential learning, Holman, Pavlica and Thorpe (1997) argue that the theory is placed within cognitive psychological tradition and tries to explain social, historical and cultural phenomena in a mechanical way: 'Rather than functioning systematically and mechanically, a person's inner life reflects interpersonal transactions, for example conversations and dialogues. In this way thinking – even when alone – always remains quasi-social' (1997: 140).

People talk to themselves; we all have an inner dialogue. Before a difficult or undesirable event this inner talk can be destructive or positive. Thinking and reflecting through the inner talk is a quasi-social phenomenon, because we have inner conversations with ourselves through these other inner people. We refer to this when considering *The Inner Game of Tennis* by Gallwey (1986) in the final chapter. Wilkes (1999) in *Intelligent Emotion* has a chapter devoted to 'The people who live within us', and recommends that people train and develop their own inner family. She suggests that 'our culture encourages us to think of ourselves as one person and no more' (1999: 39).

Psychologists have called the main personality the ego, which is Latin for 'I'. It is usually the leader of the family but if it becomes too dominant all the other family are silenced! Using positive affirming language can overcome some self-destruct language of this inner family of the self, as sometimes just one inner person takes control of the others. However, there are ways to take back control. One person inside the mind is the inner critic. It talks all day long, and seems to set many of the rules by which people operate. Challenging these unspoken rules can be very useful, as it is these rules that create many negative and destructive thoughts.

Some of the classic language of the inner critic dialogue is:

- I must never make mistakes.
- I must never look foolish.
- I must never get angry.

- I must always appear happy at work.
- I must be highly competent at all times.
- I must treat new ideas with great caution.

These same rules underpin some everyday fears. They have a powerful effect on people, and experiential learning providers can encourage people to examine them. Another list that rears its ugly head on occasions involves the rules other people set, and begins 'They should... They must...' These rules, as we have said earlier, are about control. Underlying these rules then is the fear of losing control. Many people do not change behaviours owing to the fear of what will happen. Fear of losing control or fear of finding something out that cannot be faced, about self or others, results in hesitation and apprehension. The inner voice says it is safer apparently to do it the way it has always been done. This results in compelling passion to control oneself and others, and even the environment. The Johari Window (Figure 7.2) is useful in exploring these issues. The Johari Window is used regularly by experiential providers to examine how people approach others. It was created by Joseph Luft, a psychologist, and Harry Ingram, a psychiatrist (hence the origin of the name – the Joe and Harry window!). The window shows four panes. The top left-hand window, for example, contains the aspects of self that are known to self and are evident to others. The façade covers aspects that are known to self but hidden from others.

Control brings more apparent safety, comfort and security, in a world surrounded by machines and computers that control the environment.

	Known to self	Not known to self
Known to others	arena	blind spot
Not known to others	façade	unknown

Figure 7.2 The Johari Window

Getting away from mobile phones, satellite systems and predictable, regulated environments might explain why some people stretch themselves by seeking rescue-free wilderness. High-ropes courses are now commonly used in many countries to demonstrate a range of basic emotional responses to challenges. These techniques focus on the emotional base to learning. One development centre we visited had pictures on all the walls showing exciting images that represented many of the basic emotions in life, such as fear and challenge. One image of a sailing boat had a caption that said that a boat was safe when it was in the harbour but that was not what it was designed for.

Learning providers can also help people to address fear with less dramatic methods, asking people to spring-clean the inner rules that sit in their unconscious mind with three steps. Learners can rewrite their own rules and realize that it is OK and human to make mistakes. Learners can learn to value themselves *warts and all*, loosening the grip of perfectionism:

1. The rule (the left-hand column):
   I must never show my nerves in public.
2. Which really means (the right-hand column):
   I couldn't stand the embarrassment if people saw me looking flushed and nervous.
3. So we revise the rule:
   I prefer not to show my nervous feelings in public... but if I do people will understand. Importantly it would not be the end of the world. Most people feel nervous about these things at one time or another. I might not like it but I can cope with it.

USING TRILOGIES IN EMOTIONAL WORK

Undoing and changing habitual behaviours alters our normal response to an experience. Self-control and awareness can be powerful tools to self-development in experiential learning. Benson (1987: 203) makes reference to the *I Ching* (Book of Changes) and suggests that the clever experiential group worker should 'use allegories, figures, wondrous speech or other hidden, round about ways, to convey meaning and resolve difficult situations'. Popular, well-known trilogies are also used to help to resolve difficult emotions. They help people to get in touch with the unconscious inner environment, helping them to read and interpret what is happening, especially cause and effect thinking, and so enable them to move towards positive change and transformation. Breaking down the mind processes into simple steps and grasping what is generating external actions and behaviours can be a very powerful experiential event for people. Frank (in McLeod, 1997: 25) asserts that 'certainly, it can be demonstrated that in all human societies people experience "problems in living" that are dealt with through a combination of listening, re-framing, catharsis, interpreta-tion and behaviour change'. Many writers have recommended a variety of basic steps for iterative change, which are commonly used in develop-ment training. They have a gestalt feel to them in that the steps help concentrate on the 'here and now' of feelings and so paradoxically result in change. Goleman, for example, talks of using the traffic light analogy to aid emotional self-control.

Calming and speaking the inner feelings are vital steps here. Anger as an expression of emotion is all right, but the direction in which anger is sent is more significant: how it is sent and to whom it is sent are key concerns. In dealing with our anger and other emotions we see the useful-ness of these trilogies. Anger is actually designed to protect people from a perceived threat, and so they cannot be angry unless they are also afraid. Fear then can induce anger but, when people want to try alternatives, an anger management relaxation technique can be used, as shown in trilogy two. What is so interesting is that there are many such trilogies and they are all so similar. Assertiveness, negotiating, giving and receiving feed-back, and criticism training all have common roots in three-step trilogies (see trilogy four). Significantly all of these trilogies, according to Wilkes (1999), are based on trilogy six, which is the basic trilogy.

Altering the mind: Six trilogies for change

Trilogy one: the emotional intelligence

1. **Red light**. Stop; calm down; think.
2. **Amber light**. Say the problem and how you feel.
3. **Green light**. Go ahead and try your best plan.

(Goleman, 1996)

Trilogy two: the self-anger control trilogy

1. First, say **stop**; I don't like this.
2. Second, take a **deep breath**; during exhalation, relax face, mouth, jaw, etc; take a deep breath in; during exhalation, relax hands, shoul-ders, arms.
3. Lastly, continue with a **slower, more controlled pace**, trying new, less angry behaviours.

(Lamplugh, 1991)

Trilogy three: the calming trilogy for use on others

1. **Calming** the person. Focus on calming his or her emotions not logic.
2. **Reaching**. 'Uh huh, I see...' (nodding). 'We can sort this out by...' All of this is to develop gradually a less emotional base to the talking, with open-ended questions.
3. **Controlling**. Break the issues down into their basic components and move towards solutions.

(Lamplugh, 1991)

Trilogy four: used in assertiveness, feedback and negotiating

1. **Listen** to what is being said and show that you understand – don't deny, defend or justify.
2. **Focus** on the issues and facts, and seek clarification.
3. **Move** towards a solution and agreement on the solution.

(Fritchie, 1988)

Trilogy five: to dispute the internal voice of defeat – the critic

1. **Thought stopping**. As soon as you hear it, say 'Stop it' to yourself.
2. **Challenging accuracy**. For example, 'Would I really like myself if I were so perfect?'
3. **Making the negative purposeful**. Replace 'I cannot do it' with 'This is a real challenge for me.'

(Wilkes, 1999)

Trilogy six: the basic trilogy map

1. **Revise** the past.
2. **Revitalize** the present.
3. **Redirect** the future.

(Wilkes, 1999)

USING HUMOUR AND OTHER POSITIVE EMOTIONS

We often ask new university postgraduate students if they think it is possible to have intense experiences that create a mild sense of ecstasy whilst studying! We are of course referring to flow and peak experience, and they laugh at us. But as we saw in the previous chapter endorphins can be produced by both physical and mental stimulus, as we move between the fine balance of anxiety and flow. People can release excess emotions such as anxiety through relaxation and fun. The function of ice-breakers and energizers is to do just that.

A sense of humour can be a powerful influence on learning, and studying can become a form of play. A professional trainer in a prestigious blue-chip organization once said to me that she found her postgraduate research a stressful experience at times. In one letter she jokingly said to her tutor that he need not worry as she had now put the razor blades away, but that she couldn't help but notice the length of rope in the garage! Her humour was her way of facing, making light of and communicating to others the stress she faced at times. Yet she also experienced many 'highs' and when she finished her research work she was very elated and very proud. She had entered Master's postgraduate study, and found it stressful but also exciting and adventurous. Cognitive and affective learning are not separately lived phenomena.

One reason for being interested in the role of humour as an emotion in learning was that we were concerned to encourage students to 'let go' of any obsession with grades. We wanted to encourage them instead to access and gain a greater understanding of the underlying emotions and feelings that influenced their ability to learn. We wanted them consciously to experience flow, take more risks, make learning more fulfilling and let the grades take care of themselves. Some people can connect to these emotional feelings through their use of humour. One of the authors collected examples of humour in student–lecturer correspondence on distance learning programmes, and these suggest that those who are able gently to expose some of their feelings about their work, even in a humorous way, may benefit. The following extracts are interesting.

Humour in learning

'This presentation is a vast improvement on your first assignment, from which my optic nerves are still recovering,' said my tutor on reading my attempt as a student at using a draft standard dot-matrix print-out.

'Positively my last fling! You asked for "lots of comments" – and I have surpassed myself, and I am now off to immerse myself in an extremely large gin and tonic. Not to drown my sorrows but merely to recuperate,' said my tutor on reading the last edition of my 'draft' dissertation!

Some student humour during the stressful last leg in the period of doing a dissertation:

'Would it be better to lump the data together? What do you think? Does it make sense? (Sounds like a song!) The razor blades are in a safe place (but I can't help noticing that length of rope in the garage!!!!)... I will phone you soon for some quality psychotherapy. Regards.

'PS Someone told me you can buy these [dissertations] on the world-wide web?'

(extracts from a letter to me as a tutor from a Senior Training and Development Officer at a major UK hospital studying for a Master's degree)

'Well, it's now 12.30 in the morning and I think I should go to bed. This has been a useful exercise for me, even if tedious for you. I look forward to any pearls of wisdom you may wish to cast in my direction.
'Goodnight!'

(Senior Training Manager, London Underground)

'Dear Colin, I have added to my draft in the past two weeks but still feel frustrated by a lack of real headway, combined with a growing feeling that I'm not really sure what I'm doing!!'

(Training Manager, Magistrates' Courts
(Beard and McPherson, 1999)

High energy and positive behaviour can follow positive thought. Encouraging people to look up towards the sky, put on a happy face and smile can make them feel good (Robertson, 1999: 241). People can also be encouraged to experience sad feelings by slouching their shoulders low, with head bowed and eyes looking down at the floor. In a classic Peanuts cartoon, Snoopy is advised by Woodstock that if he wants to get the most out of feeling depressed, then this is what he must do! Holding the eyebrows up high for a minute can make people feel more positive. Adopting positive physical postures does work and, for example, it is worth doing before dealing with difficult issues.

ACCESSING EMOTIONS THROUGH POPULAR METAPHORS

Metaphors present a powerful tool to access and explore feelings:
A single word can possess multiple meanings; yet as the common saying goes, one picture can be worth a thousand words. And if one

picture can be worth a thousand words, then one experience can be worth a thousand pictures. And if an experience can be worth a thousand pictures, then one metaphor can be worth a thousand experiences. But in the end, a metaphor only possesses value when:

- it is able to interpret the experience
- in a manner that provides a picture
- that produces words
- that have meaning
- for that particular person.

(Gass, 1995)

Metaphors can be used to help people to see or understand that which otherwise would remain misunderstood, unobserved or in the subconscious. *Visual–spatial intelligence*, for example, can be stimulated by metaphoric interpretations, by developing the ability to learn directly through images and thinking intuitively without the use of verbal language. Heron (1999: 102) suggests that in facilitation, theoretical inputs can be enriched by interweaving them with a variety of imaginal inputs. He offers seven examples:

- **metaphor** – the imaginative use of myth, metaphor, allegory, fable and story to convey meaning;
- **instance** – describing an illustrative incident, or dramatic case study, from real life;
- **resonance** – recounting associations and memories evoked by what is going on, in order to find meaning through resonance with the form of the other situation, which may be from some quite different field;
- **presentation** – presenting non-verbal analogies in the form of graphics, paintings, music, mime or movement;
- **dramaturgy** – combining metaphor with presentation in a creative piece of theatre;
- **demonstration** – showing in your own behaviour, both verbal and non-verbal, what it is you mean; modelling a skill in action, positively showing it well done, and negatively showing how it can degenerate;
- **caricature** – giving feedback to someone by mimicking his or her behaviour and caricaturing, in a kind way, the salient features to which you wish to draw attention.

Many of these are discussed elsewhere in this book. The experience–person match is thus a complex process and there are many methods to consider and choose from to help people interpret their experience. The imaginative use of myth, metaphor, allegory, fable and story to convey meaning is the focus of this section.

In the 1960s and 1970s environmental campaigners helped people to 'see' concerns about the earth, using titles like *Silent Spring, The Population Bomb* and *Only One Earth*. In 1993 a popular book about communication between men and women hit the headlines. It was called *Men are from Mars – Women are from Venus* (Gray, 1993). On the back of this book the promotional piece said:

> Once upon a time Martians and Venusians met, fell in love, and had happy relationships together because they respected and accepted their differences. Then they came to Earth and amnesia set in: they forgot they were from different planets. Using this metaphor to illustrate the commonly occurring conflicts between men and women, Dr. John Gray explains how these differences can come between the sexes and prohibit mutually fulfilling loving relationships.

A metaphor can provide another way of reflecting and focusing on a particular experience, so allowing us to gain new insights. A metaphor is a figure of speech that transfers meaning. The word itself is derived from the Greek *meta* (trans) and *pherein* (to carry). According to Parkin (1998), a metaphor is a comparison, a parallel between two, sometimes seemingly unrelated, terms. Metaphors tend to be used to help people to 'see' or 'connect' in their minds, to and from real or imagined inner and outer worlds. Providers of experiential learning often consider the activities as being more of a medium for learning, a means to an end, and see the value in the process of learning rather than in the nature of the activities per se. The activities employed are important though, as, in theory, they often serve as metaphors in themselves and so strengthen the potential connection between the programme and the workplace (Gass, 1992; Gass and Priest, 1998), ie metaphor is the analysis of experience.

Morgan (1997a) in his book about organizations offers a unique and original mechanism to help us to see, understand and manage organizations. He does it through a series of different metaphors. However, he also offers a word of caution and suggests that insightful learning through the use of seductive metaphors has its limitations: 'Any given metaphor can be incredibly persuasive, but it can also be blinding and block our ability to gain an overall view' (1997a: 347). In other words, metaphors can create ways of seeing and ways of not seeing. Using many different metaphors can thus help us to overcome the limitations of others. Morgan offers 'Bibliographic notes' towards the end of the book, and explains in some detail the historical use of metaphors. He describes how Aristotle suggested that the metaphor was midway between the unintelligible and the commonplace.

We can use metaphors in many ways. Feelings about work are so often expressed in metaphorical terms: 'I am just a small cog in a big machine'; 'I'm in a new team creating a work of art!' Picture-based metaphors help with a way of seeing, thought-based metaphors illustrate a way of thinking, sound metaphors guide a way of hearing, emotional metaphors access a way of feeling and activity metaphors can illustrate a way of doing things. Parkin (1998: 10) in her book on storytelling explains the use of several ingredients in a personal metaphor, using a common saying 'My head is as heavy as lead', where:

- The **topic** is head.
- The **vehicle** is lead.
- The **ground** is the feeling of heaviness.
- The **tension** is dissimilarity between the two domains, ie lead is metal and the other is head or flesh.

In therapeutic work metaphors are used to help people to surface unconscious inner thoughts and feelings and so influence the development of new behaviours. The metaphors connect the conscious mind with the unconscious mind. 'Trust' and 'fear' in participants might, for example, equal loss and exposure. In dealing with addictions, trauma or abuse, much of people's sense of existence or personality is beyond their awareness, and the therapist helps to apply the metaphor based on a client's behaviour (Stouffer, 1999). The client creates this self-metaphor with the help and guidance of the therapist, to help access his or her sense of being.

Corporate metaphors are likely to be very different. Metaphors can be used, for example, as concept-forming in a corporate event designed to connect an experiential activity to workplace production issues. High-rope challenges can represent the challenges of real life. Cliffs can represent the challenges of a giant project or that daunting change in life an individual might have to face. Finding good metaphors that enable us to see things differently requires skilled experiential providers. Benson (1987: 204) suggests that instead of coming at problems from rational deliberation and logic, which can lead to protectionism and defence, metaphors can be more intuitive and spontaneous:

Every method, exercise, or technique then as I use it, is a metaphor: a way of shifting perception and creating meaning. I am not interested in any medium or technique as an end in itself but as a means of engaging people and providing a context for work, which is directly related to the members' level of ability and willingness to act. From this perspective the value of any technique lies not in its skill or knowledge base but in what it points to, its ability to act as a sign-post, open up dialogue, and encapsulate meaning.

A metaphor can also be introduced through storytelling, or through cartoon images. These can be powerful ways to reinforce learning from experience, in both the unconscious and conscious. Cartoons, art, drama, models and conceptual frameworks are all enabling media that allow us to readjust our perceptual field, our ways of seeing and understanding the world. They can be powerful cathartic tools, simplifying and reducing complexity on the one hand, but also making emotional issues easier to grasp and comprehend. Many of these techniques were discussed in Chapter 4, where we explored the adjustment of experiential reality. In this chapter we explored the possibility of accessing, in a metaphoric sense, the 'inner family' of people within our minds. This requires careful listening and the construction of metaphors of the person, or 'self-metaphors'.

METAPHORIC INTERVENTION

In the global Outward Bound movement there has long been a debate about letting the experience speak for itself. Rustie Baillie, back in the 1960s, then a course director at Colorado Outward Bound in the USA, first coined the phrase, 'Let the mountains speak for themselves' (Bacon, 1987; James, 2000). Later Outward Bound included the 'Metaphoric Model' to raise awareness of the metaphoric nature of the activities (Hovelynck, 2000). Gass (1995) in his *Book of Metaphors* offers a clear and concise approach to the use of metaphors in adventure programmes, where the matter of letting the experience speak for itself is located alongside many other techniques. He examines the pragmatic use of metaphors in development work, building on his background in therapy, and argues that metaphoric transfer of learning takes place when parallels exist between two learning environments. A metaphor is an idea, object, process, environment, task or description that is used in place of another different idea, object, process, environment, task or description to help people to see or make a connection to reality. If the connection is through an idea, object, process, environment, task or description that is actually identical, and 'real', then the connection is said to be isomorphic (see Gass and Priest, 1998 for a description of examples). The classification offered by Gass is fashioned from the work of Bacon and Kimball in 1989 (in Gass, 1995). Gass created different facilitation techniques, based on six generations of facilitation skills that have evolved over time. In order to demonstrate the purpose and function of the six techniques, Gass uses the internationally well-known outdoor exercise called the Spider's Web. The Spider's Web is an exercise that uses a descriptive metaphor, and involves people trying to get through but not touch a mass of cord usually tied between two trees to create the spider's web. We have rearranged the six examples so that techniques that can be used prior to the event are presented first. Thus:

- *Prior to the activity* taking place the facilitator would ask questions that focus the learning that might occur. The facilitator **directly frontloads** the experience.
- *Prior to the activity* the facilitator would set the scene or context of the activity so as to relate it to the specific learning, eg to the work conditions of participants such as the problems of loading in a warehouse environment, or to the reception desk team, etc. The facilitator **frames** the experience.
- *Prior to the activity* the facilitator might deliberately but indirectly make reference to fictitious events to try to prevent certain behaviours occurring, eg 'We had a group last week that did this and failed because everyone put their "fix-it hats" on and moved straight into solutions mode, preventing discussion from...' The facilitator can **indirectly frontload** the experience.

As we remarked earlier, experiential learning programmes move from *introduction* to *action*, to *reflection* and *transfer*. These four stages all offer opportunities for various interventions and non-intervention, but choosing not to intervene can be powerful, requiring trust in the process, letting the experience or event speak for itself. There are other options to consider after the event:

- *After the activity* the facilitator might not make any insightful comment about the experience. The **experience speaks for itself**.
- *After the activity* the facilitator might provide the group with feedback about their general behaviour after the experience, such as what they did well, what they might need to work on, what they learnt, etc. The **facilitator speaks for the experience**.
- *After the activity* the facilitator would use questions to foster a group discussion about the above. The **facilitator debriefs the experience**.

Frontloading, framing and other techniques can be developed much further. Providers can include appropriate famous film clips, video footage of previous groups, TV soap extracts or cartoon images to send powerful messages. They often work well with young people. These media can reinforce key points, especially if they are seen as coming from other known or respected sources. Such media can be potent when the medium and message speaks for itself, thus providing excellent techniques that remove the scepticism associated with the facilitator who provides instant expert solutions.

CONCLUSION

This chapter explored more ways to access the feelings and emotions dimensions of learning, representing the first key tumbler in the inner cogs of the learning combination lock model. The chapter explored the states of relaxed alertness and other mood-influencing techniques, including stimulating scents and body language adjustment. Fear and perfection were seen to play key emotional roles in experiential learning, fundamentally influencing the way we communicate.

Accessing techniques included the use of 'mapping' to gain entry to the deeper levels of dialogue of the 'inner family'. Rewriting the inner rules, using trilogies, humour and metaphors were all investigated as means to access emotions. We also discuss mood-enhancing and accessing techniques in other chapters. In Chapter 8 on good practice and ethics we explore the practice of emotional engineering.

8

Good Practice And Ethics

> *Good reflective practice takes practitioners beyond mere competence*
> *towards a willingness and a desire to subject their own taken for*
> *granteds and their own activities to serious scrutiny. Competence is*
> *not enough.*
> (Jonston and Bradley, in Hunt, 1999: 235)

INTRODUCTION

This chapter explores the nature of good practice and the differing roles played by providers of experiential learning. We examine the good and bad practice of intervention, emotional engineering, the use of power and control as well as climate and value setting. Much of the second half of the chapter concentrates on the many dimensions of ethical behaviour associated with experiential learning, and case studies and scenarios are offered to explain the ethical models provided. Finally a number of codes of practice are compared to find the central themes or common ground. The focus in places is on outdoor management development. However, the themes of the chapter are applicable to all trainers and developers.

THE BOOMING BUSINESS

As spending on training and development work continues to grow and the mechanisms of delivery continue to diversify, so concerns about suitably trained and qualified people have continued to gain momentum. Ulrich and Hinkson (2001) comment that more than £20 billion are spent annually on global corporate leadership development programmes alone. The sums of money involved are very large and inevitably some sectors of the industry have seen an increase in criticism. An article in *The Times* (London) on 15 July 1998 called 'That's enough bonding, I resign' by D McGrory commented: 'Big-name companies are estimated to be spending

£550 million a year dragooning staff on to activity courses which occupational psychologists claim build team spirit and foster a more harmonious working environment.'

Williams (1996) commented on the lack of standards in the UK: 'In the last two decades management training and consultancy has mushroomed: over £2 billion each year is now spent on it, and there are about 2,700 firms specialising in it... So it seems curious that there is almost no proper evaluation of this training, no benchmarks, no criteria of success or failure.'

With growth will come the inevitable calls for standards of competence and ethical guidelines. The number of organizations delivering such programmes is increasing, as is the variety of locations used and the diversity of methods, as we have demonstrated throughout this book. Concurrently, society is becoming more litigious, governing bodies are increasingly embracing the language of competence and standards, and 'functional analysis', and the insurance industry is becoming more discerning. Consequently institutional guidance documents and inspector–watchdog roles are proliferating. In response to the increase in adventure, challenge and risk we see that: 'Training managers and others who are considering embarking on outdoor team-building and management development activities that may involve some real or perceived physical hardship or risk... have expressed concerns that there is an absence of practical and ethical guidelines to enable them to take fully informed decisions' (IPD, 1998: 1).

Experiential learning providers come from a mixture of disciplines such as traditional education, rehabilitation, therapy, corporate training and personnel development, outdoor development and adventure, and recreation-based training and development. All are involved in learning in different ways, using differing approaches, and so it is unlikely that there is any easy solution to generic, universal standards of competence.

This chapter explores ethics and good practice, and covers intervention issues, professional practice, the use of power and dependency, climate setting, ground rules and control, which are so important in determining the 'who, what, when, where and how' of experiential learning. We also review the role of reflexive practice to maintain personal and professional development. We then move on to examine a broad range of ethical dilemmas.

THE DELIVERERS

Role model. Mentor. Counsellor. Outdoor Educator. Instructor. Friend. By whichever name they are called, Outward Bound Singapore instructors are, undeniably a special breed. Their work is not merely the transfer of skills or knowledge, but, more importantly life values. They challenge participants to see the possibility in impossibilities, to dig deep within themselves for what is seemingly absent, to stretch to greater achievements.

(Outward Bound Singapore brochure, undated)

This was a message portrayed by Outward Bound Singapore in one brochure. Their experiential providers, ultimately, are the people who deliver the programmes and so interact directly with the client learners, and investment in their competence and good practice will produce a good return. To find a collective term to describe their role is clearly problematic. Living with the ambiguity is perhaps best.

The term 'trainer' is derived from the Old French *trahiner* (to drag) from the Latin *trahere* (to pull). In contrast the word 'facilitator' has a different flavour or feel to it, and comes from the Latin *facilitas* (easiness). This meaning then is to do with making it easier, to help (Bee and Bee, 1998: 1).

In the USA, the Association for Experiential Education convened a task force of 115 experiential training and development practitioners from around the world to produce a document titled *Definitions, Ethics and Exemplary Practices (DEEP) of Experiential Training and Development (ETD)* (DEEP, 1999). This task force set out guidelines for good practice, which contained a reference to definitions of trainers and facilitators. A facilitator is an 'individual responsible for managing the learning environment to assist individuals/groups to achieve value from the learning process'. A trainer however is said to be 'a practitioner who leads and directs prescribed learning for skill development, towards measurable explicit results' (DEEP, 1999: 18–19).

Boud and Miller (1996a) caution about the use of titles, and found difficulty with a whole range of terms that they considered for use in their book. They felt that the word 'facilitator' comes with much conceptual baggage, having resonance 'with humanistic psychology and work with individualistic concerns' (1996a: 7), so they opted for the French term 'animateur', but remained worried about the association of this title with 'organisation and acting'. Allison (2000a: 45) suggests careful consideration in the use of phraseology, as words portray values, and he debates a range of terms to describe the providers, advising equal caution in using terms to describe the learners, such as 'kids', 'punters', 'clients', 'youth' or 'participants'. Using the word 'client', he suggests, locates providers in the 'market of consumption'.

The UK Chartered Institute of Personnel and Development produce a guide to outdoor training (IPD, 1998), giving guidance on the choice of suitable development providers. They make reference to two kinds of training staff, and note that it is important to be aware of the distinction.

They regard tutors as 'those who should have the experience and qualifications in training, development and facilitation' (1998: 5). Instructors however 'have experience in outdoor activities – for example, canoeing or climbing – for which they will usually have qualifications from an approved body (but not always – a few activities are not covered by qualifications)'. They also suggest that a progression exists from instructor to trainer roles, and comment (1998: 5):

> tutors will often have got into outdoor training because of their interests in outdoor pursuits, and they may also be competent as instructors in one or two activities, while instructors may have ambitions to become trainers. Even if individuals are competent both as instructors and tutors, however, the distinction between these two roles is important for managing events, dealing with delegates at an appropriate level, and for health and safety reasons.

Titles can clearly also affect one's status, so, for simplicity, we have chosen to use the relatively neutral title of 'experiential providers' in this book.

FACILITATOR ROLES

What then are the key roles of providers of experiential learning? Developing people involves a qualitative change to the way individuals are, bringing out latent potential. The DEEP initiative defines experiential training and development (ETD) as 'a client centred approach to individual, group, and organisational learning, that engages the adult learner, using the elements of action, reflection, transfer, and support'. Experiential learning, they state, 'synthesises knowledge from practices of experiential learning, adult learning and organisational development' (DEEP, 1999: 8–10), and has a number of key roles:

- **Relationship development** – services that enhance interactions and motivate individuals through short-term events. Examples include energizing, incentive/reward, networking and celebration events. These events are purposeful and incorporate elements of reflection, transfer and support, as distinct from entertainment and recreation events, which do not.
- **Performance enhancement** – training in skills and competencies that result in improvement of personal, team and organizational effectiveness. Examples include communication skills, executive coaching, performance management and conflict resolution.
- **Consultation/intervention** – services addressing the interaction

between behaviour (individual, leadership and team) and business setting elements (eg reporting line structures, communication and decision-making processes, incentive/compensation systems). Activities may include analysing misalignments among these pieces, advising on possible growth/change initiatives, and coaching.

In the UK the key industrial overview body set up by the government to establish performance standards for the corporate training sector uses a key purpose statement for training: 'to develop human potential to assist organisations and individuals to achieve their objectives'. This statement has a business focus to it and it is aimed at human resource development specialists, particularly within corporate training departments. This is in contrast to the much broader, life-values approach adopted for example in therapeutic or youth rehabilitation work, where facilitators require a very different set of skills.

Power and control are also fundamental to the styles of delivery by learning providers. Back in the 1950s Carl Rogers, the eminent US psychologist, made controversial statements about teaching, declaring that anything that can be 'taught' is rather inconsequential, following his investigations into 'expert telling' versus finding out and experiencing (Rogers, 1993). His focus was concern over the intrinsic limits of what teachers can do. He explored the nature of teaching and learning, expressing concern with the ephemeral nature of what he called the 'jug and mug' approach to learning, where the so-called expert pours knowledge into the mugs, the recipients. His interest lay with the nature of 'learner-centred learning', and was concerned that the provider should not always control the agenda. Experiential learning providers regularly face such issues of power, control and intervention, as Table 8.1 highlights.

Bentley suggested that 'Facilitators concentrate on providing the resources and opportunities for learning to take place, rather than "manage and control" learning' (Bee and Bee, 1998: 2). At the heart of this dichotomy however is the issue of power and control, a subject Heron explores in *The Complete Facilitator's Handbook* (1999). Heron offers interesting views on the use of power and considers three approaches to facilitation. The first is the hierarchical mode where the trainer is leading from the front and in charge. In this mode trainers provide meaning, interpret events and take responsibility for major decisions. The co-operative mode is where power is shared and the trainer guides the group to be more self-directing and collaborative. The third mode is autonomous, where the facilitator respects the group's independence and autonomy so that people are given the freedom to find their own way.

Table 8.1 A dichotomy of power and control

Learner-centred	Provider-centred
Providers work with the natural curiosity and concerns of the learner.	Passive learning is encouraged.
There is a learning contract.	The provider has a rigid syllabus to get through.
Real issues and problems are worked on and used as vehicles for learning.	Trainees learn by memorizing, and use artificial case studies.
Feedback on self-performance is encouraged.	Learning is monitored, examined and assessed by the trainer.
Learners are considered to have a valuable contribution to make.	The trainer is the repository of knowledge.
Learners are trusted to learn for themselves.	The teacher/trainer knows best.
Responsibility for learning is shared with the learners.	Trainees wait for the trainer to lead.
The learning provider offers resources to learn.	Learning is limited to the trainer's knowledge.
Learners continually develop the programme.	The trainer dictates the flow of the programme.
Learners and providers have joint responsibility and power.	The trainer has responsibility and power.
There is a climate of genuine mutual care, concern and understanding.	Trust is low; trainees need constant supervision, and the trainers remain detached.
The focus is on fostering continuous learning, asking questions and the process of learning, and learning is at the pace of the learner.	Knowledge is dispensed in measured chunks decided by the trainer.
Emphasis is on promoting a climate for deeper, more impactful learning that affects life behaviour.	Emphasis on here-and-now acquisition of knowledge and skills to do the job.
There are no teachers, only learners.	The teacher/trainer is, and remains, the expert.

© Colin Beard, 1980, Course materials, Training the Trainer

INTRUDING COMPLICATORS OR ENABLING ANIMATEURS

Good experiential providers can help to change hearts and minds, life values, group dynamics and organizational cultures. Poor experiential providers can be seen as patronizing, and their performance can become an exaggerated ego trip, a subject explored by Rae (1995). He uses a three-dimensional grid consisting of *skills*, *concerns* and *competence* to examine a classification of trainer types. With the grid came a range of titles: professional trainer, humble expert, endearing bumbler, shallow persuader, boring lecturer, directive instructor, oblivious incompetent and arrogant charlatan! Trainers have also been variously described as martyrs, science boffins, chat-show hosts, army officers, actors, magicians and many other names.

Allison (2000a) in seeking to establish the essence of good practice, describes the six fundamental or defining characteristics of the high-quality outdoor experience, and argues that if they are not present then the experience for the individual will lack quality. One of the key ingredients is the *authenticity* of the facilitator. Similarly, work on the development of excellence in facilitation by Wickes (2000) suggests that high levels of peak experience by participants can occur more often when providers 'tread lightly'. Wickes also produces a map for facilitator excellence, where facilitators attain their peak experience. He offers 21 key ingredients including: creating the right climate; getting in – rapport; creating experiences that work; creating engaging, memorable and meaningful experiences; helping people review, articulate and share personal learning; making it easy to disclose and share experiences; maintaining a constructive atmosphere; and creating a powerful, emotional and satisfying experience.

Significantly, the choice of when or how to intervene, or when not to intervene, appears to be at the heart of good practice. To intervene at every step along the way is likely to be counter-productive. Those who facilitate behavioural changes in individuals, groups and organizations can, in their desire to deliver a showcase performance, create pressure that overrides a key principle that 'Animators need to operate in ways that make their own interventions increasingly redundant, thereby avoiding the use of their own power to create dependency and thus exercising control over the learners' (Boud and Miller, 1996b: 16).

A gradual reduction in provider control and intervention over time might help, as it allows learners to build on their experiences and confidence. Adler (1975) in his work on group psychology refers to the stages of dependency, counter-dependency, independency and finally interdependency. Whilst experiential providers continually debate these fundamental issues, the safety of learners lies not just with the physical nature of the experience, but also in the intellectual, moral and emotional domain.

DYSFUNCTIONAL AND INDIGENOUS LEARNING

Some feel about experiential education the way Hemingway felt about making love: Don't talk about it, you'll only ruin the experience. We know it's good because it feels good, and as G. E. Moore, the philosopher said: good is good, and that's the end of the matter. It can only be defined in terms of itself, it has intrinsic worth so there is no other standard to judge it by, it requires no further justification. The values are 'self-evident.' Let the mountains speak for themselves!

(Nold, in Wichmann, 1995: 113)

A number of other writers support the idea that experiential providers should simply 'let the mountains speak for themselves'. Loynes (2000) explores what he calls 'indigenous learning', which he regards as more authentic, 'real' and 'natural', and argues that learning shouldn't be overly interfered with. He notes that experiential learning can only occur when people attach meaning and value to their experience, but regards experiential learning as 'natural' when people do this themselves, or with colleagues participating in the experience. Intervention by others, he argues, especially when there is an element of imposed morality, theory or judgement, can disturb or interrupt the emergent indigenous learning and negate it as experiential learning. This can be accidental or deliberate. Underpinning this important debate about the transactive nature of experience, and the degree to which facilitators intervene, is the extent to which the learning is planned or allowed to emerge (Megginson, 1994), which we explored in Chapter 3.

Loynes (2000) takes a different approach on some planned learning, and refers to the Hitler Youth Movement and corporate team building as two very diverse and different examples of dysfunctional experiential learning using the outdoors. In a thought-provoking style, he suggests that facilitators should refrain from creating a proving ground for fixed ideas, and that experiential learning should be a source of *emerging* ideas, rather than a place to prove other people's fixed ideas. Loynes suggests that, instead of imposing pre-packaged theories or ideas to generate pre-prepared solutions, providers should allow people to build their own theory from their own action. The dualism of intervention and non-intervention is however not so simplistic. The degree to which providers intervene or deny or fail to provide opportunities for people to tell and share their experience, through their stories, is an important psychological consideration. McLeod (1997: 100) comments that 'very often the existence of a personal "problem" can best be described as a response to silencing, the unwillingness of others to hear the story that in some sense "needs" to be told'. Central to the experiential provision is this notion that individuals and organizations may need support and encouragement in order to tell their story. Neutral intervention is at the heart of a client-centred practice (Rogers, 1993), and can encourage people to tell their story.

Heron conducted extensive research into facilitator interventions, and in his book *Helping the Client* (1990) he offers a range of facilitator interventions, including echoing, selective echoing, open and closed questioning, empathetic divining, checking understanding, paraphrasing, logical marshalling, following, consulting, proposing or leading, bringing in and shutting out. These interpersonal skills, used for the benefit of learners, form the essence of good facilitation. They are similar to the behaviours identified by the Huthwaite Group (Rackham and Morgan, 1977) and used in 'behaviour analysis'. They too include proposing, building, supporting, disagreeing, defending/attacking, testing understanding, summarizing, seeking information, giving information, bringing in and shutting out. In checking understanding, for example, the facilitation phrase might be 'So can I just check this – what you are saying is...?' This gentle checking intervention encourages and checks the story, rather than redirecting it. Selective echoing involves the facilitator in selecting 'some word or phrase that carries an emotional charge or stands out as significant in its context' (Heron, 1999: 266). This is done in order to give the client space to explore, in any direction, the significance of what has been reflected or echoed back to him or her. This kind of intervention involves a degree of selective interpretation without leading the story, and it can help the client to focus. Likewise, in his therapeutic work McLeod (1997: 114) refers to similar key intervention skills:

- **Approval**. Provides emotional support, approval, reassurance or reinforcement. *Accepting or validating the client's story.*
- **Information**. Supplies information in the form of data, facts or resources. It may be related to the therapy process, the therapist's behaviour or therapy arrangements (time, place).
- **Direct guidance**. These are directions or advice that the therapist suggests for the client either for what to do in the session or outside the session. *Structuring the process of storytelling.*
- **Closed question**. Gathers data or specific information. The client responses are limited and specific. *Filling in the story.*
- **Open question**. Probes for or requests clarification or exploration by the client. *From a narrative perspective, open questioning can be used to invite the telling of a story or to explore the meaning of elements of a story.*
- **Paraphrase**. Mirrors or summarizes what the client has been communicating either verbally or non-verbally. Does not 'go beyond' what

the client has said or add a new perspective or understanding to the client's statements or provide any explanation for the client's behaviour. Includes restatement of content, reflection of feelings, non-verbal reference and summary. *Therapists using a narrative approach may wish to communicate to the client that they have 'heard' the story, or may attempt to focus attention on a particular aspect of a story.*

- **Interpretation**. Goes beyond what the client has overtly recognized and provides reasons, alternative meanings or new frameworks for feelings, behaviours or personality. It may establish connections between seemingly isolated statements or events; interpret defences, feelings of resistance, or transference; or indicate themes, patterns or causal relationships in behaviour and personality, relating present events to past events. *This response includes a wide range of narrative-informed interventions, centred on the general goal of retelling the story in different ways.*

- **Confrontation**. Points out a discrepancy or contradiction but does not provide a reason for such a discrepancy. This discrepancy may be between words and behaviours, between two things a client has said or between the client's and the therapist's perceptions. *In narrative therapy, the client is encouraged to resolve the tension or incongruity between opposing versions of a story.*

- **Self-disclosure**. Shares feelings or personal experiences. *The therapist gives an account of his or her own story, either in terms of relevant episodes from a personal life story, or framed in terms of a therapeutic meta-narrative, or drawn from a myth and other cultural sources.*

Good practice requires providers to increase intervention skills and to consider the degree to which they are open and transparent in describing their own values around which they operate; otherwise, because of the power they hold, they can have undue influence on other people's beliefs and values. Many forms of intervention exist, including *metaphoric* interventions, discussed in Chapter 4, and *gestalt* interventions. An example of the latter is described below.

Gestalt intervention

Gestalt provides a robust theory and practice of experiential learning and change at an individual, team and organization level. It is applicable in both indoor and outdoor environments, the focus being on the individual and his or her relationship to others. The 'here-and-now' approach to experience allows change to emerge naturally – the paradoxical nature of change – as opposed to planned change, which is traditional in our institutions, still largely modelled on a militaristic approach. A key outcome of change that occurs in this way is increased shared meaning between participants in an organization, because change comes through good contact and dialogue. People feel more empowered and start to create and recreate their own environments. Anybody wanting to improve the soul of the organization should take a look at what gestalt has to offer.

Individual coaching example

The individual was a senior executive in a large corporation, and the key issue was building confidence to move on to higher levels of work. Working in a global organization, she was concerned about raising her profile with a large assignment on the international stage. As I listened to her, she spoke with dissatisfaction about previous work she had done, being critical about her own performance. What I heard though was a number of key achievements where she had played a significant part. When I pointed this out and gave her some positive feedback, she shrugged my comments off and moved quickly on to something else. This had happened a couple of times already.

In the cycle of experience she was not spending time in resolution and withdrawal, enjoying the satisfaction of her achievements and celebrating her success (and no doubt that of others too). This was retroflection, turning energy in on herself, this time in a critical fashion. There was also a projection – other people were bigger and better than she was (despite her being a very tall person!). The feeling I was experiencing was sadness.

I gave her the feedback on what I observed her doing. I also pointed out that spending time in satisfaction and celebration was very confidence-building. She again shrugged this off and moved on. I stopped her and expressed my then irritation. I told her I felt as if my comments did not matter and I was not valued. This was the same process she went through to undervalue herself and probably others.

At this point she stopped and acknowledged what she was doing. I encouraged her to slow down and breathe for a few seconds. A lot emerged as a result of this. Some of the explanations were complex and interlinked – her role as a woman in this large corporation, personal difficulties balancing her work with the needs of her young son and an element of blaming herself for not doing enough with him. An underlying introject or 'rule' that emerged was around 'getting it all right'. It was very difficult for her to let herself off the hook.

Rather than trying to do anything about the specifics she was now talking about (which in any event would have meant stepping over the boundary), I felt she needed to learn how to stop just doing something and stand there! I encouraged her to spend time in resolution and withdrawal, focusing on her physical sensations more and breathing fully. This was the polarity of her busyness – taking time, relaxing and appreciating what she had achieved. I gave her some techniques to use so she could build a routine of spending more time in this relaxing and satisfying place. This process would give rise to natural change in how she approached things, rather than putting a plan in place for her to be different.

(supplied by David Willcock, Liberating Potential)

SETTING THE CLIMATE AND CONDITIONS

Wickes (2000), in a research paper titled 'The facilitators' stories', discussed aspects of facilitator excellence and peak experience management development programmes. Wickes offers a map of good practice, and we list some of the ingredients later in this chapter. The first item on his list is *creating a good climate*. How then do facilitators create a good climate for learning?

Heap (1996) in his article on the design of learning events addresses the conditions under which people learn best. He argues that people will be more motivated to learn if the events meet their particular needs. He suggests the design principles shown in Table 8.2.

Heron also addresses the climate of learning that has to be managed by providers. He creates six different dimensions of facilitation and demonstrates the broadness of the learning 'climate' (1999: 179), as shown in Table 8.3.

As Heron puts it, the challenge is 'to keep an eye on each dimension, and organise them all'. Needs, fears and anxieties can also be addressed before people enter experiential programmes, and early, sensitive communication with participants can alleviate some fears.

GROUND RULES AND VALUES

The learning climate can also be influenced by ground rules and working values. Heron (1999) creates three types of ground rules and, in a section

Table 8.2 Establishing the right climate for learning

Term	Meaning	Example
Congruence	The presenter should practise what he or she preaches.	If the course is about listening skills, the trainer should demonstrate use of listening skills.
Trust Building	Participants will work best when there is a trusting atmosphere.	If participants know how feedback will be handled, they are more likely to be more trusting and open with one another.
Clear Purposes	The purpose of each event should be clear.	Participants will know why they are undertaking the event.
Emphasize the Positive	The emphasis should be on how to get things right.	Give plenty of positive feedback.
Create Ownership	Ideas should come from participants themselves.	The trainer should ideally facilitate this learning process in a non-didactic way.
Whole People	Participants' home and non-work lives affect how people feel and learn.	The trainer should enable participants to share these whole-person concerns in a safe environment.
A Complete Process	The event should be considered as a whole.	Learners should be able and willing to put the training into practice.
Client-centredness	People find most value in the ideas they discover for themselves.	The task of the trainer is to respond to those needs flexibly and individually.

on what he calls culture-setting statements, offers advice to establish a group culture that will enable learning to flourish. *Discipline ground rules* set out the boundaries of behaviours, such as arriving on time and giving full attention when someone is working on issues in the middle of the group. *Decision mode ground rules* relate to planning and choosing what the group does, how the decision process might change at a later stage and so on. *Growth ground rules* are focused on commending sets of behaviours that will intensify personal learning and awareness, appointing self as the guardian, pointing out when someone forgets and so on. They might include listening with discernment not judgement, asking for support from others if needed and offering support if you can.

Table 8.3 The six dimensions of facilitation

The Six Dimensions of Facilitation	Facilitative Questions
1. The Planning Dimension	How will the group meet its objectives by means of an effective programme?
2. The Meaning Dimension	What meaning will be given to group experiences and actions?
3. The Confronting Dimension	How will the group's consciousness be raised in order to deal with facilitative issues?
4. The Feeling Dimension	How will emotive aspects of the group be handled?
5. The Structuring Dimension	How will the structure and methods be formed?
6. The Valuing Dimension	How will the integrity of the group be nurtured?

Example of culture setting and ground rules

Culture setting – a set of values as the basis for being and learning together:

- being co-operative and non-competitive;
- creating a safe, supportive and trusting climate;
- being experientially risk-taking and non-defensive;
- being vulnerable, and open to areas of inner pain, chaos, confusion and lack of skill;
- being open to our personal presence and power;
- exercising autonomy and the voluntary principle;
- participation in the political life of the workshop;
- adopting a spirit of enquiry without dogmatism and authoritarianism;
- exploring multi-modal, multi-stranded learning;
- having an open, transparent workshop process;
- enjoying ourselves;
- affirming confidentiality.

(adapted from Boud and Miller, 1996a: 78)

REVIEWING SELF-PRACTICE

The term 'reflection' is evocative of a number of images: mirrors, tranquil scenes in still waters, thinking idly about past times, and forms of meditation come immediately to mind. In the context of education and training, though, the term is often used specifically to signify an important stage in the learning cycle where a complex and deliberate process of thinking about and interpreting an experience is undertaken in order to arrive at a new understanding of events and our part in them.

(Hunt, 1999: 221)

Much of the theory and practice of learning that we introduce throughout the book applies to both participants and providers. Here we simply explore reflection for the purpose of self-review.

Learning from doing is the basis of good practice for experiential providers, but doing is not the same as learning, and the importance of the reflective process is that it is a deliberate, conscious act. From this we find out more about our own learning and working relationships (Hunt, 1999). Hunt reviews the nature of unspoken, 'tacit knowledge', where practitioners 'just know' even though it cannot be described or written about, and considers the dangers of not defining and bounding practice. In offering practitioners something to reflect on, Hunt asks what responsibility the reflective provider has for encouraging participants to reflect on their own work and/or learning processes. She quotes Johnston and Bradley (Hunt, 1999: 235):

Reflective practice at its best is neither just a set of operational techniques nor a clearly identifiable group of academic skills, but is rather a critical stance. Good reflective practice takes practitioners beyond mere competence towards a willingness and a desire to subject their own taken for granteds and their own activities to serious scrutiny. Competence is not enough. The reflective practitioner has to become, if not an *agent provocateur*, an educational critic who is willing to pursue self and peer appraisal almost to their limits.

Hunt, whilst offering an interesting theoretical and historical perspective on reflective practice, also examines her own personal experience on the subject of writing as opposed to merely thinking about practice. She focuses on (1999: 236):

- a particularly positive experience;
- an occasion when her interventions seemed to have made a real difference to someone's learning;
- a negative experience where things seemed to go badly wrong;
- an experience she found hard to handle;
- something trivial but which made her think, 'What's going on here?'

Continuous professional development (CPD) involves a systematic maintenance, improvement and broadening of knowledge, skills and personal qualities necessary for execution of professional and technical duties in professional working life. Self-review is an essential element in day-to-day experiences. Maintaining and developing professional competence and sharing expertise are recommended by Benson (1987) in *Working More Creatively with Groups*. In a chapter called 'Keeping your practice going', Benson advises that such reflection and reviewing requires concentration, persistence and hard work. He acknowledges that there is a client/participant expectation that deliverers are whiter than white, and so sometimes it is important that facilitators are also allowed to feel the pain of growing and failing and learning. Benson advises a system of ongoing recording as essential to developing powers of observation. This would enable facilitators to examine individual and group behaviour and to become reflective practitioners, creating dialogue with ourselves, to clarify thoughts, review practice, express feelings, gain a deeper awareness and thus improve. He also offers some survival procedures, as shown below.

Survival procedures for creative group workers

- Avoid crucifixions – do not try to save, rescue, or work it out for everyone all of the time... avoid being seen as a saviour, guru, or charismatic leader because we crucify our messiahs, shoot our presidents, and forget our pop stars more quickly than you would find comfortable.
- Don't push the river upstream – the more you do the less they do... what is required is the light and sensitive touch... learn to work from where the group is and go with the flow...
- Wait quietly until the mud settles – learn to wait and watch and listen. In this way your awareness is focused on the group and not just on your needs. Do not feel that you must intervene immediately.
- Learn to forgive yourself... make mistakes, and feel inadequate at times... be compassionate with yourself...
- Cultivate goodwill – help to explore self-defeating behaviours. And discover more positive ways of being.
- Make up your own rules – no book can give you the rules or the prescription... each group is different... do not be afraid to improvise... use your imagination... and intuition.
- Do your best and that is that.

(adapted from Benson, 1987: 249–51)

ETHICAL BEHAVIOUR

Like every other professional, training professionals work by assessments and value judgements. Training implies certain dealings in which one has to make a choice among various options. A choice, which implies solving a certain problem, implies formulating a value judgement about the available alternatives. Such a choice is generally based upon an ethical decision.

(Bergenhenegouwen, 1996: 26)

Helping people to learn is seen as intrinsically good, a virtuous activity that, until recently, has avoided some of the more serious debates about ethical practice. *Good practice* and competence come with good judgement born out of experience, and to an extent depend on the maturity of the profession. *Ethical practice*, however, is seen as different; whilst underpinning good practice, it is also regarded as being concerned with morality and integrity.

The nature of an ethical decision, as opposed to any other decision, is problematic, and the word 'ethics' actually covers a very broad range. The process of defining ethics is difficult, and dictionary definitions variously portray ethics as involving the science of morals, dealing with a branch of philosophy concerned with human character and conduct, or embracing rules of good behaviour and the principles of professional conduct. The principles of ethical conduct and professional practice move beyond legal compliance or satisfying customer needs. We now scrutinize the deeper, fundamental choices trainers face in everyday practice that are of an ethical nature, and analyse how ethical issues are constructed within a social, political and environmental context, and guided by principles of virtue and moral conduct, all of which change over time.

There is of course an ethical dimension to all that an experiential provider does, and one could therefore reason that all choices have something to do with ethics; it is only in their relative importance that they differ. The choice, for example, of deciding to take a contract or decline it and leave it to someone else, deciding which training methods would be most suitable for a set of clients, or how much or how little preparation needs to be done could involve ethical dimensions. At the most simplistic level, ethics might be considered as 'moral relativism', involving a set of choices between right and wrong behaviour, intentional or unintentional. There may not be a 'right' or a 'wrong' answer, but choice is inexorably linked with morality.

Petrick and Quinn (1997) regard ethics as the study of individual and collective moral awareness, which relates to judgement, character and conduct. In attempting to define ethics these writers embrace personal and institutional issues, fairness, exploitation, morality and right or wrong conduct. They introduce the breadth of the ethical debate that we now analyse in more detail. But first we consider a simple scenario. Read this and then reflect on what you might do.

Practical case study: Facing difficult choices – a scenario

This is an account of a management development event that actually happened, with many factors altered to disguise the identities of the people involved.

The incident

On the last evening of a three-day team-building event, following the evening meal, many of the delegates from a creative computer design company stayed up drinking in the bar into the early hours. This culminated in a fire extinguisher being set off at around 5 am, a vacuum cleaner being left switched on outside someone's room, and generally lots of noise and disturbance right through the night. Many of those involved in these 'high-spirited games' were high-profile individuals in the company, including the CEO, and the most senior instructor representing the outdoor management development company.

The next day

This was the final day of the programme. At breakfast there were two distinct camps: those who thought that the previous evening had been 'a good laugh' (ie those who had participated in the late-night pranks) and those who were extremely upset at the goings-on, owing to the disturbance, the lack of consideration for others and the image that it presented of the organization. Some delegates were sufficiently upset to be all set to abandon the remaining day of the programme and return to work. 'If that's what you call team building, you can forget it,' one person was heard to say. One group of two or three delegates were particularly offended by some of the language used towards them and others the previous night, and felt that 'apologies were in order'.

The programme for the final day was as follows:

9 am	Travel to water park (about 45 minutes drive by minibus)
10 am – 12.30 pm	Land-/water-based activity, culminating in giant raft build
12.30 – 1.45 pm	Final review; formal end of programme
1.45 – 2.30 pm	Return to hotel; delegates depart

The antics of the previous night had resulted in a 'team' that was now worse off than when the programme had started. The group were just about to leave for the last morning of events. A few people, including the facilitators and the managing director, were left in the hotel breakfast room. If you were one of a number of facilitators hired to work on this event by the outdoor management development company...

What would you do to rescue this event?

The answer to the scenario might be, 'It depends.' It depends on whether you hold the view that the outdoor instructors in this scenario were simply contracted to help on the management development programme. The situation might have been avoided by a company policy on alcohol, or adherence to a code of conduct. Were the instructors involved guilty of unprofessional conduct or was it really a corporate managerial issue for their senior staff to deal with? Did the instructors get involved in the drunken party at the request of the director, or is that not significant? Should the instructors involved have courteously bowed out early on that evening? These are some of the many moral decisions about the conduct of the clients and facilitator alike.

Ethical relativism is reflected in the nature of one's personal style of operating. Margerison (1988: 103), for example, refers to four consulting role models: detective, doctor, travel agent and salesperson. Margerison describes the consulting styles in detail, and suggests, 'We all have an approach to giving advice based upon a consulting model. It may not be written down, but it reflects itself in the way in which we consult and give advice.' The key words associated with these four consulting styles, when examined, give an indication of mindsets that can occur in the consultation process. The medical analogy is of a doctor approaching the client or organization as having an *illness* to be cured, and the consultant would be looking to generate normal good health. The consultant looks for *symptoms*, uses a form of *diagnosis* and then suggests the *medicine* to be *prescribed*. Occasionally *surgery* might be required in order to *cut out* unhealthy bits. If trainers and facilitators examine their own preferred methods of interacting with people in the consultation process, we see that people do say that they like to operate in one way more than in others. The travel agent approach is question-based and client-centred, where customers get what they ask for. The idea that consulting is a form of detective work or investigation generates a consulting style based on finding the *culprit* who committed the *offence*, apportioning *blame* and instigating punitive solutions.

Personal and organizational styles and cultural differences may occasionally be difficult to separate from the notion of integrity. Jones (2001) conducted research into ethical practice and interviewed trainers who anonymously admitted to placing bets on consulting and training sales outcomes, and competing with one another to get contracts. As a result they felt they were guilty of unethical practice. They wanted clients to take as many contracts as they could possibly sell in order to win bets. This, they claim, was due to the organizational culture that they worked in, one they found difficult to resist, and their description of events potentially locates them as *victims*, blaming the *organizational vow* for this ethical erosion. Personal integrity has a high value placed on it, yet an organizational pressure to perform can result in inexcusable behaviour (see Whyte, 1960) and some organizations have set up confidential phone 'hotlines' for employees to report ethical concern anonymously.

Block (2000) in *Flawless Consulting* refers to the shadow side of consulting, and argues that the negative reputation of some consultants is more to do with ethics than competence. Part of the problem, Block suggests, is due to promises made and the commercialization of the 'service', which can become too packaged and standardized. Block makes reference to a number of tensions between care and commercialization; of promising magic through re-engineering or the excellence movement; of entertainment rather than learning; of collusion between top management and consultants; of buying fashion trends. He also cautions that all consultants will have stepped over the moral line at one time or another, and that people must not try to solve all the problems in becoming what he calls the 'super-someone'. Four key combinations to consider are what learners want and do not get, what learners want and get, what learners do not want and do not get and finally what learners do not want but get anyway!

A QUESTION OF BALANCE

The imbalance between work life and personal life is increasingly under scrutiny, and experiential providers regularly detect these issues in development work. The UK Department for Education and Employment (2000) address the issues of work–life balance in their guidance code for employers. This publication by the UK government notes that organizations that are committed to work–life balance will:

- recognize that effective practices to promote work–life balance will benefit the organization and its employees;
- acknowledge that individuals at all stages of their lives work best when they are able to achieve an appropriate balance between work

and all other aspects of their lives;

- highlight the employer's and employees' joint responsibility to discuss workable solutions and encourage a partnership between individuals and their line managers;
- develop appropriate policies and practical responses that meet the specific needs of the organization and its employees.

Such organizations, it is suggested, concern themselves with fairness and consistency, valuing employees for their contribution to the business, not their working pattern. Monitoring and evaluation are recommended, and a good business communicates its commitment to work–life strategies to its employees, demonstrates leadership from the top of the organization and encourages managers to lead by example.

Learning providers working with corporate clients encounter conflicting views on how 'workers' should be looked after by 'management', and this can result in a climate within a programme being potentially at odds with the everyday world of the participants. The same issues can arise with any programme provider and client, such as 'youth' and 'youth workers'. Phillips and Fraser (1982) argue that if such programmes encourage people to develop skills that are not supported or valued by the organization, then the scene is set for a battlefield of recriminations.

Money also underpins the climate and operating behaviour. Dybeck (2000) debates the balance of commercialism and altruism, and illustrates his discussion with reference to the history of Brathay, a charitable organization based in the UK Lake District National Park. Dybeck describes how financial pressures during the history of the organization meant that it was difficult to maintain youth development initiatives, an area of work on which Brathay was founded. He argues that the charitable roots of many experiential providers like Brathay influence their operational culture and can create a tension with some aspects of private sector commercialism. Scott, the founder of Brathay, stated in 1967 that 'the idea that... good fortune called for a share of the family wealth to be allocated for charitable purposes has no doubt been the origin of most of the existing charitable trusts' (Dybeck, 2000: 113). There are also fundamental differences between the public sector and the private sector in terms of accountability, to the public or shareholders. These dualities create a wide range of ethical issues, for example:

- client-centred and organization-centred;
- workers and management;
- needs and wants;
- work and life;
- soft and hard skills;

- commercial and charitable;
- business and environment;
- corporate loyalty versus personal values;
- whistle blowing or keeping quiet.

Many ethical issues simply involve the careful balancing of the needs of those involved. However, ethics can also encompass a broader raft of organizational issues such as health and safety, balancing the needs of individuals as well as the organization and the selection of consultants. Ethical decisions might also involve training practice, confidentiality, sexuality, copyright issues, cultural issues, dishonesty and improper behaviour. Ultimately all providers have to decide what makes sense to them, and in so doing construct their own moral code. Some decisions are more difficult than others, as we shall now explore, and this requires all facilitators to take responsibility to review and learn from past experience.

A different kind of ethical issue arises in youth development programmes, where the 'highs' experienced on outdoor wilderness adventures can be temporary, and later prove debilitating. Euphoric adventures can leave young people vulnerable in the longer term, with subsequent feelings of disappointment, feeling low and feeling let down on return to their home environment (Davis-Berman and Berman, 1999). However, such disillusionment and potential crisis can be avoided by good practice, and Barrett and Greenaway (1995) suggest ways to overcome these negative effects, recommending a four stage realignment approach to change:

- close to home introduction;
- Outward Bound away-from-home experience;
- city-bound – working on preparation for the last stage;
- homeward-bound – for supported transfer of learning.

Tragedies and accidents also generate considerable deliberation on the subject of ethics. On 9 May 1996, five expeditions launched an assault on Everest. Twenty-four hours later one person had already died and 23 other men and women, mainly amateurs and paying clients, were struggling for their lives. In all, eight climbers died that day. Climbing protocol on the crucial turnaround time on the summit attempt was ignored, and three guides, with very high levels of professional practice, lost their lives. Speculation took place over the reason for the tragedy. The media spotlight, the competitive nature of the business, the commercial impact of a successful summit, personal reputation and oxygen deprivation all entered the ethical arena in the debate that followed. The event has been extensively analysed in books and journals (see, for example, Dickinson, 1998; Krakauer, 1997), and it is used as a case study in ethics by Hunt and Wurdinger (1999: 129). They point out that one guide:

[who] died as a result of his attempting to aid his stricken client rises to an extremely high level of a key moral virtue – courage. Similar acts of courage evidenced themselves throughout this expedition both by guides and by clients. Thus one can see that this case is extremely complex in its mix of virtues and vices. Internal and external goods germane to the practice are interwoven in a manner that defies simple judgement and analysis.

EMOTIONAL ENGINEERING

The negative use of personal skills is to be found in all stakeholders. Experiential providers occasionally witness individuals who use their newly acquired interpersonal skills, such as assertiveness training, to sustain negative attitudes towards work, confidently yet dishonestly defending their negative 'can't be bothered' behaviours with assertive vigour. Likewise corporate interest in emotional intelligence can be used for dubious reasons, as a form of emotional engineering. Teaching people the 'corporate smile', for example, might be interpreted as emotional engineering, and this raises ethical issues concerning the authenticity of imposed and artificially generated positive moods.

Fineman (1997: 13) argues: 'learning is inextricably emotional and of emotions. The traditional cognitive approach to management learning has obscured the presence and role of emotion… we need more explicit frameworks, derived from the literature on emotion, to place emotion as both a product and a process of learning. Special attention is required to the growth of corporate emotion engineering.'

Fineman (1997: 18) talks of the management of McDonaldized jobs that 'have been subjected to fine-tuned routines of emotion control and programming', and refers to the work of Hochschild (1983), who writes about the psychological 'work' done and the corporate 'feeling rules', in personally maintaining the corporately desired impressions. The term 'emotional labour' is used. Emotion in this sense is seen as something in the human machine to be controlled and learnt, in a neo-Tayloristic form. Emotion-as-performance is a competency that does not really require an ability to read or express emotion in any depth or variety. Fineman argues in contrast to Goleman (1996: 18), that the gung-ho view is that 'In an era of tough love it is the emotionally lean who are most likely to survive.' Hopfl and Linstead (1997: 9) are also critical of the scientific analytical approach by Goleman, and they suggest (1997: 5) that 'rationality has led to a relative neglect of emotional issues in organisational life'.

Emotions are dealt with in a functional way so that we 'discount our feelings, deny them to ourselves, project them on to others, rationalise them away or keep them private... treatments of emotions in the workplace concentrate on handling at the surface level what is apparent in conflict, or the encouragement of more open displays of the more positive emotions...' (Hopfl and Linstead, 1997: 8).

The corporate demand for staff training in emotional intelligence creates ethical issues for learners and experiential providers alike. Boud and Miller (1996a) describe a 'stripping down' of emotional intelligence so as to reshape employee attitudes for corporate profit. Fineman (1997: 19) in a similar vein argues that the ability to feel 'shame, embarrassment or guilt' is crucial to making ethical judgements, and that the push for business profits can easily override personal conscience. Fear of being 'caught out' and 'public pressure', he suggests, shapes management actions, rather than the conscience of the organization. Reid and Barrington (1999: 142–43) argue that loyalty to the organization should take priority over and above personal beliefs or 'favoured causes'. These suggestions can create tensions and emotional conflict. In having concern for the environment, Greenpeace comment that too often they have to act as the 'active conscience of industrial society' (Rose, 1996).

In exploring ethics we conclude that the subject is essentially about choices that concern practice and conduct. The broad and boundless nature of ethics means that models and guidelines can be appropriate to help providers solve ethical problems.

ETHICAL MODELS

Priest and Gass (in Barnes, 2000) divide ethical issues into two types: *principle ethics* and *virtue ethics*. Others refer to these respectively as *coded ethics* and *situation ethics* (Scott Peck, 1997). Principle or coded ethical issues are answered by predetermined rules or principles. Many of these are to be found in the codes of good practice we examine in detail next. A well-known example is the Ten Commandments. Decisions become a matter of principle, and as such they can be seen as relatively independent of the specific situation. A facilitator looks to these externally set codes or rules to inform judgement. External agencies often create these socially constructed, de facto sets of basic tenets. Virtue or situation ethics on the other hand involve *de jure* (it depends) ethical issues. Here the answer has to be considered in the light of each specific situation or scenario as it occurs. It might for example depend on personally held values and beliefs, or be culturally determined. Here the facilitators have to look inside themselves to find the answers.

Choices and judgement are value-laden and so involve axiology and morality, but holding the moral high ground is always risky. Hunt (1995) refers to the internal and external success of the goods and services provided. If the contracting organization believes that a good service has been provided, but the provider knows that corners were cut and that the work was not of a high standard, the external goods were successful but the internal goods were less successful. The facilitator did not have the satisfaction of a job well done. The latter then is one of virtue, where standards of excellence are set internally by each professional facilitator. Hunt (1995: 335) quotes McIntyre as saying 'a virtue is an acquired human quality, the possession and exercise of which tends to enable us to achieve these goals which are internal to practices and the lack of which prevents us from achieving such goals'. Hunt argues that it is not just technical skills and interpersonal skills that make up ethical practice; intellectual virtue and moral virtue also make up ethical practice. Knowing how to perform technically and interpersonally is intellectual virtue, but this has to be guided and propelled towards a proper end by moral virtue.

The ethical subjects operate at three levels, and all stakeholders share some responsibility for setting and maintaining the ground rules, climate and behaviour. The negative consequences of not doing so can incur differing degrees of harm. We create a tier system (see below), similar to a risk management approach.

Ethical models

Ethical subjects – three levels:

1. **meta issues** – societal, trends, contextual, future;
2. **organizational-level issues** – culture, state actions and interventions;
3. **personal issues** – methods and behaviours.

Ethical decision making – three tiers:

1. **most serious** – because they affect large numbers of people, cause greatest harm, are on the verge of illegality;
2. **less serious** – for example, deliberately misleading people;
3. **less harm** – might include unintentional actions that negatively affect people.

Similarly Kitchener (in Hunt, 1995) offers a model that creates a five-step approach to help facilitators find the answer to ethical questions, suggesting the issue is moved on up through each layer if the answer is not reachable at the previous layer:

1. **intuitive** – gut reaction as to what is right;
2. **option listing** – options, ramifications and outcomes are considered and weighed up;
3. **ethical rules** – written in established codes of conduct;
4. **ethical principles** – autonomy, fidelity, justice, choice, loyalty, respect;
5. **ethical theory** – either: a *balancing* approach, taking action that has less harm to clients, with the greatest positive outcomes to the greatest numbers; or a *universality* approach, creating a decision that might be applied to all similar situations.

Thus we see that ethical choices can be made by individuals and under-pinned by their own culture, styles of operating, philosophy, concerns and moral values. They are internally set. Now we explore the nature of exter-nally decided, institutionally set codes of practice.

CODES OF PRACTICE

Ethics then is the application of moral standards to good practice. The more experienced that providers are, the more the decision-making process becomes intuitive. Hunt argues that ethics should have a central role in the maturing profession of experiential education and offers two scenarios to illustrate his central debate about the role of virtue between and within professions. One involves a person who is under the control of psychiatric care; the other involves a person who faces a corporate edict. At a basic level both scenarios described by Hunt revolve around client decisions to participate in experiential activities, and the consequent use of coercion and intervention by others. In the first scenario the decision to come down from a high-ropes course appears to involve three people. The participant is a patient at a psychiatric hospital, and he wishes to come down. The instructor, in adopting a principle of 'challenge by choice' agrees to bring the client down, but is asked not to do so by the psychia-trist from the hospital, who informs the instructor that the youth is about to face an important psychological breakthrough. The facilitator is reminded that she is merely the employee of the hospital and is therefore under the supervision of the psychiatrist. Hunt then presents scenario two as a corporate scene where a woman refuses to participate in an activity, claiming that it has nothing to do with management skills. The CEO inter-venes and suggests that non-participation will reflect badly on the company. The facilitator decides that the decision to intervene with staff of the company is ultimately the decision of the CEO.

Hunt portrays these scenarios to unravel the deeper and more profound issue of whether practitioners set their own standards that govern their work, and the extent to which they merely act as technicians, providing a service to organizations. The extent to which the experienced practitioner is *permitted* to intervene in this relationship between the organization and its members, or *morally obliged* to is embodied in the notion of 'professional practice'. The relationship hinges on power, consent and respect for the individual, and the extent to which this is dealt with within the profession or left to others who contract the service.

Ethical responsibility might then lie with individuals, organizations or, at a higher level, the profession or the state. What then do professional bodies regard as the basic guidance required for the development of professional codes of good practice?

PROFESSIONAL BODIES AND THE PROFESSIONAL CODES OF PRACTICE

The professional bodies regard facilitator responsibility as stretching beyond the boundaries of caring for participants or clients. There are other considerations outlined in numerous codes of conduct for development trainers and facilitators, produced by many associations and institutions, and they have many common ingredients. The globally constituted members of the DEEP initiative explore five main responsibilities, whereas the Institute for Outdoor Learning (formerly the Association for Outdoor Learning) in the UK examines four areas (see Table 8.4). The latter code is detailed in the box below.

Table 8.4 Broad categories of responsibility

Global DEEP Initiative	UK Institute for Outdoor Learning
1. Responsibility to self.	1. Professional integrity.
2. Responsibility for professional development and conduct.	2. Professional responsibilities and relationships.
3. Responsibility to clients/customers.	3. Professional standards.
4. Responsibility to profession.	4. Environmental and cultural responsibilities.
5. Global responsibility.	

Institute for Outdoor Learning Code of Professional Conduct

A fundamental principle of membership is an understanding that the conduct of each member can be justified ethically and morally at all times and will bring credit to themselves and the Institute and the outdoor profession.

The purpose of this Code is to set out the standards of behaviour agreed to and upheld by members of the Institute as they cultivate and promote special values and importance of outdoor learning experiences. The revision, updating and use of the Code shall be the responsibility of the Trustees.

1. Professional integrity

- Members should maintain the highest of standards and values. Members should demonstrate fairness, consistency, honesty, tolerance, compassion, truthfulness and discretion during their work out of doors.
- The Institute may be judged by the conduct of its Trustees, Officers and Members. Consequently all members of the Institute should conduct themselves in a befitting manner.
- The logo of the Institute may not be used for personal or commercial purposes.

2. Professional responsibility and relationships

- Members have a duty of care to each participant and should accept their responsibility to protect the dignity, privacy and safety of all those for whom they are responsible. Members should define and respect the boundaries between personal and working life and never misuse a leadership position whatever the age of the client.
- When dealing with other members, agencies, clients, students, sponsors or the general public, members should present themselves as responsible persons and in a manner that inspires confidence and trust.
- Members should manage the activities for which they are responsible with due regard to student, client and staff emotional and physical welfare, complying with all legal requirements and Health and Safety guidelines.
- Members should accept that discrimination on the grounds of race, gender and sexual orientation have no place in outdoor learning and should be challenged if displayed.

- Members should safeguard confidential information relating to participants and use discretion when there is a particular need to share essential information with professional colleagues.
- Where a member delegates any activity or welfare responsibilities they should understand that the ultimate responsibility remains with themselves.
- Members should respect fellow members. Public or private reference to the conduct, integrity or quality of service of another member should be expressed with due care, accepting that there is a clear moral obligation to challenge unprofessional conduct.

3. Professional standards

- Members should work only within the limits of their competence and experience, acknowledging and adhering to commonly accepted, current best practice and standards.
- Members should maintain and develop their personal, professional competence and when possible share their expertise with other members and contribute to the debate on professional matters.
- Members should respect the needs, traditions, practices, special competencies and responsibilities of other institutions, associations, agencies and professions that share a common interest in Outdoor Learning.

4. Environmental and cultural responsibilities

- Members should conserve the natural environment, endorsing the principles of sustainable use and minimum impact.
- Members should be sensitive to the impact of their operation on the local community and cultural setting within which they work and minimize any adverse effect.
- Members should encourage knowledge, understanding and respect for the cultural setting within which they work.

GOOD PRACTICE: THE ENVIRONMENT

Most ethical codes of practice embrace environmental concerns, and the reduction of environmental impact can take place in many ways. Cooper (1998: 90–91) classifies the negative impact we have as *ecological* (disturbance to wildlife, trampling, etc), *physical* (damage to property, footpath erosion, etc), *psychological* (lack of respect for others, when one group or person affects the enjoyment of another) and *social* (noise, litter, dangerous driving, etc). The position people take towards environmental issues varies considerably (see Figure 8.1). Environmental impact reduction requires the right attitude, a degree of environmental education and understanding and, ultimately, a preparedness to take action. All three are important.

Support for the improvement of the natural environment by experiential providers who use the outdoors might include a whole range of new ideas, utilizing a broader range of instruments of change:

- carrying out experiential activities that contribute to the environment;
- stating environmental support through policy or on letterheads or products;
- encouraging the education and awareness of learners;
- signing up to and working with voluntary codes or charters of conduct towards the environment;
- reducing waste and dumping by using recycled materials creatively;
- directing tasks and practical action towards a productive end – such as tree planting or restoration;
- making donations to direct practical action groups;
- encouraging governing bodies to support environmental research;
- using annual access agreements or licences to caves, land or water to create fees for environmental repair;
- where possible purchasing environmentally friendly clothing and outdoor equipment;
- considering carbon debt repayments and other innovative schemes.

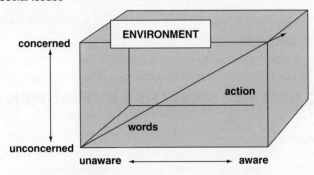

Figure 8.1 Environmental issues: people and responses

Ironically a great deal of experiential learning takes place in the natural outdoors, yet few recognize and fully value this free resource. Sadly, corporate environmental awareness training rarely utilizes the powerful attributes of the natural environment as a learning medium, as we discussed in Chapter 5. Environmental awareness training still takes place predominantly in classroom settings, and environmental concern is largely seen to be the domain of engineers, scientists, and health and safety specialists. The innovative use of the natural environment as the location for learning is described in many sections of this book. We hope some of our thinking will offer you new ideas.

CONCLUSION

It is not possible to create a once-and-for-all set of rules to guide good practice and behaviour, as the subject remains under continuous debate and negotiation from all stakeholders. Acting in a befitting manner, creating high standards and values, demonstrating fairness, consistency, honesty, tolerance, compassion, truthfulness and discretion, all form the underpinning conduct of good providers of experiential learning. We might look elsewhere, to external institutions, for codes of behaviour and guidance, or we might look within ourselves to find the answers.

> If people live with criticism, they learn to condemn,
> If people live with hostility, they learn to fight,
> If people live with ridicule, they learn to be shy,
> If people live with shame, they learn to feel guilt,
> If people live with tolerance, they learn to be patient,
> If people live with encouragement, they learn confidence,
> If people live with praise, they learn to appreciate,
> If people live with fairness, they learn justice,
> If people live with security, they learn to have faith,
> If people live with approval, they learn to like themselves,
> If people live with acceptance and friendship,
> He or she learns to find love in the world.

9

Ways Of Learning

> *Any experience that does not violate expectation is not worthy of the name experience.*
>
> (Hegel)

INTRODUCTION

In this chapter we will investigate the final tumbler of the learning combination lock, by briefly considering the ways in which people learn. An understanding of learning theories will enable us to select the appropriate elements from the various tumblers and thus make strategic choices regarding the manner in which we can encourage learning. The main theories of learning all involve experiential learning to some degree. We will then progress to the development and nature of reflective practice and action learning. These two practical forms of individual and organizational learning attempt to identify solutions to the challenges and problems that are faced and use the process of experiential learning.

THEORIES OF LEARNING

We are all unique and each of us has likes and dislikes, and effective and ineffective methods of learning. In this respect there is an almost endless list of individual learning theories. Take a moment to consider where and when you think best. Perhaps it is in the shower in the morning. Is it late at night just before you go to sleep? Individual variations such as these influence the success or failure of learning. In order to make the understanding of learning more manageable we need to provide some categorization of the main theories.

In essence, the main distinction involves the long-running debate about nature and nurture. The view of the authors is that there is an interactive dependency between the uniqueness of the individual and the specific influences that interact from the surrounding environment. It is the sum of these characteristics and the experiences that occur that shape the person. Wilson (in an article entitled 'Harsh words can deform children's brains for life' by Jason Burke, published in the *Observer* (London), 31 December 2000) stated, 'The nature versus nurture debate is being seen as increasingly outmoded. We are talking now about a complex interaction between genetic disposition and experience.'

The strategies that we use for our learning and that of others are based upon our conscious or subconscious philosophies about how people learn and their ability to learn. For example, if we believe that there is almost unlimited potential within human beings we may be encouraged to help them achieve their targets. If, on the contrary, we believe that some people are intelligent and others 'do not have it', we may be less inclined to support them. The influence of personal philosophies and more general ones is pervasive and can inhibit the learning process. It is important to be aware of the value of learning philosophies that can provide insights into the learning process but we should also understand the 'flip side' in that they can constrain our thinking and thus limit our potential to help people learn.

It is beyond the scope of this book to go into detail about the various learning theories that are noted in Table 9.1. More detailed information may be found by referring to the authors mentioned for each learning theory category. One important fact should be noted, which is that experiential learning would appear to be involved with all of these theories and thus provide a unifying theme.

THE DEVELOPMENT OF REFLECTIVE PRACTICE

While human beings have reflected on their actions for as long as we know, the circumstances described next are drawn from Kolb's writings about Lewin, and led to the formalization of the process of reflective practice. In 1946 Lewin and a number of colleagues worked on the development of training approaches in leadership and group dynamics for the Connecticut State Interracial Commission. Group discussion was encouraged between the participants and the staff, and records of the meetings were kept and later discussed by the staff without the involvement of the participants. However, the participants were concerned that they were not involved with this discussion and approached Lewin requesting permission to attend, and he agreed. Lippit, who was present, observed that a remark made by an observer was challenged by one of the participants who disagreed with the interpretation of events:

Table 9.1 Learning theories

Learning Theory	Description	Exponents
Action Learning/Research	Theory and practice inform each other as the individual applies theories in the environment.	J Locke, J Dewey, R Revans, K Lewin, D Kolb
Cognitivist	A person perceives stimuli and consciously interprets them in relation to his or her own mental frameworks.	J Bruner, J Dewey, K Lewin, G Kelly
Cognitive Development	Children pass through a number of stages of cognitive development.	J Bruner, J Piaget, L Vygotsky
Computational	The development of ICT has provided parallels with how the brain operates. Likewise, computers are being designed to operate more closely to the operation of the brain, eg parallel processing.	G Moore, R Kurzweil, A Turing
Conditioning – Classical	The greater the frequency and recency of a stimulus, the stronger the bond between stimulus and response.	I Pavlov, J B Watson
Conditioning – Reinforcement	Thorndike built on Watson's work but emphasized that after the response there was a satisfier or annoyer: thus S–R–S or S–R–A. The former encouraged and the latter discouraged behaviour.	E L Thorndike
Conditioning – Operant	Skinner argued that although a stimulus produced some automatic responses (respondent behaviour), operant behaviour in response to stimuli is dependent to some extent on the individual or organism.	B F Skinner
Gestalt	Wertheimer used the term gestalt to indicate pattern or configuration. He maintained that we see the whole picture, eg the relationship of notes in music or the relationship between a figure and background in a picture.	W Köhler, M Wertheimer
Human Development and Self-actualization	People develop at particular rates and need to be supported and encouraged.	F Froebel, A H Maslow, M Montessori, J J Rousseau
Humanist	The belief that knowledge resides within the mind of the individual and that the role of the teacher is to question the student carefully and thereby draw out this knowledge.	Aristotle, Plato, Socrates, C Rogers

Table 9.1 continued

Learning Theory	Description	Exponents
Hereditary	Our ability to change and our genes influence our development.	C Darwin, S Fraser, R Herrnstein
Neuroscience	The use of brain scanning of injuries, and operations on the brain illustrate how brain cells respond to stimuli.	R Carter, S Pinker
Theistic	Mental discipline is necessary to train the mind towards good rather than allowing evil to develop.	St Augustine, J Calvin

NB The concept of experience may be applied to all the theories above

At the end of the evening the trainees asked if they could come back for the next meeting at which their behaviour would be evaluated. Kurt [Lewin], feeling that it had been a valuable contribution rather than an intrusion, enthusiastically agreed to their return. The next night at least half of the 50 or 60 participants were there as a result of the grapevine reporting of the activity by the three delegates.

The evening session from then on became the significant learning experience of the day, with focus on actual behavioural events and with active dialogue about differences of interpretation and observation of the events by those who participated in them.

(Lippit, in Kolb, 1984: 9)

Kolb (1984: 9) stated that this incident demonstrated that 'learning is best facilitated in an environment where there is dialectic tension and conflict between immediate concrete experience and analytic detachment'. To put it rather less academically, the learner was freed to think about events that happened in order to make sense of them.

This leads us to the question, what do we mean by reflection? Dewey (1938: 9) defined reflective thought as, 'Active, persistent and careful consideration of any belief or supposed form of knowledge in the light of the grounds that support it and further conclusions to which it leads... it includes a conscious and voluntary effort to establish belief upon a firm basis of evidence and rationality.'

USING PROBLEMS AND CHALLENGES

In Chapter 2 we discussed Freire's (1982) concept of banking education in which the teacher 'narrated' and pupils were passive receptacles into which information could be poured. Freire was very critical of this approach, saying that not only did it dominate the pupils with a way of thinking but it inhibited them from thinking and learning properly.

To counteract the banking concept Freire (1982: 54) proposed 'problem posing education'. Rather than banking education with its anaesthetizing effect, 'problem posing education involves a constant unveiling of reality' and it 'strives for the *emergence* of consciousness and *critical intervention* in reality'.

Freire (1982: 54) stated that the teacher 'does not regard cognizable objects as his private property, but as the object of reflection by himself and the students. In this way, the problem posing educator constantly reforms his reflections in the reflection of the students. The students – no longer docile listeners – are now critical co-investigators in dialogue with the teacher.' This approach involved the teacher and the pupils working alongside one another rather than being divided by desks and more importantly being divided by didactic and organizational barriers. By reflecting together he believed learning was best achieved through providing pupils with problems rather than solutions. Freire (1982: 54) stated:

Students, as they are increasingly faced with problems relating to themselves in the world and with the world, will feel increasingly challenged and obliged to respond to that challenge. Because they apprehend the challenge as interrelated to other problems with a total context, not as a theoretical question, the resulting comprehension tends to be increasingly critical and less alienated. Their response to the challenge evokes new challenges, followed by new understandings; and gradually the students come to regard themselves as committed.

This approach to using problems to encourage reflection is a form of Socratic investigation. Through the process of challenge from either a problem or alternative perspectives from other people, reflection can lead to learning. This is a fundamental part of human nature, and Freire (1982: 56) maintained, 'Problem posing education bases itself on creativity and stimulates true reflection and action on reality, thereby responding to the vocation of men as beings who are authentic only when engaged in inquiry and creative transformation.'

Problems and problem solving are at the essence of human development, and this theme will be revisited in our consideration of action learning and also in the final chapter. The same principle of problem or challenge is incorporated in Chapter 5, 'Places and elements', where we consider how different environments can be chosen for their impact on the learning objectives.

REFLECTION-IN-ACTION AND REFLECTION-ON-ACTION

One of the main books on the subject of reflection is *The Reflective Practitioner* by Donald Schon (1983). He distinguished between what he termed reflection-in-action and reflection-on-action as a means of investigating how people used their experience to analyse and frame problems, propose action and then re-evaluate the experience as a result of the action.

Reflection-in-action considers the consequences of action whilst one is within the process. Thi~ ' what we term concurrent learning, and is discussed in Cʰ~ 'ection-on-action (Schon, 1987) involves thinkin~ ~al experiences, analysing them and then develo₁ ~f action; and this we call retrospective learninɡ ~orm of learning is prospective learning, ie explo~ ~ues, which is discussed in the next chapter.

Not o~ ~ reflection occur in a structured environment with formal support from the organization; it can also occur as a form of unstructured reflection where people gather together when they meet a challenging experience. This reflection occurs as managers attempt to make sense of the circumstances in which they find themselves.

Making sense of what is happening to themselves by professionals has been termed reflection-in-action by Schon (1983). This form of reflection occurs particularly where people face unusual and different experiences that they find difficult to structure and make sense of. Reflection-in-action does not necessarily require support or coaching because it happens spontaneously. However, for deep learning to occur there is a danger in relying on reflection-in-action happening, especially when time constraints put a premium on people making time to analyse what is happening. It is for this reason that many organizations have coaching, counselling and mentoring structures to support the development of their employees. Seibert (1999) called reflection-on-action coached reflection and illustrated the differences between the two (see Table 9.2).

SINGLE AND DOUBLE LOOP LEARNING

Allied to the process of reflective practice is Kolb's learning cycle and also Argyris and Schon's (1974) single loop learning and double loop (or deutero) learning. They drew on the work of Bateson's (2000) *Steps to an Ecology of Mind*, which discussed single loop learning and deutero learning. Single loop learning involved planning the action, undertaking it, evaluating it and finally learning from the previous stages (see Figure

Table 9.2 Reflection-on-action and reflection-in-action

Coached Reflection (Reflection-on-Action)	Reflection-in-Action
Planned intervention to support learning from an experience.	Spontaneous reflection that occurs as a result of a need to understand and respond to experience.
Learner(s) supported by a facilitator.	Learner(s) organize reflection themselves.
Is planned for specific times.	Can occur at any time but usually when understanding of the circumstances is necessary and when time is available.
Usually happens with learner(s) away from the immediate workplace.	Usually happens in the workplace.
Involves contemplation.	Reflection is an active process.

9.1). Essentially, it is not too different from the learning cycle and quality improvement cycle, which we saw in Chapter 2. What the learner asks is, 'Am I doing the thing right?'

Double loop learning or deutero learning is similar to single loop learning. However, in this case the learner steps out of the single loop in order to assess whether the activity he or she is involved with is appropriate and asks, 'Am I doing the right things?' (see Figure 9.2). For example, a traditional watchmaker might be operating within the single loop learning process and progressively improving what he does. However, it may be that he should have been asking himself whether he should consider digital technology. It was this single loop learning that caused the Swiss watchmaking industry so much trouble until they asked themselves, 'Are we doing the right things?' This may be a historical example but when looking through the financial pages of newspapers it is not too difficult to find illustrations of industries and organizations that have failed to reflect more widely on what they are doing.

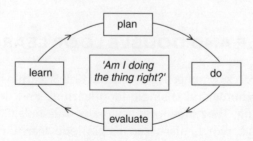

Figure 9.1 Single loop learning

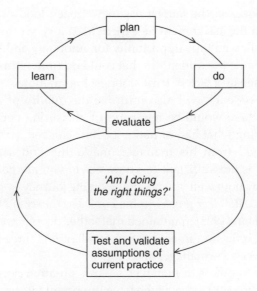

Figure 9.2 Deutero or double loop learning

ENCOURAGING CONDITIONS FOR REFLECTION

Although reflection-in-action can occur spontaneously within an organization, the possibility of it happening is conditional upon the variety of factors occurring at the time, eg work pressures may minimize the opportunity for reflection. In the research conducted by Seibert (1999) one manager described how, owing to a heavy workload, his reflection was momentary. This does not necessarily minimize the potential for reflective learning from the experience since there may still be potential for profound insights. However, constraining the opportunities for reflection may also severely limit the degree and quality of the reflection and therefore the degree of learning. It is hard both to do and to reflect at the same time when the issues are complex and may not be related.

Five main factors that encourage reflection were identified by Seibert (1999) and are described below:

1. *Autonomy*. Where people work autonomously they are personally responsible for their actions and therefore must think things through and decide for themselves. Where people operate within the responsibility of others there is a danger that they will abdicate the responsibility for thinking and just follow instructions. The degree of autonomy is the responsibility of the organization. Seibert described a manager, Ted, who was given a considerable degree of autonomy

while working on the launch of a new frozen food product. On his return from the assignment he experienced a very directive environment that allowed little opportunity for autonomy and reflection. It is easy to imagine the difficulties that could occur in terms of demotivation and a sense of lack of trust amongst his emotions.

2. *Feedback*. Feedback will also improve the quality of reflection, for without it there would be few ways of measuring performance and benchmarking what had or had not been achieved. For Ted feedback was received from his manager, marketing and sales staff, and retailers. It is not sufficient to know where you are going; you need also to know how well you are doing on the journey.

3. *Interactions with other people*. In his book *The Career is Dead, Long Live the Career*, Hall (1995) maintained that 'other people' were essential to supporting reflection-in-action. Seibert identified three types of interaction between the manager and others:

   - Access to others: a manager's work situation needs to provide interaction with others who have important information.
   - Connections to others: this category is not the same as 'access to others' since it concerns a 'meaningful supportive relationship' (Seibert, 1999: 60) in which bosses, peers, mentors and even spouses give emotional support.
   - Stimulation by others: the need for others to provide information, new ideas and perspectives, which encourage the development of ideas.

4. *Pressure*. Promotive pressure is the situation in which managers have a high workload with little time in which to complete it. 'Not surprisingly, this reflection was highly concentrated and of brief duration, often lasting for only a few moments' (Seibert, 1999: 61). Directive pressure is related to the pressure people experience as a result of undertaking a highly visible assignment that focuses attention on their project.

5. *Momentary pressure*. This refers to those few occasions managers have when they can reflect on their work. These occasions are often when the person is involved with other activities such as walking to a meeting, waiting for an answer on the telephone, or even in the lavatory! The categories described by Seibert above illustrate some of the circumstances when people reflect in the workplace. However, he does not discuss the quality of the reflective process and in particular how effective the insights are. The finding that managers have significant time pressures is nothing new and their limited time to reflect, sometimes in the toilet, indicates that personal management of time and the creation of thinking time is an essential ingredient if reflection-in-action is to deliver satisfactory results.

THE DANGER OF FORMAL EDUCATION AND TRAINING

It is only in the past 150 years that we have handed over the responsibility for learning to the educational system. Before then individuals were more responsible for what they learnt. Today, the result of the abdication of responsibility is that there is a dependence on the teacher. Expressions such as, 'I have never been taught or attended a course so I can't do it', are far from uncommon. In many instances, 'I need to go on a course' provides an excuse to avoid learning. Attending a course is not the only way to learn. This mindset needs to be discouraged because deep and permanent learning is often more likely to occur in the workplace or the home rather than in formalized situations.

Research at the Centre for Creative Leadership and at Honeywell Inc indicated that managers learn more from structured and challenging work experiences than from sitting in the classroom (Seibert, 1999). Five types of experience were found to encourage learning among managers and these are regularly used intentionally by organizations to encourage the development of their managers:

- project or task force – temporary work on a project;
- increase in responsibility – significant increase in size of people, budget or job functions;
- transfer from line to staff responsibilities;
- start-up – creating and developing an area of responsibility from scratch;
- fix-it – resolving a problem in an organization.

The human resource development departments of numerous organizations including PepsiCo, Hoechst Celanese and General Electric took managers out of their work environment for workshop-based coached reflection. This reflection occurred both at fixed intervals during a period of work and at its conclusion. The learners were provided with formal tools and structured processes to stimulate reflection.

CRITICAL REFLECTION

The term critical reflection is not to be confused with reflection used in the individual or organizational context. Critical reflection emerged from the work of the Frankfurt School and is often known as critical theory, which encourages emancipation and the development of a just and democratic society. It is illustrated in the work of Habermas (1972), which challenges 'the dominant, science-influenced rationality which privileges means over ends, facts over values, and which perpetuates arid intellectualism at the expense of people's feelings' (Reynolds, 1998: 187). Critical reflection is concerned largely with social issues while reflective practice is predominantly concerned with individual and organizational learning.

Case study: The case of Pegasus Transport

Background

Pegasus Transport Ltd, the firm at the centre of this case study, was started in spring 1988 by a husband and wife team engaged in a small-scale domestic removal operation. Initially, the business was run from the garden shed of a small cottage located in a rural village in the West Midland region of Great Britain. Neither Elisa nor Alexander Jones had any previous entrepreneurial experience. Before leaving full-time employment to start a family Elisa worked as a sales clerk in the accounts department of a large manufacturing firm in Birmingham. Alexander worked for nine years as the regional manager of a well-known vehicle rental organization. At the end of 1987, following the rationalization and centralization of hire operations and the relocation of the company to Wales, Alexander Jones found himself out of work. In his late 30s, he decided to invest most of his redundancy money in a new venture, which he could develop and grow into a successful family business.

Experiential learning as a proactive HRD strategy

Both husband and wife were aware of their skills limitations in relation to the intended growth path of the new enterprise but, by starting from basics, they hoped to learn 'on the job' whilst trying not to make too many costly mistakes. In their own words, 'learning from experience proved to be an acceptable and, at times, enjoyable way to progress from self-employment to micro-business status'. Initially, the chosen growth strategy presented Alexander and Elisa with many challenges but relatively few problems. However, by 1999 business growth started to accelerate in line with prevailing economic trends and staffing problems and related skills shortages multiplied accordingly. It soon became obvious that there was a shortage of qualified and experienced individuals in the local labour market and that the business could not support the expense of searching for and moving staff from other localities. It became imperative that a proactive rather than a reactive human resource development (HRD) strategy should be adopted. An accept-

---

able solution was hit upon when the oldest of their children left school and decided to join the family business. Dylan Jones was employed as a trainee and soon other school leavers were recruited in similar positions within various departments. It appears that a proactive HRD approach, based on experiential learning, supported and also contributed to the rapid growth and diversification of the transport business.

A number of different experiential learning interventions were adopted, most of which proved to be very successful. For example, mentoring became an important method of initiating and furthering experiential learning as well as transferring related knowledge. The use of both tacit and explicit knowledge to arrive at learning-based experiential outcomes proved equally successful as trainees began keeping personal learning logs, which, as they progressed through various jobs and positions, became increasingly available throughout the organization. Interestingly, both formal and informal training interventions were used to improve and widen learning interventions at all levels of organizational hierarchy. The choice of which intervention or the mixture of approaches was determined either by a 'mentor' or by a 'minder' as the informal trainers were known to staff. Furthermore, it appears that such choices were made in conjunction with the prospective trainee and on the basis of an extensive skill needs analysis, both at personal and organizational levels. It is often stated that experiential learning and related knowledge management act as important motivators and retainers of staff. Unusually in this case study, detailed training, development and attendance records appear to corroborate such claims. All leavers are offered an exit interview and the knowledge gained from departing employees has often been used to improve the retention rates of employees across the organization.

The original business has grown into a multi-site, nationwide operation and staff development became formally recognized as central to the future success of the corporation. A national training manager was appointed to lead and consolidate this important strategic function. Each location has a training station where new recruits are formally inducted to the organization and where they can take advantage of an extensive ICT-based local and national development database. Much of the material is based on multi-perspective experiential outcomes. The most important HRD strategic challenge for Pegasus Transport Ltd relates to graduate employment and development, which consistently proved more difficult and less successful in terms of staff retention. Several HRD options were tested in relation to graduate trainees yet only a small proportion of starters actually completed their training period. Even fewer achieved their mutually agreed medium- and long-term individual development targets. Some of the past failures were blamed upon the educational system and its perceived lack of relevance to working environments. The current training manager, a graduate and professionally qualified former trainee himself, is more realistic about the future of experiential learning within the group. He feels that most graduates have learnt how to learn at university but have unrealistic expectations in regard to their immediate impact upon strategy and outcomes. In his view, the right experiential learning intervention – when correctly identified and applied – can contribute significantly to graduate retention and development.

Dr Harry Matlay
Knowledge Management Centre
University of Central England Business School

ACTION LEARNING

Action learning is a not dissimilar process to that of reflective practice. The main difference is that action learning is generally located in the workplace. It was originally developed by Reg Revans, a former Olympic long-jumper and Cambridge physicist, who began the process in 1938 whilst investigating the entry of women into the nursing profession. His main concern was with the divide that occurred between the consultants and administrators (scribes) and the nurses (artisans).

Revans, being a scientist, applied an evolutionary model to individual and organizational learning and stated that learning needs to be equal to or greater than the surrounding change:

Learning $\geq$ Change

Revans also stated that learning consisted of two elements: programmed knowledge (traditional teaching and instruction) and questioning insight:

Learning = f (programmed knowledge + questioning insight); $L = f(P + Q)$

There has been a significant amount of cross-fertilization among many of the contributors to experiential learning. In his book *Developing Effective Managers*, Revans (1971) described an approach to succeeding in managerial objectives, which he called System Beta. This approach he acknowledged was based on the scientific method that he used as a researcher at the Cavendish Laboratories:

1. a stage of observation;
2. a stage of hypothesis or theory;
3. a stage of experiment;
4. a stage of inspection;
5. a stage of consolidation.

Revans (1971: 105–06) explained that this System Beta was a cycle that contained the following elements:

1. an attention-fixing event occurring within a framework of experience;
2. a new constructive relationship perceived in or around this event;
3. an attempt to exploit this relationship for some desired purpose;
4. an audit or inspection of the results of this exploitation;
5. the incorporation (or not) of the relationship into the experience of the manager, namely, a process of learning.

This cycle is very similar to Kolb's learning cycle, which was published two years after a visit to Kolb at MIT from Revans and 21 Belgian managers in February 1969. In addition, illustrating this interconnection of ideas, Revans's early work on action learning has also been credited by Professor Naoto Sasaki, in his book *Management and Industrial Structure in Japan*, with being the foundation for the quality circle concept in Japan. Interestingly, the work of Deming paralleled that of Revans in the form of his quality circle.

In addition to System Beta, Revans developed a contrasting perspective called System Gamma, which considered the 'pre-disposing mental set', ie the subjective consciousness of the manager. Linking the objective System Beta and the subjective System Gamma is System Alpha, which involved personal values, the external environment and internal resources. It asked (Lessem, 1982: 11):

- By what values am I guided?
- What is blocking their fulfilment?
- What can I do against such blockage?

This consideration of values leads to the core of Revans's work. Pedler (1996: 91) in analysing Revans's writings concluded:

Revans is a radical and it is clear from his writings that he intends Action Learning to be a deeper, more revolutionary process than just a training method for 'learning by doing'. Action learning, being about individual and organizational development, contains a *moral philosophy* involving:

> honesty about self
> attempting to do good to the world
> for the purpose of friendship.

One source of Revans's inspiration was the writings of John Locke (1968: 335). Locke argued in *Essay Concerning Human Understanding* that ideas originated from experience:

> Our observations may be employed either about external sensible objects, or about the internal operations of our minds. The former is the source of most of the ideas that we have, and, as it depends 'wholly upon our senses', is called 'sensation'. The latter is a source of ideas which 'every man has wholly in himself', and it might be called 'internal sense'; to it he gives the name 'reflection'.

Another writer to whom Revans referred was Piaget. Revans viewed the following quotation by Piaget (1977: 28) as a definition of action learning:

> knowledge is derived from action, not in the sense of simple associative responses, but in the much deeper sense of the assimilation of reality into the necessary and general co-ordinations of action. To know an object is to act upon it, in order to grasp the mechanisms of that transformation as they function in connection with the transformative actions themselves. To know is therefore to assimilate reality into structures of transformation, and these are the structures that intelligence constructs as a direct extension of our actions.

This integration of the self and external reality is illustrated in the dialectic of what Lessem (1982: 11), in describing the work of Revans, called 'the interactions between thought and action, intellect and faith, scientific method and personal conviction'. These dualities are very similar to those identified by Dewey: person–nature, subject–object, knowing–doing and mind–body (see Chapter 2).

Defining action learning is not an easy task. Pedler (1996) explained that defining action learning was very difficult and he referred to the fact that Revans never provided a one-sentence definition. Pedler (1996: 13) stated, 'Although the idea may be essentially simple, it is concerned with profound knowledge of oneself and the world, and cannot be communicated as a formula or technique.' Revans (1982: 626–27) did in fact provide a long definition, part of which is reproduced here:

> Action learning is a means of development, intellectual, emotional or physical, that requires its subject, through responsible involve-

ment in some real, complex and stressful problem, to achieve intended change sufficient to improve his observable behaviour henceforth in the problem field. 'Learning-by-Doing' may be perhaps a simpler description of this process, although action learning programmes assume a design and organization unnecessary in the every day actions that supply the learning of young animals and of small children.

A clearer definition is given by McGill and Beaty (1992: 17):

Action learning is a continuous process of learning and reflection, supported by colleagues, with an intention of getting things done. Through action learning individuals learn with and from each other by working on real problems and reflection on their own experiences. The process helps us to take an active stance towards life and helps to overcome the tendency to think, feel and be passive towards the pressures of life.

McGill and Beaty (1992: 17) explained, 'We all learn through experience by thinking through past events, seeking ideas that make sense of the event and help us to find new ways of behaving in similar situations in the future.' They described how we all use reflection to connect past actions with improving our behaviour in the future. In addition, through the use of reflection we can improve action and 'learning from experience can be enhanced through deliberate attention to this relationship'.

The focus of action learning is mainly on the individual although, of course, the person is operating within an action learning set containing other people. Revans (1982: 632) argued, 'It is development of the self, not merely development by the self of what is known of the external world.' Through the process people actively challenge one another's ideas, encourage people to espouse theories and perceptions that they may not have voiced before and help people consciously to think about other ideas and concepts that might be applied.

Pedler (1996) built on these ideas and his interactions with Revans, and explained that the purpose of action learning was:

- Voluntarily to work on problems of managing and organizing.
- To work on problems that involve the set members.
- To analyse individual perceptions of the problem in order to provide other perspectives and identify courses of action.
- To take action after which it is reported back to the learning set to allow further reflection.
- To support and challenge members to encourage effective learning and action.

- To raise awareness of group processes and encourage improved team-work. The learning set sometimes has a facilitator who helps members develop the skills of action learning.
- To encourage three levels of learning:
  - about the problem;
  - about oneself;
  - about the learning process and 'learning to learn'.

Case study: The Rolls-Royce plc Lean Transformation Programme – learning by doing!

The concept of 'lean thinking' (Womack and Jones, 1996) would suggest that the manufacturing world is moving toward continuous improvement or *Kaizen*, as the Japanese put it. *Kaizen* can be translated by splitting the word into its two components, *Kai* – to improve, and *Zen* – goodness (Joynson and Forrester, 1995), and it can now be found in many world-class companies following its inception in the Toyota Production Systems, created by Taiichi Ohno in 1953 (Ohno, 1978). Ohno's work was the base on which the 'just-in-time' (JIT) manufacturing philosophy was born. So, what is JIT? 'A system developed at Toyota Motors in the 1950's. The goal is to produce what the customer wants, when they want it, in the quantity they want, using the minimum amount of material, machinery, manpower, minutes and money' (Joynson and Forrester, 1995).

Womack and Jones appear to be the first to illustrate the introduction of 'lean production', another name for JIT, in their collective research study of the automobile industry. Womack and Jones uncovered the further adaptation of lean production into the aerospace business. Their book *Lean Thinking* (1996) embodied a catalyst subject that has energized manufacturing companies around the world into looking at how they can dramatically change the way their business performs.

In my role as the Improvement Trainer within one of the operation units of Rolls-Royce plc I have developed a Lean Transformation Programme (LTP), which addresses the principles of lean production. The application of the lean production principles is based on 'action – learning by doing', the basis of experiential learning. The LTP was originally developed as a five-day residential course during which a learning environment was created to allow the delegates to experience the changes that lean production engenders, eg changes in organizational and individual culture, production area layout and external relationships within the supply chain.

Lean production is based on the supply of a product or service to a customer, as they demand it – based on a 'pull signal'. The emphasis of a lean production system relies on the continuous elimination of waste (*muda* in Japanese) while flowing the product to the customer in an ever-decreasing lead time.

The training programme needed to engender a sense of excitement in the delegates, to the point at which they were not learning solely from the delivered material, but from the interaction between one another. The presenter's function was to generate enthusiasm within the delegates whilst facilitating them through the four stages of Kolb's experiential learning cycle to allow them to test the skills as they were learning. In so doing, the presenter needed to contend with the different learning styles that were present in the class.

The programme was designed to give the delegates as many opportunities as possible with the learning cycle and, to help achieve this, the training method remained varied. Firstly, the delegates were exposed to a 'taught input', which lasted for approximately 30–60 minutes. It is now policy for the presenter to be a current practitioner of the subject, eg Single Minute Exchange of Dies (SMED). This policy was to ensure that the transfer of knowledge to the delegates was of the highest quality. Having practitioners who deliver the subject helps to reinforce the key learning points through the generation of positive examples. This delivery method was designed to bring about an experience that could be grasped through apprehension, knowing 'instantaneously without the need for rational enquiry or analytic confirmation' (Kolb, 1984: 43).

In order to build on the more theoretical input, the delegates were provided with an opportunity really to experience the subject for themselves in a 'safe' environment, the classroom. Throughout the LTP the delegates have to apply the tools that they are learning to a 'simulated supply chain model'. The simulation model is called 'Plastic Parts plc' and was developed specifically for this programme. The simulation encompasses all of the frustrations found in a traditional manufacturing organization:

- long lead times;
- erratic customer schedules;
- lack of motivation within the employees;
- high levels of inventory;
- badly designed production areas.

During the five days, the delegates deploy their new skills whilst acting as members of the production team for the simulated factory, experiencing all of the stages of the team alignment model (Tuckman and Jenson, 1977). Feedback sessions are held at the end of each day, providing an opportunity for the delegates to voice their opinions on the validity of the course material. Each feedback session allows the facilitators (lead trainer and support trainer) to ensure that the delegates have gained maximum benefit from each of the subjects presented.

The LTP has been delivered on numerous occasions in support of strategic improvement plans. It has been presented to businesses ranging from 250 employees to two programmes involving all the companies from the entire supply chain of particular aerospace components, and has been enthusiastically received.

It is important to conclude that this programme of learning has created a number of 'raving fans', who have been inspired enough to go back to their own organizations and apply these tools from the moment they walk back into work. However, this type of enthusiasm can only be sustained by educating the senior management of an organization in the lean principles before educating the 'troops'. Experience has shown that the troops pick up the lean tools exceedingly quickly – management are less likely to accept the new order of things unless they first attend the LTP and experience the power of 'learning by doing'.

Milto J Hopkins
Rolls-Royce plc

THE ACTION LEARNING SET

Action learning may occur and be found in self-help groups, support groups, quality circles and learning sets. Learning sets provide a formalized structure within which to encourage learning. In essence there are four main elements in the action learning situation:

- the person – who joins the group voluntarily;
- the learning set – the group of people who meet;
- the problem(s) – which each person brings to the meeting;
- the action – which is taken and learnt from.

Many of the activities that occur within an action learning set also occur naturally in the work situation and it is not uncommon for people to say that they learn through discussing things with colleagues. The main difference is that action learning is formalized and thus legitimizes the process and provides a clear focus on a specific problem or group of problems. It also occurs with a specific group of people who meet on a regular basis and not in an ad hoc manner. The latter can lead to insufficient time and focus being given to the problems and learning opportunities.

Much of the reflection-in-action learning occurs through the dissection and examination of experience within the group and by the various individuals concerned. The 'action' part of the action learning is concerned with a project, the extent of which is decided by the group. This can be small and discrete, or as large and complicated as the group choose it to be.

There is no fixed duration for an action learning set or a project. On many occasions a project is brought to a group and may continue after the group has disbanded. In the reality of working life, problems are rarely completely solved; instead they change shape and/or lead into other related problems. As each issue is explored and addressed, so another surfaces ad infinitum.

Through reflection we are able to ensure that rather than having one year's experience 10 times, we have 10 years' experience where each year builds upon the learning that occurred in the previous year. That is to say, action learning enables us to build on what we have experienced.

It is not necessary in an action learning set that the people know each other, nor do they need to be experts on the subject in question. Their role is not to provide advice, albeit this can be of value; rather it is to act as devil's advocates and question and challenge the assumptions that underpin the reflections of others in the learning set.

The nature of the issues that are brought to the set can be placed on a spectrum from the very personal to those of concern to the organization. In order for the set to function effectively it is necessary for there to be trust and confidence among the members. Through this supportive environment, feelings and emotions can be explored, as well as practical issues, in a confidential environment. This takes time to establish and as confidence builds in the group so more will be shared. Action points may be minuted but the discussion is not normally included in any record of the meeting.

Whilst one objective of the meeting is the production of better action and results within the organization, probably the main purpose is the development of the individual. The impact of this learning is then likely to have a longer-lasting impact than the transitory influencing of a project. This reflects the adage, 'Give people a fish and they can eat for a day. Teach them to fish and they feed themselves for life.'

There are two roles in an action learning set: the presenter and the set member. Whilst the presenter is providing information about the project, it is the 'contractual duty' of the other set members to explore the project and help the presenter to discover new insights and strategies with the intention of resolving the problem.

Some action learning sets have facilitators and this can provide a number of advantages. Facilitators normally possess much more experience than the other members of the set and thus ensure that the process is more effective and applied to achieving learning. The facilitator also does not have concerns of her or his own and can give more attention to the projects of the other members.

Members of the set are encouraged to use the word 'I' in order to indicate not only that it is the person him- or herself who is involved but also that the person is responsible for his or her actions. It also avoids confusion about the use of the words 'you' (indicating I or me) or 'one' (people in general).

It is important, too, that the members carefully analyse the project to identify the 'problems' of the presenter. It is not uncommon for the initial problem to be underlain by a more fundamental problem that is different to the original one. Likewise, the presenter may think he or she has a specific problem and depart from the meeting with a very different one. Feedback techniques such as rephrasing and gently probing can enhance the quality of the interaction between the presenter and the other members of the set.

As with counselling there is much to be said for each presenter discovering his or her own solutions and new perspectives on the projects. To be provided with an answer dilutes the learning process and may result in the presenter not buying into the solution. The process may take much longer when the answer is not directly provided. Furthermore an answer may not be the answer that is most appropriate to the situation since the presenter is often the most knowledgeable person about his or her situation.

Specific instances of the culture of learning hindering the learning of individuals include: providing answers too readily and allowing certain individuals to coast through the process without really examining their circumstances; allowing members to be too vague and not specific with their action plans and presentations; members receiving support when they make their presentations but not contributing to the process when others make their presentations.

In addition to the identification of more effective ways of working and also perceiving issues there are other benefits from undertaking the process of action learning. McGill and Beaty (1992: 190) stated that these include:

- enhanced effectiveness in working with the range of relationships at work, including teamworking, developmental roles such as mentoring, and working with and encouraging cultural and transpersonal change;
- capacity to learn, reframe and empower self and others;
- ability to live with uncertainty and ambiguity;

- enhanced capacity to undertake project management;
- developing skills of active facilitation that can be utilized to manage group processes.

In summary the basic elements of an action learning set are:

- Ground rules may be developed by the members.
- Ground rules may be changed following discussion by the members.
- Equal time should be allotted to each member.
- Action plans should be agreed.
- All members should make a commitment to attend.
- Each member's project is dealt with in turn.
- Members need to develop the skill of listening and receiving information.
- The presenter should clearly explain what he or she is looking for from the presentation so that the other members can focus their attention.
- Feedback should be conducted in a constructive and supportive spirit, which may require the development of these skills.
- Issues discussed in the set should be confidential.

The action learning set should also regularly review how effective it is in the process of encouraging development among its members. It should reconsider its ground rules and the culture that is operating in order to identify constraints and limitations that are holding back learning.

Learning bays in German industrial enterprises

Background

Since the middle 1980s industrial production processes have changed fundamentally. The most noticeable of these changes to strike one's eye are the information and communication technologies, which have altered the principles of production.

Accompanying these technological innovations, new concepts and theories of organizational development have also emerged. Among these is the concept of a 'learning enterprise' promising new liberty and expanding the scope for personal and professional learning and development in the field of skilled work on the shop floor. Contrasting this, a return of Tayloristic labour structures has been observed in some parts of industrial production (Springer, 1999). The term 'learning enterprise' runs the risk of becoming merely a persuasive slogan. If learning is to

---

become a central interest of enterprises, new organizational forms of work and learning need to be implemented because 'organisational learning calls for... new social forms of learning, specifically, comprehensive functions and hierarchies including learning processes' (Novak, 2000: 104).

To address this need for new social forms of learning in Germany, the Federal Institute of Vocational Training and Education established a 'decentralized learning' programme in the 1990s. The objective of the programme was to discover how companies and employees might adapt to the new demands. The concept of 'learning bays' was developed for a truck and car assembly plant of Daimler-Benz (now DaimlerChrysler). Following the success of this model project, the learning bay principle has been applied to several other enterprises.

Integrating formal and informal learning

Traditional forms of learning in enterprises may be categorized as either formal or informal. Formal learning usually takes place in in-company training centres 'outsourced' from the production process. Learning in training centres is aimed at imparting fixed content and objectives, and usually leads to theoretical and sometimes rather abstract knowledge. Unfortunately, this knowledge often vanishes owing to the transfer gap. Although training interventions may incorporate pedagogical and didactic considerations they remain, nonetheless, different from the actual work experience. Additionally the complexity of work reality and its tasks is usually divided into a series of acts and learning steps. As in Tayloristic working structures, different actions and skills often stand in loose relation. If, however, high-quality production standards are to be met, process orientation by the employees is needed.

The shortcomings of formal learning together with rising costs have led to a greater interest in informal learning. However, when informal learning is integrated into specific work tasks on the shop floor it is often constrained by the production process. The objective of current vocational training, ie the acquisition of comprehensive action competence, can be achieved by the integration of formal and informal learning in learning bays.

How are learning bays designed? What are their principles?

In order to develop an adequate organizational response to the new demands, the model of learning bays was developed. Learning bays are separated areas integrated within the work process, to which a small group of trainees might be allocated for a certain time – from a few weeks to several months. In the learning bay the same work is done by the trainees as that by the skilled workers in the surrounding work areas but there is also time and room for learning. Essentially, the learning bay is situated alongside the production line, and vehicles may be removed from the line, worked on and then returned to the line. Therefore, learning bays are supplied with a double infrastructure, which includes learning facilities, ie flip charts, noticeboards, multimedia and respective software, books, papers and drawings, as well as learning tasks, contents of learning, the assistance of a learning bay trainer and the opportunity for group interaction. The work infrastructure establishes the work conditions and tasks, including work resources like machines, computers and tools, as well as process organization, company structures and qualification demands. Consequently, the term infrastructure is meant not only in a material sense; it also encloses the non-material work and learning setting.

In addition to this double infrastructure, the integration of formal and informal learning in learning bays is accomplished through group learning. The trainees work in a team of four to six learners similar to the model of a half-autonomous group work. Each trainee rotates through all the respective work tasks, including the role of group leader. All work processes of planning, performing tasks and checking outcomes are done by the group, collectively and in co-operation.

A learning bay trainer assists the group. He or she is usually a skilled worker from the respective department, who has the ability to train. The trainer establishes a framework within which the trainees can acquire the desired skills through self-managed learning and working. All costs of the learning bay, including the pay for the learning bay trainer, are assigned to the department where the learning bay is situated. This, therefore, encourages the department to have an interest in the learning process.

Another important feature of learning bays is the opportunity to acquire knowledge and skills through first-hand experience by means of job tests, and trial runs of machines and operations. Mistakes and faults provide a motive and reason for learning.

What are the outcomes of implementing learning bays in the work process?

In learning bays trainees gain action competence: technical, social and methodical skills are learnt by experience in combination with theoretical instruction. The trainees coordinate the different tasks, and they learn how to conduct consultations and write protocols. They work as a team and experience group dynamics, which may occasionally result in conflict with other group members, the learning bay trainer or even the chief of the department. In an exemplary way trainees learn how to deal with these 'working problems' in a structured setting and acquire theoretical knowledge about communication processes. Moreover, they learn how to use presentation and visualization techniques.

Learning bays, as a new organizational tool, encourage participation, self-responsibility and process-directed action and learning orientations (see Dehnbostel, 2001). They enable self-directed learning and working processes by enhancing the ability for decision making. As a result of task diversity and process orientation, trainees acquire comprehensive knowledge and skills through first-hand experience.

Further research into the new forms of combining informal and formal learning has shown that informal learning in enterprises can be identified and encouraged through reflective learning by experience and subconscious implicit learning (see also Dehnbostel and Molzberger, 2001).

Possible future development and enhancement needs

Although learning bays were originally developed for initial vocational training, they are nowadays also used for further vocational training. They can be observed in action in more than 50 industrial companies and have been set up within shift production, for axle assembly, maintenance, customer and after-sales service and also commercial training.

Newly developing professional job and task profiles can be addressed as part of formal general training schedules. In addition, the principle of learning bays could meet qualification demands up to and including the advanced further education and higher education sectors. Integrating theory and practice in the workplace promises to be a rich source of development for organizations internationally as the process is exported and adopted.

Peter Dehnbostel and Gabriele Molzberger

TIMING AND DURATION OF LEARNING SETS

The frequency and duration of action learning set meetings is dependent on the particular circumstances and those involved. McGill and Beaty recommend that the presenter has half an hour to discuss his or her project although more can be allocated. The frequency and duration may be dependent upon the organizational commitment to this learning process and many meetings occur on a monthly basis and continue for a period of between six months and a year.

Time needs to be dedicated and timetabled; otherwise other work pressures may squeeze out the time for the meetings. The use of the time should be carefully allocated in order that it is not wasted in general discussion and being sidetracked. A businesslike approach will provide momentum to the presentation and discussions, and ensure that people receive an equal consideration of their project.

Essentially, each meeting normally consists of a series of presentations from each of the members. This is likely to be the case even where all the people are working on the same project since they each have specific tasks and, more importantly, they all have different perceptions and feelings about the project and therefore will benefit from a personal examination of their own circumstances. The process for each individual at each meeting might be:

- action points from the last meeting;
- points completed and deferred;
- objectives to be achieved from this presentation;
- what the presenter learnt from completing and not completing action points.

PROBLEMS AND ACTION LEARNING

The main starting point for action learning is for each member of the group to bring a problem to the meeting. It is only by being challenged and through engagement with the problem that people will find the opportunity for learning. For some people the word problem is a difficult one to use because of its negative connotations. Thus, it is quite satisfactory to call it a concern, an issue, an opportunity, a project or a task. The important thing is that this problem is the beginning of the investigation towards discovering solutions to the difficulty and identifying new personal perceptions about it and oneself.

Revans distinguished between what he called problems and puzzles. A puzzle is an issue about which there is already some knowledge or solution that might provide an answer. A problem is an issue to which there is no direct source to which we can go for an answer. He also identified three key questions (Pedler, 1996: 73):

1. Who knows about the problem?
2. Who cares about the problem?
3. Who can do anything about the problem?

Pedler emphasized the fact that much management education concentrates only on the thinking about the problem and very little on the emotional aspects of willingness and commitment to resolving the problem.

There are six main areas to consider in the identification of a problem:

1. It is valuable when identifying a problem to be used for action learning to be clear what it is about and what measures are going to be used to judge the level of achievement. One approach to this can be to write down the problem in one sentence. This will crystallize the issue and allow focus by yourself and the other members of the set.
2. Identify the benefits associated with addressing the problem. If you cannot identify any then there will be little motivation to resolving the issue and the energy will dissipate.
3. Choose a problem that is important to you and your organization. If the problem is perceived to be trivial then it will not occupy your attention and energies nor will it be something the organization will actively support in terms of time and resources.
4. Set yourself benchmarks to assess your progress in resolving the problem; this may also be done through consultation with other people who may have a vested interest in your quest.
5. Try and forecast possible difficulties that might arise, and work out strategies for overcoming these. One of the reasons the problem exists is probably that there are a number of difficulties that have previously prevented any action being taken on the problem.
6. Will the culture of the organization support action learning? Accepting that problems exist within an organization is an awkward one for some individuals and organizations since it may challenge the status quo and cast doubt on the abilities of people. It is not an easy situation to manage if notions of infallibility exist and egos are placed on the line. For this reason it is essential to the success of the action learning programme that there is commitment and openness across the organization and particularly from the top. Without support, attempts to address problems will be stifled and pushed to the periphery where they will be forgotten about. For action learning to be successful, as with almost all organizational development initiatives, there is a need for full organizational support in a trusting atmosphere, which is easy to talk about but difficult to deliver.

The action learning cycle is shown in Figure 9.3.

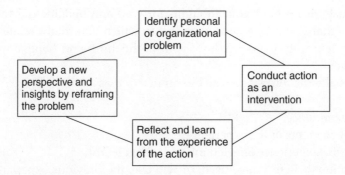

Figure 9.3 The action learning cycle

STRATEGIES FOR LEARNING FROM EXPERIENCE

With the learning cycle there are four distinct stages, which involve a concrete experience, thinking about the experience, generalizing and conceptualizing about the experience and finally applying these ideas and thoughts to new situations. It can be argued that if we do not get as far as stage three then we have not really learnt from the experience. In stage three we make links and connections to our previous experience and knowledge held in our heads. Without the links the experience may have little value in learning.

The learning cycle is used by the Learning from Experience Trust (1987) to construct a learning approach. Firstly, they recommend that we draw upon our life history and draw a life chart that chronicles all the major incidents in our life. The next step is to categorize the various experiences under headings such as education, work, relationships, travel, etc. By doing this, other experiences will emerge and these can be added to the categories.

The next stage is to ask who, what, when, where, why and how about one of the experiences. Also, did it involve someone else and did it happen as predicted? When this is done, describe your thoughts before, during, after and much later after the event. Then do a similar exercise with your feelings before, during, after and much later after the event. It may prove to be helpful to discuss the event with another person and reflect on how it changed your thoughts and feelings. What did you learn from the event and how have your expectations changed as a result of the experience?

The final stage is to analyse a subsequent event where your learning was applied. In what ways were you more able to deal with these circumstances as a result of your learning?

You may also project your thoughts forward and imagine the various scenarios that you might encounter and to which you might relate your previous learning. Consider how you might think and behave in this future event.

Essentially the four stages can be summarized as:

1. the experience;
2. main elements of the experience;
3. how the experience affected me and what I learnt;
4. situations where I have used, or will use, the previous experience to better effect.

Learning from experience is often more effective than traditional learning for children. At Raleigh Hunter Elementary School in the USA, children were not very successful in learning and the school was perceived to be a 'sink' school. As a result of a change in philosophy, greater emphasis was given to experiential and practical learning. This change had a major impact on the school – children's concentration levels increased, test scores improved and behavioural problems decreased. In addition, the turnaround in the overall school performance began to attract children from other families in neighbouring districts. The school is now perceived as a success and a role model for other schools.

It is not only in schools that experiential learning can improve performance. Universities, businesses, the probation service, etc also have problems in preparing students for work demands and difficulties in the real world. Hall *et al* (1978: 1) stated, 'Universities have trouble preparing their students for the job demands and problems they will encounter in the "real world"… most academic courses do a better job of providing theory than action.' To ameliorate this problem, Hall *et al* proposed redressing the balance between theory and action through the use of personal experience and action exercises.

Experiences in Management and Organizational Behaviour, written by Hall *et al* (1978: 2), consisted of many experiential exercises that were designed to encourage the transfer of learning from the university to the workplace. It is based upon a number of assumptions:

1. Learning is more effective when it is an active rather than a passive process.
2. Problem-centred learning is more enduring than theory-based learning.
3. Two-way communication produces better learning than one-way communication.

4. Participants will learn more when they share control over and responsibility for the learning process than when this responsibility lies solely with the group leader.
5. Learning is most effective when thought and action are integrated.

CONCLUSION

Reflective practice and action learning are very similar approaches to the development of individual and group learning. They can be used in the work situation but are equally effective in other circumstances. What becomes clear from the chapter is that it is experience that unifies these approaches to learning and gives us greater insight into how we can structure our own personal learning. Another factor arising from the chapter is the value of problems. They can be used to reflect on actions and oneself to develop new ways of thinking and behaving. Without problems it is unlikely that we would change what we do. The other clear theme is that many of the developers of learning theories and learning strategies have drawn from one another and cross-fertilized their ideas. Throughout all these concepts lies, once again, the notion of experience.

10

Imagining And Experiencing The Future

> Faith in the power of intelligence to imagine a future that the projection of the desirable in the present, and to invent the instrumentalities of its realisation, is our salvation. And it is a faith that must be nurtured and made articulate.
>
> (Dewey, 1917:69)

INTRODUCTION

In Chapter 2 we investigated the nature of learning and how it was possible to look back on a past experience and learn from the events that occurred. We called this form of learning *retrospective learning*. An example of retrospective learning is when we reflect on a previous incident that we didn't fully understand and we attempt to understand and make sense of what happened.

Another dimension of retrospective learning is when we revisit events from our past and consider, once more, our thoughts and feelings. It is possible to reframe what we once thought to be a negative experience into a positive one, and vice versa, by changing our perspective. An illustration of this might be when we burnt our finger on a stove as a child and were very upset. The benefits of this negative experience were probably only appreciated years later when we realized that it may have discouraged us from more reckless actions and prevented us from undergoing more extreme trauma.

We also discussed the possibility of learning at the same time as we were undergoing an experience, and named this *concurrent learning*; for instance, when we interact we exchange our own thoughts and feelings with those of other people who see things in different ways to ourselves. This disparity means that when we engage in conversation we must continually take into account and adjust our communication, if we are sensitive, to what the others say and do.

The third and final stage in this chronological consideration of learning is to look at how we can learn by using past experiences to reflect on the future. This is achieved by imagining various possibilities and the strategies that are required to achieve them; we call this *prospective learning*. The quotation by Dewey above illustrates the importance of using experiences from the past and the present to help shape the future. By imagining what might be possible we are then able to develop operational strategies that hopefully will deliver the concrete reality. Our terms of retrospective and prospective learning are combined in Dewey's (1916: 140) explanation:

> To 'learn from experience' is to make a backward and forward connection between what we do to things and what we enjoy and suffer from things in consequence. Under such conditions, doing becomes a trying; an experiment with the world to find out what it is like; the undergoing becomes an instruction – the discovery of the connection of things.

In Chapters 6 and 7, which investigate emotions, it can be seen that these three forms of learning – retrospective, concurrent and prospective – are brought together in one of the trilogies by Wilkes (1999: 24), who described the need to 'Revise the past. Revisit the present. Redirect the future.'

In this final chapter we will look at prospective learning and draw together some of the main messages that have been addressed in earlier chapters. We will begin with an examination of imagination and in particular the work of Gareth Morgan. We will also look at the nature of problems and challenges, a recurring theme in this book, and how they are a necessary catalyst for change. We will then look at how the different parts of our brains can be in conflict with one another and thereby reduce our performance – we draw on examples from playing tennis.

IMAGINATION

Imagination is one of the most powerful mental tools we have at our disposal. Without this ability to speculate about what might be, we would be imprisoned in a world of fatalism waiting for whatever might befall us. We would be buffeted by whatever forces with which we came into contact and just react rather than attempting to shape our destinies at least to some degree.

Without the ability to project our thoughts into the future we would be like a ship without a rudder; there could be no direction other than drifting at the mercy of the tides. And, if we take this metaphor further, we would soon end up shipwrecked with the vessel on the rocks and no hope of rescue from this predicament of living life only in the present.

If we lacked the ability to imagine the future there could be no plans, no hopes, no aspirations, no wants, no dreams and no desires. There would only be ennui and a nihilistic approach to living life now with no regard to the consequences for the future. This would be a very negative existence and indeed it is hard to think how the human species could have survived without the power to investigate the myriad futures that might be possible.

Fortunately, the world is not as bleak as that which has been described in the preceding paragraphs. We are able to use our imagination; we can speculate about possible alternatives; and we are able to select a course of action that can lead towards the achievement of our goals and objectives. Circumstances may intervene to hinder or prevent the achievement of our goals, not least our own limitations. But, at least we have the ability to weigh up the possibilities of success by taking into account our own strengths and weaknesses. Sailing around the world like Ellen MacArthur may be a dream for those who are more adventurous, but the majority would recognize their limitations and fears, and opt for something more achievable such as sailing a dinghy on a relatively calm lake, or taking a sightseeing boat along the River Seine in Paris.

This book is titled *The Power of Experiential Learning*; however, it might also have been called *The Power of Imagination*. It is only through imagination that individuals and society have advanced and prospered. It enables us to learn from the future, and Dewey (1934: 267), recognizing this importance, stated:

> [Imagination] designates a quality that animates and pervades all processes of making an observation. It is a *way* of seeing and feeling things as they compose an integral whole. It is the large and generous blending of interests at the point where the mind comes into contact with the world. When the old and familiar things are made new in experience, there is imagination. When the new is created, the far and strange become the most natural inevitable things in the world. There is always some measure of adventure in the meeting of mind and universe, and this adventure is, in its measure, imagination.

When we imagine or speculate about ideas and the ways people or things might be in the future, we are exploring the possible consequences and the potential to achieve them. This speculation is often driven by desires and impulses to improve upon current circumstances and they have a clear purpose, eg to find a more effective way of achieving work targets; to plan a holiday that takes into account as many of the family members' desires as possible; or perhaps to examine which is the best response when our boss asks why a certain task has not been undertaken.

There is a relatively clear process through which we investigate and act on our intentions. Dewey (1938) maintained that when we become aware of an impulse it becomes translated into a desire – something that we wish to achieve. However, neither an impulse nor a desire is the same thing as a purpose, which represents an achievement or outcome. Acting on an impulse or desire requires an examination of the potential consequences to determine whether they will have a positive or negative result. This examination requires the frontal cortex of the brain to assess whether desires and emotions that feed through the amygdala (which activates the emotional parts of the brain) are appropriate (Goleman, 1996). Dewey (1938) explained that a purpose is a complex operation and involves three main stages:

- Observation of the circumstances and environmental factors in operation at the time.
- Knowledge of what has occurred in similar circumstances in the past is applied to the observation of current factors. This knowledge is based upon personal experience and that of others together with advice and what we have read and learnt about second-hand.
- Application of judgement. This takes into account the observations and recollections to assess their importance and determine which is the most appropriate course of action. Judging what is realistic and achievable, and the potential consequences of a course of action is a critical part of the process.

In 1938, Dewey was aware of the importance of thinking about a desire or impulse before acting upon it. This use of judgement was an important one from an educational perspective, and he (1938: 81) stressed, 'The crucial educational problem is that of procuring the postponement of immediate action upon desire until observation and judgement have intervened.'

The process of thinking about the consequences of a desire before acting upon it is increasingly important. We often talk about the difficulty of choosing between 'heart' and 'mind', ie the distinction between what our emotions are encouraging us to do and the more analytical reasoning of the brain. Drawing on neurological research we now know that the emotions originate in the limbic system, while the neocortex allows us to think more rationally about the facts before responding. Evolutionary physiology suggests that it was the emotional parts of the brain that developed first, thus allowing us to respond with alacrity to threats from the likes of sabre-toothed tigers. However, as the threats diminished it became more important to think through a course of action about a possible threat before responding. For example, our boss attempting to bully us may cause an instinctive desire to punch him or her, but in most cases, hopefully, reason will take over and we will address the issue through more appropriate means, eg a grievance procedure.

This use of emotional maturity to control impulsive urges and temper them with reason is one of the indicators of future educational success. Goleman (1996) in his work on emotional intelligence drew attention to the importance of postponing immediate gratification in order to achieve longer-term objectives. This requires the ability to project ideas into the future – in other words to use our future learning or imagination.

IMAGINATION VERSUS ACTION

If someone is accused of daydreaming it is usually in a pejorative sense, ie he or she is wasting time doing nothing or idly speculating about things that could never have any concrete reality. There is a danger that we can become lost in daydreams and desires that are unattainable, as happened to Billy Liar. In some respects this may be a waste of mental energy since the brain might be used for more constructive purposes. Indeed, perpetually wishing for things that are highly unlikely to materialize may be demotivating and harmful in its effects. Dewey (1938: 81) succinctly summed up this potential for wasting mental energy with the statement, 'If wishes were horses, beggars would ride.'

Alternatively, the process of daydreaming may be viewed more positively because it allows the brain to relax and enables it to structure, and store in the memory, information that might be used at a future date. Furthermore, daydreaming may be a means of energizing and exercising the brain when external stimuli are limited.

The notions of daydreaming and imagination are not too disparate and may sometimes be interchangeable. However, on investigating them more closely it can be argued that daydreaming in its more negative sense implies futile speculation about unachievable objectives. Imagination, on the other hand, is perceived as being much more positive; hence the accusation that someone lacks imagination is seen as rather critical.

We saw earlier how the stages of an impulse may be translated ultimately into an action through a consideration of the requirements and demands needed to achieve an objective. Unfortunately, as we know, not all learning experiences are positive ones and these can mentally scar the individuals concerned. We described in Chapter 2 three types of behaviour by people who have made a mistake: some people recognized the mistake, learnt new behaviour and so avoided the mistake in the future; some didn't learn and continued to make the same mistake time after time; and some were so traumatized by an experience that they avoided any potential of involving themselves in a similar experience again.

Staying within a safe and familiar comfort zone does have its benefits in the short term, but in the longer term it can also cause claustrophobia and stagnation. The lack of challenges minimizes the chances we have to learn new things and develop new conceptual frameworks. Failing to move from the comfort zone into the challenge zone removes most of the opportunities for learning. Postle (1993: 35) stated that:

> we often cling, with the intensity of addiction, to the comfort that comes from staying with our preferred mode and keeping away from the other modes. I remain convinced that this is usually because at some point in our history, one or another, – or all – of the four modes of learning may have become debilitated or ruined. If this debilitation or damage was severe, whether locally or generally, then staying with the preferred mode may also successfully defend us against the feelings associated with that early hurt. If so, then our interest in action, *or dreaming up futures* [our emphasis], or caring, or arguing, whichever most keeps quiet our painful history, can indeed come to have the intensity of addiction.

It would appear, therefore, that we should add an element of caution to the use of imagination. Whilst it fires our motivation it can also constrain our activity by locking us into idle speculation that may achieve very little. However, on the whole, the limitations of imagination are relatively small in comparison to the numerous benefits that can accrue from attempting to chart our future.

MENTAL FITNESS FOR THE FUTURE

Have you ever broken an arm, leg or some other part of your anatomy and had it bound up in a plaster cast for a period of time? When the plaster was removed you would probably have noticed that the muscles surrounding the break were much weaker than before. Neurological researchers have discovered that not only are the muscles weaker but so too is the brain tissue associated with the movement of those muscles. The longer the body part is encased in plaster the greater the shrinkage of the brain.

As the development of scanning and imaging technology has grown so too has our knowledge of how the brain operates. In one experiment, research was conducted into the effect of physical and mental practice of tensing a finger in the left hand. During a four-week period involving five sessions per week half the participants carried out physical exercises. The other people undertook a similar number of exercises but this was all done mentally. At the end of the period the ones who had done the physical exercises had increased their strength by 33 per cent. A control group who had done nothing showed no change. And the virtual exercisers improved their finger strength by 22 per cent! (Robertson, 1999). The increase in strength had resulted from changes in the brain.

In another exercise, participants mentally rehearsed a five-finger piano exercise for two hours a day over five days. Brain scans revealed that the area of the brain associated with the fingers had expanded over the period of the exercises. Thus, it becomes clear that if we project ideas into the future we are likely to increase the number of connections within the brain and thereby increase the chances of us being more effective. When we consider imagination in this light it is possible to view it as a form of mental exercise designed to increase the chances of success in a future activity.

IMAGINING THE FUTURE

Imagination is more important than knowledge.

To raise new questions, new possibilities, to regard old problems from a new angle, requires creative imagination and marks a real advance in science.

(Albert Einstein)

One of the main contributors to the subject of imagination was Gareth Morgan (1997b) in his book, *Imaginization*. Morgan (1997b: 2) explained, 'Imaginization is about improving our abilities to see and understand a situation in new ways.' The book provided a number of strategies to develop the mind and encouraged the development of new perspectives and ways of thinking.

In the most basic sense, imaginization invites a way of thinking. It encourages us to become our own theorists and to feel comfortable about acting on the basis of our insights. It invites us to develop a skill that I believe we all have, even though we may not realize that this is the case. By recognizing this, and thinking creatively and intelligently about ourselves and our situations, we can 'push the envelope' on our realities and reshape them positively.

(Morgan, 1997b: 16)

To push the envelope on our realities and positively reshape them requires us to reflect and see past experiences in a new light – in other words this is a form of retrospective learning. It also requires us to place ourselves in new situations that present new challenges and opportunities for learning, ie prospective learning.

The difficulty is that we frequently fail to push the envelope and become entrapped in repetitious behaviour or habit, which Dewey described as 'the great flywheel of society' (Miettinen, 2000: 68). Revans expressed the danger of getting trapped in a particular routine or habit of which we were not aware and thus being unable to see or comprehend other ways of acting. Both our thought and language are closely interlinked and provide us with lenses with which we view the world. In this way our understanding is significantly influenced by the language we have at our disposal and the experiences that we have undergone. This perspective is endorsed by Sapir (1987) who maintained that 'language and our thought grooves are inextricably interwoven, [and] are, in a sense, one and the same'.

It would appear that our ability to comprehend is related to our use of language, which can liberate us or imprison us. The difficulty when we are trapped within a groove is that we are unable to recognize this and thus are unable to take action to remedy the problem. To avoid getting tramlined within a habit we need to be able to take a new and fresh perspective that allows us to learn in different ways. One of these approaches is through the use of metaphors, which Morgan (1997a) discussed in *Images of Organisations*. He (1997a: 4–5) stated, 'The use of metaphor *implies a way of thinking* and *a way of seeing* that pervade how we understand our world generally', and perhaps more significantly, '*all theory is metaphor*'. Chapters 4 and 7 discuss the nature of storytelling and metaphors.

Through his research, Morgan identified a number of metaphors that allowed us to think about issues from a variety of perspectives. Each metaphor provided insights and also constrained our ways of thinking. For example, if we think of the organization as a machine and the people working in it as the cogs, then when there is a problem we may conclude that the best solution is to replace the cogs. On the other hand, if we envisage an organization as an organism then it is difficult to think of replacing parts of it through amputation. Rather, we will encourage the organism to grow, which might mean investing in educating and training the workforce. The types of metaphors Morgan identified were:

1. the organization as a machine;
2. the organization as an organism;
3. the organization as a brain;
4. the organization as a culture;
5. the political organization;
6. the organization as a psychic prison;
7. the organization as a flux and transformation;

8. the organization as an instrument of domination.

Through the use of metaphors we can gain different understandings on the world and ourselves. Aristotle in his *Rhetoric* (1946) was the first to discuss the value of metaphors and stated, 'midway between the unintelligible and the commonplace, it is metaphor which most produces knowledge' (cited in Morgan, 1997a: 379). When we use different metaphors they provide us with different perspectives, in other words different dimensions of the truth. As we discussed in Chapter 2, it is difficult to understand completely what we mean when we discuss the concept of a chair. This dilemma about the nature of knowledge is discussed by Morgan (1997b: 279), who stated:

> Knowledge as objective or literal truth places too much emphasis on the *object* of knowledge and not enough on the paradigms, perspectives, assumptions, language games, and frames of reference of the observer. The challenge before us now is to achieve a better balance, by recognizing that all knowledge is the product of an interpretive process. To achieve this, we need fresh metaphors for thinking about the process through which knowledge is generated. Instead of placing emphasis on the need for 'solid,' 'literal,' 'foundational,' 'objective Truth,' we need more dynamic modes of understanding that show how knowledge results from some kind of implicit or explicit 'conversation,' 'dialogue,' 'engagement,' or interaction between the interests of people and the world in which they live.

THE VALUE OF PROBLEMS

If we do not face problems and challenges to our *Weltanschauung*, our philosophy of life, that make us question whether the world is truly as we see it, then we will become more and more entrapped within our mental and linguistic grooves. We will become more resistant to change and will eventually atrophy and become fossilized.

It becomes apparent that problems, paradoxically, have both a negative and positive aspect. From a negative perspective a problem implies that we have a current state of affairs that is unsatisfactory and needs to be resolved. From a positive perspective, a problem provides us with the opportunity to improve upon the current situation. It is here that the enormous value of problems and difficulties to our personal and social development becomes more apparent. Without awareness of a problem we will continue with our unenlightened interaction with the world. Recognizing a problem allows us to advance and improve on the current circumstances. A problem might be that we are hungry and we need to eat; it might be that we want promotion at work, which encourages search activity to achieve this advancement; it might also be an argument we have had with a partner, which requires us to assess what we think and how we behave.

Revans talked about the notion of there needing to be a problem that exercises the mind to finding commitment to a solution. The presence of a problem indicates a challenge to the mental status quo. Morgan (1997b: 13) recognized the value of these challenges and stated:

> Ambiguity, uncertainty, questioning, instability, risk, chance encounter, crisis, openness, quest, challenge: these seem to be the characteristics of situations in which innovation thrives, and which systems of shared meaning need to support... One needs, in short, to encourage understandings that generate capacities for learning and continuous self-organisation and an ability to deal with crisis and opportunity positively. Our capacities for imaginization can serve us well here, helping us to mobilize the power of shared understanding in fluid, creative ways.

In attempting to deal with problems we may have emotional blocks that prevent us from seeing things in a different way and thus from developing new schemas or conceptual frameworks. In Piaget's terms we reject a situation because we cannot incorporate it within our way of seeing the world. By not adjusting to the problem it continues to remain. These emotional blocks consist of various types, and Adams (1987: 42) includes the following:

1. fear that we may make a mistake, fail or risk;
2. inability to tolerate ambiguity; overriding desires for security or order; 'no appetite for chaos';
3. preference for judging ideas, rather than generating them;
4. inability to relax, incubate and 'sleep on it';
5. lack of challenge (problem fails to engage interest) versus excessive zeal (overmotivation to succeed quickly);
6. inability to distinguish reality from fantasy.

Facing up to problems

We can often solve problems we face if we are aware of our negative reactions. These negative reactions may constrain us with our comfort zones and restrict us from exploring and learning from new experiences.

Bransford and Stein (1984) described how a muscular friend went on

---

a sports psychology workshop that was designed to address feelings about winning and losing. Initially the activities involved the use of power, eg arm and leg wrestling, most of which the friend won. He explained that he was a 'humble winner' and that his ego would have stood up to losing.

Later, emphasis was given to coordination activities, one of which was dance instruction, which the friend found to be problematic. Indeed, he believed that he 'couldn't dance'. His frustration became so much that he exploded, 'This workshop has gotten ridiculous; I'm going to leave.' The instructor, who was alert to such concerns, encouraged the friend to remain and receive special classes with other people who felt challenged. Bransford and Stein (1984: 5) stated, 'According to our friend, this was a significant experience. It made him realize that he had been avoiding a number of situations because they were initially difficult. As a result of this experience, our friend resolved to increase his "courage span" when dealing with uncomfortable situations.'

The next time you explode from frustration about an event, take time out to assess your thought patterns and whether they are inhibiting you from learning something new rather than trying to enforce your perspective of the world on someone else.

Revans argued that when we are in situations where we perceive that there is nothing really new we are just reliving an older experience. In effect, if we do not learn from something that we undergo then arguably it cannot be called an experience. We therefore have to look for differences that challenge our way of seeing things. In other words we are looking for problems or challenges to our conceptual frameworks. Lumsdaine and Lumsdaine (1995: 37) offer advice on how to learn from the ordinary and mundane:

if a new experience, fact, or situation is very much like something already in our memory, the mind will not pay much attention, and the new information will not be retained. Thus we must develop a habit of looking for differences, for something odd in the 'new' input, to prevent forgetting. In addition, attention comes from the outside through strong stimuli. Intense experiences are unforgettable. The classic example is the John F. Kennedy assassination. People clearly remember what they were doing when they heard this shocking news: 'It was a hot, sunny afternoon and I was outside in the backyard, ironing this blue and white striped dress while listening to the radio.'

IMAGINATIVE STRATEGIES

Thinking perspectives

In order to break out of these habitual straitjackets a number of strategies can be used to view the world in different ways and thereby experience and learn so that we get closer to the truth about an object or concept. Edward de Bono (1986) recognized the limitations of the ways in which different people view the same issues and situations. He maintained that by putting on different metaphorical hats conflict between individuals who see things in different ways would be minimized because the process would legitimize the way things were discussed. Moreover, it allowed a systematic approach to how the thought processes in meetings were organized.

He identified five main benefits from adopting this approach:

1. **Role playing**. In many cases the ego prevents one from seeing the other person's point of view and only defends its own perspective. Giving people the freedom of playing a role enables them to discard the egotistical posturing.
2. **Attention directing**. The hats enable us to direct our attention to a specific interpretation rather than being reactive to the views of others.
3. **Convenience**. It allows people to change perspectives in an efficient manner.
4. **Brain chemistry**. The chemicals that exist in our brains are neurotransmitters, which enable thinking, and the creation of certain chemicals may encourage certain kinds of ideas.
5. **Rules of the game**. The hats procedure may be used with a group of people to enable them to operate in clear and understandable ways.

The six thinking hats have the following colours:

- **White hat**. This represents a neutral perspective, which only considers objective facts and information.
- **Red hat**. This symbolizes anger and allows people to express emotions.
- **Black hat**. This hat suggests negativity and allows people to discuss why a particular proposal is inappropriate or likely to be unsuccessful.
- **Yellow hat**. This symbolizes a bright and sunny view, which encourages people to think positively.

- **Green hat**. Like fertile vegetation, the green hat encourages the development of creative ideas.
- **Blue hat**. Like the sky, this hat provides an overview and enables the discussion to have order and control.

Experience and the inner game

The Inner Game of Tennis by Timothy Gallwey (1986), a tennis coach and former junior tennis champion in the United States, has become a classic. Through the medium of tennis, Gallwey has made a number of observations about the nature of learning and experiencing.

His first observation was that the secret of winning a game of tennis was not to try too hard, with the result that the mind became more relaxed and it became easier to make better shots. As a new coach he had also noticed some apparent anomalies when he tried to coach some pupils. Namely, some of the errors his pupils made seemed to correct themselves without his intervention or the pupils being aware of the improvement. Gallwey was also conscious of sometimes overteaching his pupils and the fact that on occasions his attempts to improve a particular stroke resulted in a deteriorating performance from the pupil. Telling pupils to lift their shoulder might result in other errors creeping into their game with the result that they concentrated even more, causing further deterioration.

Gallwey theorized that there would appear to be two elements of the self involved with the game of tennis or other activities, ie the conscious self and the unconscious self. Self 1 is the part of the brain that is the conscious teller, which instructs the body and says such things as, 'Keep the racquet head closer to the ground in order to give the ball more topspin.' Self 2, the unconscious automatic doer, carries out the various movements needed to play a game of tennis. It is important to be aware that this part of the brain operates all the bodily functions that are needed to live – it ensures that our heart keeps beating and that our lungs keep breathing without us needing to be consciously aware of it. In many ways our brain is like an iceberg: the conscious brain is like the tip of the iceberg above the water; the unconscious brain, which conducts most of the processing and which we are rarely aware of, is like the greater part of the iceberg, which is under water.

Every time a person hits or doesn't hit a ball, Self 2 is gathering the information and storing this information in the memory. It is aware of how high the ball is bouncing, where the head of the racquet is positioned, where the feet are, how fast the ball is travelling and so on. For a beginner, the most effective way to learn is to experience hitting the ball and avoid detailed instructions that put Self 1 and Self 2 into opposition.

Gallwey suggests that the basic language of Self 2 is not words since we were learning as infants before we could speak. He maintains that an activity is learnt through feelings and visual images. This consists of stages:

1. **Observation**. In this stage, you see, feel and hear what is happening as you make a stroke.
2. **Programming**. You use visioning to see yourself serving and using supportive elements, such as the sound of the ball as it is hit, how smooth it feels to swing the racket, and the trajectory of the ball as it flies through the air and lands in the service box.
3. **Let it happen**. This stage is just to allow your body to do what is required without concentrating and using Self 1.
4. **Observation**. The cycle is complete and the server continues to be aware of what is happening from the various sources of sight, sound and touch that are available.

When sportspeople make several mistakes they evaluate their performance, recognize that it was weak and then sometimes call themselves bad players. You can see this phenomenon on tennis courts, golf courses, football fields, etc where people are talking and chastising themselves as they play. Not only does this self-criticism undermine their confidence but it encourages Self 1, the conscious brain, to try and impose itself on Self 2, the unconscious brain, with destructive effect.

Gallwey recommended that we use Self 1 to support Self 2 by being alert and aware of what is happening. With a serve many muscles are used, and the coordination of all the elements is very complicated; it is extremely difficult for us to concentrate on all these elements at the same time. All Gallwey advised is that when we attempt to serve into the opposite court we are aware and note where the ball landed, ie was it long or short, and was it to the left or the right? Through just letting it happen rather than concentrating hard on what is going on and making it happen the serve will become fluent and accurate. This simple feedback of being aware then allows Self 2 to make the necessary corrections unconsciously, and our game improves. Gallwey (1986: 50) stated, 'It is important not only to understand intellectually the difference between *letting* it happen and *making* it happen but to *experience* the difference.'

The more we practise the easier it becomes to repeat the task because the neural connections have been increased and developed. Gallwey (1986: 67) described this in slightly different terms:

One hears a lot about grooving one's strokes in tennis. The theory is a simple one: every time you swing your racquet in a certain way, you increase the probabilities that you will swing that way again. In this way patterns, called grooves build up which have a predisposition to repeat themselves. Golfers use the same term. It is as if the nervous system were like a record disk. Every time an action is performed, a slight impression is made in the microscopic cells of the brain, just as a leaf blowing over a fine-grained beach will leave a faint trace. When the action is repeated, the groove is made slightly deeper. After many similar actions there is a more recognizable groove into which the needle of behaviour seems to fall automatically.

Peak experience

One of the key skills in playing tennis is the use of concentration. By concentrating we are able to focus more clearly on what is happening within ourselves as well as what is happening around us. This develops our consciousness and allows us to experience even more deeply. Gallwey (1986: 85) explained:

> Whatever we experience on a tennis court is known to us by virtue of awareness – that is, by the consciousness within us. It is consciousness that makes possible awareness of the sights, sounds, feelings and thoughts that compose what we call 'experience'. It is self-evident that one cannot experience anything *outside* of consciousness. Consciousness is that which makes all things and events knowable. Without consciousness eyes could not see, ears could not hear, and mind could not think. Consciousness is like a pure light energy whose power is to make events knowable, just as an electric light makes objects visible. Consciousness could be called the light of lights because it is by its light that all other lights become visible.

Gallwey suggests that our focus can be developed in a progressive manner, moving from awareness, to attention, to concentration, to one-point concentration. The more we focus our attention the more we can experience. For instance, your concentration is on the words in this book, but if you disconnect from this stimulus and concentrate on what you can hear you may be able to pick out the sound of a bird or other sounds, and if you listen even more closely you may be able to identify what type of bird and where it is singing.

Similarly, concentrating on an experience and even reflecting on it will often provide us with a deeper and more satisfying sensation through increased understanding and increased awareness of the details that we might have overlooked when it did not fully occupy our consciousness.

Thus concentration heightens the experience and enables us to benefit more significantly from events. Gallwey (1986: 125) asserted:

> What makes it possible to learn more from ordinary experience? Two people witness the same sunset; one has a deep experience of beauty, and the other, perhaps because his mind is preoccupied, has a minimal experience. Two people read the same lines in a book; one recognizes a profound truth while the other finds nothing worth remembering. One day we get out of bed and the world looks full of beauty and interest; the next day everything appears drab. In each case the difference lies in our own state of consciousness. In the final analysis it is our state of consciousness that is the determining factor in our appreciation of the beautiful, the true, or the loving.

Appreciation and recognition of beauty may lead to an advanced state of well-being. Most of us will have experienced occasions when we felt totally in tune with ourselves in some activity, perhaps at work, participating in a sport or being with another person. No major effort was required; there was no need to concentrate very hard because everything was very clear and understood. This heightened form of awareness is sometimes called peak experience and equates to Maslow's (1954) self-actualization. A good example of peak performance is given in Orlick's description of night-time skiing below.

Peak performance and skiing

One winter night, the sky was clear, the moon was full, the night air crisp. The snow sparkled like dancing crystals under the moonlight. It was a majestic evening as we set out to ski up the mountain trail to a small log chalet nestled in among the trees. We had a fire, had some wine, a bit of stew, joked a little and set out back down the mountain. As I skied down, I became one with the mountain, not knowing where it ended and where I started. I was so close to it, hugging it, it hugging me, as I flowed along that tiny snow packed trail. I moved in shadows and out of shadows as the moonlight darted through the trees. I was totally absorbed in the experience... it was novel, challenging, sensual, fun, exciting, physically demanding, a meaningful trip with nature... a peak experience, the kind that makes it great to be alive.

(Orlick, 1975: 12)

Orlick's description of being fully absorbed in the experience illustrates how he was fully aware of everything around himself and how he understood it so much that he became part of the mountain. In other words he was learning to the fullest extent possible. Similarly, the inner game that Gallwey described is really a quest for the person on a journey of self-discovery and actualization. When we experience something very deeply we also know it to the maximum extent and this is a form of peak experience. It becomes very clear that if we wish to maximize learning we should involve people cognitively, affectively and behaviourally in the experiential learning event.

IMAGINATION AND THE CHILD

The power of imagination is strong, especially in children, who are sometimes unable to distinguish between fact and fantasy. As we saw in Chapter 4, 'Exploring reality', the value of play enables children to rehearse skills and thoughts in a safe environment before venturing out into the real world where lessons are learnt in harder ways. Using their imagination allows children to project ideas into the future to test their viability. Imagination also allows the development of creativity. Developing the ability to imagine can unleash a powerful tool, as Alison Uttley (1943: 199), the children's writer, illustrated:

> 'Have you any toys? Toys! We play with anything, with sticks, stones and flowers, and we run about and look at things and find things and sing and shout. We don't have toys.'
> The fields were our toyshops and sweetshops, our market and our storehouses. We made toys from things we found in the pastures. We ate sweet and sour food of the wild. We hunted from hedge to hedge as in a market, to find the best provisions, and we had our wild shops in corners of fields, or among the trees.

The benefits of prospective learning or imagination can be very powerful for the child and far exceed the testing of ideas and the development of creativity. Cohen (1987: 136) summarized the cognitive benefits:

> The well-imagining child would learn to integrate experience, work out what was inner and outer, learn to organise information better, become more reflective, elaborate perceptions and cognitions, recognise mistakes quicker and develop better concentration... The 'social benefits of imagery' included becoming more sensitive to others, increased empathy, poise, acculturation, self-entertainment, reducing fear and anxiety, improved emotional well-being and self-control.

Parents encourage their children to become more mature. However, children have a great ability to live for the moment and experience the joy of just being, whereas adults often say that they will be happy when they own a new car or house, have completed a piece of work, etc. We need to remember as adults that this also means that we need to travel in the opposite direction and meet the child in us to appreciate fully the nature of being.

Tower and Singer's (1980: 36) perspective is very similar:

> When a child engages in imaginative play with a parent, a very special phenomenon is taking place: the child is generating and executing ideas based on its own experience in a context of mutual respect, interest and absence of criticism. Parent and child are free to experience each other in terms of possibilities. Constraints inherent in the usual roles they play in relation to each other may be temporarily put aside. The give and take of laughter and of shared 'dangers' and 'rescues' may enhance a positive sense of communion. Parents often have lost touch with their own childhood joys in fantasy play and can regain some of that excitement through play.

A child's development begins at a very early stage, and the case study below demonstrates this clearly and shows how this may have significant implications for the future.

Case study: Antenatal and post-natal development

During my pregnancy with twins we had an interesting experience. In one of my antenatal visits to the hospital I had an ultrasound scan, which showed that one of the babies was a girl. (We later found that the other was a boy.) Calum, the boy, was very active throughout the pregnancy while Eilidh, the girl, was quiet and slept a lot.

During the scan Calum was moving around and kicking vigorously while Eilidh was quite passive. As we were watching, Calum kicked out and came into contact with Eilidh who responded by spinning 180 degrees to turn her back on him, all the while continuing to suck her thumb.

Now that they are born I can observe them more closely and take note of their personalities. One year on, Eilidh still loves her sleep whilst Calum is a very early riser. Calum enjoys the rough-and-tumble of play while Eilidh likes more gentle play.

We tried to ensure that both babies were given equal care and stimulation, even alternating which parent put each baby to bed at night.

They also shared the same toys. Despite this, both Calum and Eilidh are developing in quite different ways. Eilidh courts attention from others, especially adults. She treated me to her first real smile when she was less than four weeks old and learnt at a very young age that a smile would get the reaction and attention that she loves. Eilidh was first to recognize and sing along with her favourite songs. Calum, on the other hand, prefers things to people. He treats strangers with indifference, preferring to play with his toys. He quickly became very adept at recognizing and sorting shapes and exploring the mechanisms of his toys.

Although the twins were very close and became upset when they were separated, they behaved as if the other was an extension of themselves. They sucked each other's thumbs and toes but they did not interact with each other in the same way as with ourselves and other adults until one incident when they were around five months old. They were lying side by side on the floor and Eilidh had her hand in Calum's mouth. Calum sneezed and Eilidh pulled away, giggling. She put her hand back and he sneezed again, eliciting another giggle. For the next 20 minutes, both babies watched, smiled, touched and giggled with each other. It appeared to me that each baby suddenly recognized the other as a separate person. From that day, they became a team, interacted, played and communicated with each other, often sharing a private joke which nobody but themselves could understand.

One day I was teaching them to give me a kiss by kissing each of them in turn. A few minutes after the game was over, they started giggling and kissing each other. Since then, without any prompting from ourselves, they spontaneously give each other a kiss and cuddle every morning, as we do with them.

Although the only evidence I have is observing just two babies, from their behaviour I can only conclude that their learning is not driven solely by nature, nurture or environmental factors but a combination of all three.

Rosie MacIntyre

CONCLUSION

Throughout this book we have emphasized the importance of using the concept of experiential learning as a means of drawing together theory and practice. It is probably the single unifying feature that integrates the neurological processes of the brain with the various theories and strategies for encouraging learning. It involves action learning and reflective practice; it involves the emotional aspects of learning, and incorporates the various environmental factors that add to the learning experience.

In this final chapter we have investigated the nature of prospective learning and the use of imagination to investigate future possibilities. We also discussed the value of problems that challenge our way of seeing the world. If we were not challenged we would tend towards inertia and gradually atrophy and fossilize. As a consequence we would fail to progress, and follow the route of the dinosaurs. We will leave the final words to Freire (1982: 57) who linked problem solving with the development of our future and thus all our hopes:

Problem solving education is revolutionary futurity. Hence it is prophetic (and, as such, hopeful), and so corresponds to the historical nature of man. Thus, it affirms men as beings who transcend themselves, who move forward and look ahead, for whom immobility represents a fatal threat, for whom looking at the past must only be a means of understanding more clearly what and who they are so that they can more wisely build the future.

References

Adams, James L (1987) *Conceptual Blockbusting: A guide to better ideas*, Penguin, Harmondsworth

Adler, P S (1975) The transitional experience, *Journal of Humanistic Psychology*, **15** (4), pp 13–23

Allison, P (2000a) Authenticity and outdoor education, *Values and Outdoor Learning*, Association for Outdoor Learning, Cumbria

Allison, P (2000b) Research from the ground up, *Brathay Occasional Papers*, 1, Brathay Hall Trust, Cumbria

Applebaum, S, Bregman, M and Moroz, P (1998) Fear as a strategy: effects and impacts within the organisation, *Journal of European Industrial Training*, **22** (3), pp 113–27, MCB University Press, Bradford

Argyris, C (1994) Good communication that blocks learning, *Harvard Business Review*, July–August, pp 77–85

Argyris, C and Schon, D (1974) *Theory in Practice: Increasing professional effectiveness*, Jossey-Bass, San Francisco

Aristotle (1946) *Rhetoric*, Oxford University Press, Oxford

Arran, A (1998) Personal communication on the design of Spider Club awards

Assagioli, R (1980) *Psychosynthesis*, Wildwood House, London

Attard, P (2001) The use of drama-based training as a learning medium, Unpublished Master's thesis, Department of Continuing Education, Sheffield University, Sheffield

Attarian, A (1999) Artificial climbing environments, in *Adventure Programming*, ed J C Miles and S Priest, pp 341–45, Venture Pubishing, USA

Bacon, S (1987) *The Evolution of the Outward Bound Process*, Greenwich Outward Bound, USA

Badger, B, Sadler-Smith, E and Michie, E (1997) Outdoor management development: use and evaluation, *Journal of European and Industrial Training*, **21** (9), pp 318–25, MCB University Press, Bradford

Bagshaw, M (2000) 17 tried and tested activities for understanding the practice and applications of emotional intelligence, *Using Emotional Intelligence at Work*, Fenman Ltd, Cambridgeshire

Baldacchino, G and Mayo, P (1997) Adult education practice: alternatives to chalk and talk, pp 85–88, in *Beyond Schooling: Adult education in Malta*, Mireva Publications, Malta

Bank, J (1994) *Outdoor Development for Managers*, 2nd edn, Gower, Aldershot

Barnes, P (2000) *Values and Outdoor Learning: A collection of papers reflecting some contemporary thinking*, Association for Outdoor Learning, Cumbria

Barrett, J and Greenaway, R (1995) *Why Adventure? The role and value of outdoor adventure in young people's personal and social development*, Foundation for Outdoor Adventure, Coventry

Bateson, Gregory (2000) The logical categories of learning and communication, *Steps to an Ecology of Mind*, pp 279–308, Essay written in 1964, University of Chicago, Chicago

Beard, C (1998) The outdoor leisure industry and the environment, *Horizons*, **2**, Cumbria

Beard, C (1999) Unpublished course materials, Master's degree in outdoor management development, School of Sport and Leisure Management, Sheffield Hallam University, Sheffield

Beard, C and McPherson, M (1999) Design and use of group-based training methods, in *Human Resource Development: Learning and training for individuals and organizations*, ed J P Wilson, Kogan Page, London

Beard, C, Rhodes, T and Waller, J (in press) *Artificial Environments: An exploration of trends in the UK artificial urban adventure sites*, School of Sport and Leisure Management, Sheffield Hallam University, Sheffield

Beard, C M (1996) Environmental awareness training: three ideas for greening the company culture, *Eco-Management and Auditing*, **3**, pp 139–46

Beard, C M (2000) A brave new environmental vision for the millennium, Euro Environment 2000 Conference: Visions, strategies and actions towards sustainable industries, 18–20 October, Aalborg Congress and Culture Centre, Denmark

Bee, F and Bee, R (1998) *Facilitation Skills*, Institute of Personnel and Development, London

Benson, J (1987) *Working More Creatively with Groups*, Routledge, London

Bergenhenegouwen, G L (1996) Professional code of ethics for training professionals, *Journal of European Industrial Training*, **20** (4), pp 23–29

Berger, P and Luckmann, T (1985) *The Social Construction of Reality*, Penguin, Harmondsworth

Berne, E (1973) *Games People Play*, Penguin, Harmondsworth

Binstead, D and Stuart, R (1979) Designed reality into management learning events, *Personnel Review*, **8** (3)

Black Mountain Ltd (1996) Developing your human dimension, Commercial publicity brochure

Block, P (2000) *Flawless Consulting*, 2nd edn, Jossey-Bass Pfeiffer, San Francisco

Bloom, B S *et al* (1956) *Taxonomy of Educational Objectives: The classification of educational objectives, Handbook 1:* Cognitive Domain, Longmans, Green & Co, London

Bolton, G (1985) Changes in thinking about drama in education, *Theory into Practice,* **24** (3), Summer, pp 151–57

Boniface, M (2000) Towards an understanding of flow and other positive experience phenomena within outdoor and adventurous activities, *Journal of Adventure Education and Outdoor Learning,* **1** (1), pp 55–68

Booth, B F and Moss, I (1994) *A Social History of Sport,* HPA Inc, Ottawa

Boud, D, Cohen, R and Walker, D (1993) *Using Experience for Learning,* Open University Press, Buckingham

Boud, D and Miller, N, eds (1996a) *Working with Experience: Animating learning,* Routledge, London

Boud, D and Miller, N (1996b) Synthesising traditions and identifying themes in learning from experience, in *Working with Experience: Animating learning,* ed D Boud and N Miller, pp 14–24, Routledge, London

Boud, D and Walker, D (1990) Making the most of experience, *Studies in Continuing Education,* **12** (2), pp 61–80

Boud, David and Walker, David (1993) Barriers to reflection on experience, in *Using Experience for Learning,* ed D Boud, R Cohen and D Walker, pp 73–86

Bransford, John D and Stein, Barry S (1984) *The Ideal Problem Solver: A guide for improving thinking, learning, and creativity,* W H Freeman & Co, New York

Bryson, B (2000) An introduction, *The English Landscape,* pp 1–2, Profile Books, London

Butcher, G B (1991) Creating the right environment for training managers, *Training and Development,* **9** (6), pp 26–30, The Institute of Training and Development, UK

Buzan, T (2000 edn) *The Speed Reading Book,* BBC Worldwide Ltd, London

Buzan, T (2001) *The Power of Spiritual Intelligence,* Thorsons, London

Carlson, R (1998) *Don't Sweat the Small Stuff with Your Family,* Hyperion, New York

Charlton, C (1992) Developing leaders using the outdoors, in *Frontiers of Leadership: An essential reader,* ed M Syrett and C Hogg, pp 454–61, Blackwell, Oxford

Child, G (1993) *Mixed Emotions,* The Mountaineers, USA

Chisholm, A (2000) A time for change, *Achievement,* September, p 5, Achievement Publishing, Kent

Chopra, D (1996) *The Seven Spiritual Laws of Success: A practical guide to the fulfilment of your dreams,* Bantam, London

Cohen, David (1987) *The Development of Play,* New York University Press, New York

Collison, C and Mackenzie, A (1999) The power of story in organisations, *Journal Of Workplace Learning*, **11** (1), pp 38–40, MCB University Press, Bradford

Consalvo, C (1995) *Outdoor Games for Trainers*, Gower, Aldershot

Cooper, G (1998) *Outdoors with Young People: A leader's guide to outdoor activities, the environment and sustainability*, Russell House Publishing, Dorset

Cornell, J (1989) *Sharing the Joy of Nature*, Dawn Publications, California

Covey, Stephen R (1990) *The Seven Habits of Highly Effective People*, Simon & Schuster, New York

Crosby, A (1995) A critical look: the philosophical foundations of experiential education, in *The Theory of Experiential Education*, ed K Warren, M Sakofs and J Hunt, Association for Experiential Education, Kendall/ Hunt Publishing, Dubuque, IA

Crowder, R G (1976) *Principles of Learning and Memory*, Erlbaum, Hillsdale, NJ

Cuffaro, Harriet K (1995) *Experimenting with the World: John Dewey and the early childhood classroom*, Teachers College Press, New York

Curriculum Corporation (1994) *Statements and Profiles for Australian Schools*, Melbourne, Australia

Dainty, P and Lucas, D (1992) Clarifying the confusion: a practical framework for evaluating outdoor development programmes for managers, *Management Education and Development*, **23** (2), pp 106–22

Daudelin, M (1996) Learning from experience through reflection, *Organizational Dynamics*, **24** (3), pp 36–46

Davis, J R (1993) *Better Teaching, More Learning*, Oryx Press, Arizona

Davis-Berman, J and Berman, D (1999) The use of adventure-based programs with at-risk youth, in *Adventure Programming*, ed J C Miles and S Priest, pp 365–72, Venture Publishing, USA

de Bono, Edward (1986) *Six Thinking Hats*, Viking, Harmondsworth

DEEP [accessed March 1999] *Definitions, Ethics and Exemplary Practices (DEEP) of Experiential Training and Development (ETD)*, http://rogue.northwest.com/icg/deep.htm

Dehnbostel, P (2001) Lernorte, Lernprozesse und Lernkonzepte im lernenden Unternehmen aus berufspädagogischer Sicht, in *Berufliche Bildung im lernenden Unternehmen: Zum Zusammenhang von betrieblicher Reorganisation, neuen Lernkonzepten und Persönlichkeitsentwicklung*, 2nd edn, ed P Dehnbostel, H-H Erbe and H Novak, pp 175–94, Edition Sigma, Berlin

Dehnbostel, P and Molzberger, G (2001) Combination of formal learning and learning by experience in industrial enterprises, in *Perspectives on Learning at the Workplace: Theoretical positions, organizational factors, learning processes and effects*, ed J N Streumer, pp 77–85, University of Twente, Enschede

Department for Education and Employment (DfEE) (2000) *Work–Life Balance*, September, HMSO, Department for Education and Employment, London

Dewey, John (1916) *Democracy and Education*, Macmillan, New York

Dewey, John (1917) A recovery of philosophy, in *Creative Intelligence*, ed J Dewey *et al*, pp 3–69, Henry Holt, New York

Dewey, John (1925) *Experience and Nature*, The Paul Carus Foundation Lectures 1, Open Court Publishing Company, Chicago

Dewey, John (1934) *Art as Experience*, Allen & Unwin, London

Dewey, John (1938) *Experience and Education*, The Kappa Delta Pi Lecture Series, Macmillan, New York

Dickinson, M (1998) *The Death Zone*, Arrow Books, London

Dybeck, M (2000) Commercial considerations, in *Values and Outdoor Learning*, ed P Barnes, pp 113–19, Institute for Outdoor Learning, Cumbria

Elgood, C (1984) *The Handbook of Management Games*, Gower, Aldershot

Experience Creative Development (2000) Promotional leaflet, Leatherhead, Surrey

Ferrucci, P (1982) *The Visions and Techniques of Psychosynthesis*, Turnstone Press, Wellingborough

Fineman, S (1997) Emotion and management learning, *Management Learning*, **28** (1), pp 13–25, Sage, London

Fox, Rebecca (1999) Enhancing spiritual experience in adventure programs, in *Adventure Programming*, ed J C Miles and S Priest, pp 455–61, Venture Publishing, USA

Freire, Paulo (1982) *The Pedagogy of the Oppressed*, Penguin, Harmondsworth

Fritchie, R (1988) in *Working with Assertiveness*, BBC training video booklet, BBC Enterprises Ltd, London

Gabriel, Y (1998) The use of stories, in *Qualitative Methods and Analysis in Organisational Research*, ed G Symon and C Cassel, Sage, London

Gallwey, Timothy (1986) *The Inner Game of Tennis*, Pan Books, London

Gardner, H (1983) *Frames of Mind: The theory of multiple intelligences*, Basic Books Inc, New York

Gardner, Howard (1986) Originally in conversation with Daniel Goleman and reported in Rethinking the value of intelligence tests, *New York Times Educational Supplement*, 3 November, and also in Goleman (1996: 37)

Gass, M (1992) WebCare international: using the Spider's Web with business populations, in *Book of Metaphors*, M Gass and C Dobkin, AEE, Boulder, CO

Gass, M (1995) *Book of Metaphors*, vol II, Kendall/Hunt, Dubuque, IA

Gass, M and Priest, S (1998) Using metaphors and isomorphs to transfer learning in adventure education, in *Outdoor Management Development*, ed C Loynes, Adventure Education, Cumbria

Gilley, J W (1991) Demonstration and simulations, in *Adult Learning Methods: A guide for effective instruction*, M Galbraith, Kreiger Publishing Company, FL

Gold, G (1996) Telling stories to find the future, *Career Development International*, 1st quarter, pp 33–37, MCB University Press, Manchester

Goleman, D (1996) *Emotional Intelligence*, Bantam Books, London

Gray, J (1993) *Men are from Mars – Women are from Venus*, Thorsons, London

Gray, J (1999) *Children are from Heaven*, HarperCollins, New York

Greenaway, R (1996) *Reviewing Adventures, Why and How*, NAOE, Sheffield

Greenaway, R [accessed 14 July 1999] http://www.users.globalnet.co.uk/-rogg/activities/outdoor_ indoor.htm

Gura, P (1992) *Exploring learning: Young children and blockplay*, Paul Chapman, London

Habermas, J (1972) *Knowledge and Human Interests*, Heinemann, London

Hall, *et al* (1978) *Experiences in Management and Organizational Behaviour*

Hall, Douglas and Associates (1995) *The Career is Dead, Long Live the Career*, Jossey-Bass, San Francisco

Handy, C (1989) *The Age of Unreason*, Business Books, London

Handy, C (1994) *The Empty Raincoat*, Hutchinson, London

Hartmann, R and Beard, C M (2000) Environmental training: a strategic tool in an organisation's environmental management, *Proceedings of the Euro Environment 2000 Conference: Visions, strategies and actions towards sustainable industries*, 18–20 October, Aalborg Congress and Culture Centre, Denmark

Hawking, Steven (1988) *A Brief History of Time: From big bang to black holes*, Bantam, London

Heap, N (1993) Bridging the learning gap, *Training and Development*, January, pp 16–17

Heap, N (1996) The design of learning events, *Industrial and Commercial Training*, **28** (12), pp 10–14

Heron, J (1990) *Helping the Client: A creative, practical guide*, Sage, London

Heron, J (1999, 2000 reprint) *The Complete Facilitator's Handbook*, Kogan Page, London

Higgins, P (1996) Connection and consequence in outdoor education, *Journal of Adventure Education and Outdoor Leadership*, **13** (2)

Higgins, P (1997) Outdoor education for sustainability: making connections, *Journal of Adventure Education and Outdoor Leadership*, **13** (3)

Hochschild, A (1983) *The Managed Heart*, University of California, Berkeley

Holman, D, Pavlica, K and Thorpe, R (1997) Rethinking Kolb's theory of experiential learning in management education, *Management Learning*, Sage, London

Honey, Peter and Mumford, Alan (1992) *Manual of Learning Styles*, 3rd edn, Honey Publications, Maidenhead

Hopfl, H and Linstead, S (1997) Learning to feel and feeling to learn: emotion and learning in organisations, *Management Learning*, **28** (1), pp 5–12, Sage, London

Hovelynck, J (2000) Recognising and exploring action-theories: a reflection-in-action approach to facilitating experiential learning, *Journal of Adventure Education and Outdoor Learning*, **1** (1), pp 7–20, Association for Outdoor Learning, Cumbria

Hunt, C (1999) Reflective practice, in *Human Resource Development: Learning and training for individuals and organizations*, ed J P Wilson, pp 221–40, Kogan Page, London

Hunt, J S (1995) Ethics and experiential education as professional practice, in *The Theory of Experiential Education*, ed K Warren, M Sakofs and J Hunt, pp 331–38, Association for Experiential Education, Kendall/Hunt Publishing, Dubuque, IA

Hunt, J and Wurdinger, S (1999) Ethics and adventure programming, in *Adventure Programming*, ed J C Miles and S Priest, pp 123–32, Venture Publishing, USA

Illich, Ivan (1973) *De-schooling Society*, Penguin, Harmondsworth

IPD (1998) *The IPD Guide on Outdoor Training*, Institute of Personnel and Development, London

Irvine, D and Wilson, J P (1994) Outdoor management development – reality or illusion?, *Journal of Management Development*, **13** (5), pp 25–37

James, T (2000) *Can the Mountains Speak for Themselves?*, Scisco Conscientia, **2** (2), pp 1–4, USA

Johnson, B (1996) Feeling the fear, in *Working with Experience: Animating learning*, ed D Boud and N Miller, pp 184–93, Routledge, London

Jones, L (2001) Ethical issues for trainers, Unpublished Master's thesis in education training and development, Department of Adult Education, Sheffield University, Sheffield

Joynson, S and Forrester, A (1995) *Sid's Heroes*, BBC Books, London

Kellert, S R (1993) The biological basis for human values of nature, in *The Biophilia Hypothesis*, ed S R Kellert and E O Wilson, Island Press, Washington, DC

Kirk, P (1986) Outdoor management development: cellulose or celluloid?, *Management Education and Development*, **17**, pp 85–93

Kolb, David A (1984) *Experiential Learning*, Prentice Hall, Englewood Cliffs, NJ

Krakauer, J (1997) *Into Thin Air: A personal account of the Everest disaster*, Pan Books, London

Krouwel, B and Goodwill, S (1994) Achieving your aims in the outdoors, *Training Officer*, September, pp 220–21

Kuhn, Thomas S (1970) *The Structure of Scientific Revolutions*, University of Chicago Press, Chicago

Lamplugh, D (1991) *Without Fear: The key to staying safe*, Weidenfeld & Nicolson, London

Learning from Experience Trust (1987) *Handbook for the Assessment of Experiential Learning*, LfET, London

Lessem, Ronnie (1982) A biography of action learning, in *The Origins and Growth of Action Learning*, R W Revans, pp 4–17, Chartwell-Bratt, Bickley, Kent

Lewis, C S (1980) *The Chronicles of Narnia: The lion, the witch and the wardrobe*, Collins, London

Lippit, R (1949) *Training in Community Relations: A research exploration toward new group skills*, Harper & Brothers, New York

Locke, John (1968) *The Educational Writings of John Locke*, Cambridge University Press, London

Loynes, C (2000) The values of life and living: after all, life is right in any case, in *Values and Outdoor Learning*, ed P Barnes, Association for Outdoor Learning, Cumbria

Lumsdaine, Edward and Lumsdaine, Monika (1995) *Creative Problem Solving: Thinking skills for a changing world*, McGraw-Hill, New York

Macala, Joan C (1986) Sponsored experiential programs: learning by doing in the workplace, in *Experiential and Simulation Techniques for Teaching Adults*, ed Linda H Lewis, pp 57–70, Jossey-Bass, San Francisco

Mallia, G (1997) The use of comic strips in adult education practice, in *Beyond Schooling*, ed G Baldacchino and P Mayo, Mireva Publications, Malta

Mallinger, A and De Wyze, J (1993) *Too Perfect*, HarperCollins, London

Margerison, C (1988) *Managerial Consulting Skills: A practical guide*, Gower, London

Maslow, A (1971) *The Farther Reaches of Human Nature*, Viking, New York

McGill, Ian and Beaty, Liz (1992) *Action Learning*, Kogan Page, London

McLeod, J (1997) *Narrative and Psychotherapy*, Sage, London

Megginson, D (1994) Planned and emergent learning: a framework and a method, *Executive Development*, **7** (6), pp 29–32, MCB University Press, Manchester

Miettinen, Reijo (2000) The concept of experiential learning and John Dewey's theory of reflective thought and action, *International Journal of Lifelong Education*, **19** (1), January–February, pp 54–72

Miles, J (1995) Wilderness as a healing place, in *The Theory of Experiential Education*, ed K Warren, M Sakofs and J Hunt, Association for Experiential Education, Kendall/Hunt Publishing, Dubuque, IA

Miller, N and Boud, D (1996) Animating learning from experience, in *Working with Experience: Animating learning*, ed D Boud and N Miller, pp 3–13, Routledge, London

Mohawk, J (1996) A nature view of nature, *Resurgence*, **178**, pp 10–11

Morgan, G (1997a) *Images of Organisations*, Sage, London

Morgan, G (1997b) *Imaginization: New mindsets for seeing, organising, and managing*, Sage, London

Morris, D (1969) *The Human Zoo*, Corgi Books, London

Mortlock, C (1984) *The Adventure Alternative*, Cicerone Press, Cumbria

Mumford, A (1991) Individual and organisational learning: the pursuit of change, *Journal of Industrial and Commercial Training*, **23** (6), pp 24–31

Newell, Allen (1990) *Unified Theories of Cognition*, Harvard University Press, Cambridge, MA

Novak, H (2000) Zur Re-Formulierung und Erweiterung der Aufgaben der betrieblichen Berufsbildung im lernenden Unternehmen, in *Zum Zusammenhang von betrieblicher Reorganisation, neuen Lernkonzepten und Persönlichkeitsentwicklung*, 2nd edn, ed P Dehnbostel, H-H Erbe and H Novak, pp 95–110, Edition Sigma, Berlin

Ogilvie, K (1993) *Leading and Managing Groups in the Outdoors*, NAOE Publications, Sheffield

Ohno, Taiichi (1978) *Toyota Production System*, Diamond Publishing Company, Tokyo

Orlick, Terry (1975) *In Pursuit of Excellence*, Human Kinetics Publishers/Coaching Association of Canada, Champaign, IL

Parkin, M (1998) *Tales for Trainers*, Kogan Page, London

Parr, J (2000) *Identity and Education: The links for mature women students*, Ashgate Publishing, Aldershot

Peard, G (1999) Spirit of the Earth: Chief Seathl's speech, *Horizons*, **4**

Pedler, Mike (1996) Action Learning for Managers, Lemos and Crane in association with The Learning Company Project, London

Petrick, J A and Quinn, J F (1997) *Management Ethics: Integrity at work*, p 43, Sage, London

Phillips, K and Fraser, T (1982) *Ethical and Professional Issues: The management of interpersonal skills training*, Gower Press, Farnborough

Piaget, J P (1927) *Conditioned Reflexes*, Oxford University Press, Oxford

Piaget, J P (1950) *The Psychology of Intelligence*, Routledge Kegan Paul, London

Piaget, J P (1977) *Science of Education and the Psychology of the Child*, Penguin, Harmondsworth

Pirsig, Robert M (1976) *Zen and the Art of Motorcycle Maintenance: An inquiry into values*, Corgi, London

Plato (1953) Laws, in *Plato's Modern Enemies and the Theory of Natural Law*, J D Wild, University of Chicago Press, Chicago, Il, p 24

Pollock, L (2000) That's infotainment, *People Management*, 28 December, pp 19–23

Porter, T (1999) Beyond metaphor: applying a new paradigm of change to experiential debriefing, *Journal of Experiential Education*, **22** (2), pp 85–90

Postle, Dennis (1993) Putting the heart back into learning, in *Using Experience for Learning*, ed D Boud, R Cohen and D Walker, pp 33–45, Open University Press, Buckingham

Priest, S (1995) An international survey of outdoor leadership preparation, in *The Theory of Experiential Education*, ed K Warren, M Sakofs and J Hunt, Association for Experiential Education, Kendall/Hunt Publishing, Dubuque, IA

Priest, S and Ballie, R (1995) Justifying the risk to others: the real razor's edge, in *The Theory of Experiential Education*, ed K Warren, M Sakofs and J Hunt, pp 307–16, Association for Experiential Education, Kendall/Hunt Publishing, Dubuque, IA

Priest, S and Rohnke, K (2000) *101 of the Best Corporate Team-building Activities We Know!*, Kendall/Hunt Publishing, Dubuque, IA

Proudman, S (1999) Urban adventure in 1989 and reflections ten years after, in *Adventure Programming*, ed J C Miles and S Priest, Venture Publishing, USA

Rackham, N and Morgan, T (1977) *Behaviour Analysis in Training*, McGraw-Hill, London

Rae, L (1995) *Techniques of Training*, 3rd edn, Gower, Aldershot

Randall, R and Southgate, J (1980) *Co-operative and Community Group Dynamics*, Barefoot Books, London

Reed, C (1999) A weekend in the country: the outdoors, the earth and drama therapy, *Horizons*, **3**

Reid, M and Barrington, H (1999) *Training Interventions*, IPD, London

Revans, Reginald W (1971) *Developing Effective Managers: A new approach to business education*, Longman, London

Revans, R W (1982) *The Origins and Growth of Action Learning*, Chartwell-Bratt, Bickley, Kent

Reynolds, M (1997) Learning styles: a critique, *Management Learning*, **28** (2), pp 115–33, Sage, London

Reynolds, M (1998) Reflection and critical reflection in management learning, *Management Learning*, **29** (2), pp 183–200, Sage, London

Robertson, I (1999) *Mind Sculpture: Unleashing your brain's potential*, Bantam Books, London

Rodwell, J (1994) *Participative Training Skills*, Gower, London

Rogers, A (1996) *Teaching Adults*, Open University Press, Buckingham

Rogers, Carl (1983) *Freedom to Learn for the 80's*, Merrill, London

Rogers, C (1993) *The Carl Rogers Reader*, Constable, London

Rose, C (1996) The Greenpeace campaigning strategy: who we are, what we campaign for and why, Greenpeace Business Conference: Brent Spar... and after, 25 September, London Marriott Hotel

Salaman, G and Butler, J (1990) Why managers won't learn, *Management Education and Development*, **21** (3), pp 183–91

Samra-Fredericks, D (1998) Conversation analysis, in *Qualitative Methods and Analysis in Organisational Research*, ed G Symon and C Cassel, Sage, London

Sapir, Edward (1987) Quoted in *Conceptual Blockbusting: A guide to better ideas*, James L Adams, p 84, Penguin, Harmondsworth

Sasaki, Naoto, *Management and Industrial Structure in Japan*, Mentioned in Foreword, *The Origins and Growth of Action Learning*, R W Revans (1982), Chartwell-Bratt, Bickley, Kent

Saunders, D (1988) Simulation gaming: three aspects, *Training Officer*, May

Schank, R C (1992) Story-based memory, in *Minds, Brains and Computers*, R Morelli *et al*, Ablex Publishing Corporation, NJ

Schetter, M (1992) Comic strips in Belgium, in *Belgium, Economic and Commercial Information*, ed. Borgerhoff *et al*, Belgium Foreign Trade Office, Brussels, Quoted in Mallia, G (1997) The use of comic strips in adult education practice, in *Beyond Schooling*, ed G Baldacchino and P Mayo, p 89, Mireva Publications, Malta

Schoel, J, Prouty, D and Radcliffe, P (1988) *Island of Healing: A guide to adventure-based counselling*, Project Adventure Inc, Hamilton, MA

Schon, Donald (1983) *The Reflective Practitioner*, Basic Books, New York

Schon, Donald (1987) *Educating the Reflective Practitioner*, Jossey-Bass, San Francisco

Schueller, G (2000) Thrill or chill, *New Scientist*, **2236**, 20 April, pp 20–24

Scott Peck, M (1997) *The Road Less Travelled and Beyond*, Rider, London

Seibert, Kent W (1999) Reflection in action: tools for cultivating on-the-job learning conditions, *Organizational Dynamics*, Winter, pp 54–65

Senge, Peter (1992) *The Fifth Discipline: The art and practice of the learning organisation*, Century Business, London

Smith, P K *et al* (1986) Play in young children: problems of definition, categorisation and measurement, in *Children's Play: Research developments and practical applications*, ed P K Smith, pp 37–54, Gordon & Breach, New York

Snell, Robin (1992) Experiential learning at work: why can't it be painless?, *Personnel Review*, **21** (4), pp 12–26

Springer, R (1999) *Rückkehr zum Taylorismus? Arbeitspolitik in der Automobilindustrie am Scheideweg,* Campus Verlag, Frankfurt am Main

Stouffer, Russell (1999) Personal insight: reframing the unconscious through metaphor-based adventure therapy, *Journal of Experiential Education,* **22** (1), June, pp 28–34

Strangaard, F (1981) *NLP Made Visual,* Connector, Copenhagen

Surtees, M (1998) New frontiers in outdoor development: evaluating the personal development outcomes of expeditions, Unpublished Master's thesis in HRD, Sheffield Business School, Sheffield

Swarbrooke, J *et al* (in press) *Adventure Tourism: The new frontiers,* Butterworth-Heinemann, London

Taylor, H (1991) The systematic training model: corn circles in search of a spaceship?, *Journal of the Association for Management Education and Development,* **22** (4), pp 258–78

Terrell, C (2000) Cartoon review cards, *Horizons,* **12**, Winter, AfOL, Cumbria

Thayer, R (1996) *The Origin of Everyday Moods: Managing energy, tension and stress,* Oxford University Press, Oxford

Tower, R B and Singer, J L (1980) Imagination, interest and joy in early childhood, in *Children's Humour,* ed P E McGhee and A J Chapman, Wiley, Chichester

Tuckman, B W and Jenson, M A C (1977) Stages of small group development revisited, *Group and Organizational Studies,* **2**, pp 419–27

Ulrich, D (1974) Aesthetic and effective responses to natural environments, in *Behaviour and the Natural Environment,* ed I Altman and J Wohlwill, Plenum Press, New York

Ulrich, D and Hinkson, P (2001) Net heaps, *People Management,* pp 32–36, Chartered Institute of Personnel and Development, London

Uttley, Alison (1943) from *Country Hoard,* Faber & Faber, pp 199–201, in Jerome S Bruner, Alison Jolly and Kathy Sylva (1976) *Play,* Penguin, Harmondsworth

Van Matre, S (1978) *Acclimatisation,* American Camping Association, IN

Van Matre, S (1979) *Sunship Earth,* American Camping Association, IN

van Ments, M (1994) *The Effective Use of Role Play,* Kogan Page, London

Vanreusel, B (1995) From Bambi to Rambo: towards a socio-ecological approach to the pursuit of outdoor sports, in *Sport in Space and Time,* ed O Weiss and W Schulz, Vienna University Press, Vienna

Walker, R (1999) Fire in the sky: from big bang to big money, *Horizons,* **4**

Walter, G and Marks, S (1981) *Experiential Learning and Change,* John Wiley & Sons, New York

Warner Weil, Susan and McGill, Ian (1989) *Making Sense of Experiential Learning: Diversity in theory and practice,* SHRE and Open University Press, Buckingham

Whyte, W H (1960) *The Organisation Man*, Penguin, London

Wichmann, T (1995) Babies and bath water: two experiential heresies, in *The Theory of Experiential Education*, ed K Warren, M Sakofs and J Hunt, pp 109–19, Association for Experiential Education, Kendall/Hunt Publishing, Dubuque, IA

Wickes, S (2000) The facilitators' stories, *Organisation Development*, Brathay Topical Papers, **2**, pp 25–46, Brathay, Cumbria

Wildemeersch, Danny (1989) The principal meaning of dialogue for the construction and transformation of reality, in *Making Sense of Experiential Learning: Diversity in theory and practice*, ed Susan Warner Weil and Ian McGill, pp 60–77, SHRE and Open University Press, Buckingham

Wilkes, F (1999) *Intelligent Emotion*, Arrow Books, London

Wilson, J P, ed (1999) *Human Resource Development: Learning and training for individuals and organizations*, Kogan Page, London

Wilson, P (1997) *Calm at Work*, Penguin, London

Womack, J P and Jones, D T (1996) *Lean Thinking*, Simon & Schuster, London

Woodruffe, C (2001) Promotional intelligence, *People Management*, 11 January, Chartered Institute of Personnel and Development

Yaffey (1993) The value base of activity experience in the outdoors, *Journal of Adventure Education*, **10** (3), pp 9–11

Yardley-Matwiejczuk, K (1999) *Role Play: Theory and practice*, Sage, London

Yerkes, R M and Dodson, J D (1980) The relation of strength of stimulus to rapidity of habit formation, *Journal of Comparative Neurological Psychology*, **18**, pp 459–82

Zohar, Dana and Marshall, Ian (2001) *Spiritual Intelligence: The ultimate intelligence*, Bloomsbury, London

Further Reading

Beard, C M (1996) Environmental training – emerging products, *Journal of Industrial and Commercial Training*, **28** (5), pp 18–23, MCB University Press, Bradford

Beard, C M (1997) Sustainable design: re-thinking future business products, *Journal of Sustainable Product Design*, **3**, October, pp 18–27

Boydell, T (1976) *Experiential Learning*, Department of Adult and Higher Education, University of Manchester, Manchester

Brookfield, S D (1986) *Understanding and Facilitating Adult Learning*, Open University Press, Buckingham

Campbell, J (1990) Outdoor management development: a fad or a phenomenon?, *Training Officer*, **26**, pp 218–20

Cremona, V A (1997) Creating community theatre, in *Beyond Schooling: Adult education in Malta*, ed G Baldacchino and P Mayo, pp 213–28, Mireva Publications, Malta

Everard, B (1997) Establishing the competence of outdoor training staff, *Horizons*, pp 20–21

Fritchie, R (1990) Biography work: the missing part of career development, *Industrial and Commercial Development*, **22** (2), pp 27–31

Gass, M (1999) Accreditation and certification: questions for an advancing profession, in *Adventure Programming*, ed J C Miles and S Priest, pp 247–51, Venture Publishing, USA

Gass, M and Dobkin, C (1992) *Book of Metaphors*, AEE, Boulder, CO

Heron, J (1989) *The Facilitator's Handbook*, Kogan Page, London

Heron, J (1996) Helping whole people learn, in *Working with Experience: Animating learning*, ed D Boud and N Miller, pp 75–91, Routledge, London

James, T (1995) Kurt Hahn and the aims of education, in *The Theory of Experiential Education*, ed K Warren, M Sakofs and J Hunt, pp 33–43, Association for Experiential Education, Kendall/Hunt Publishing, Dubuque, IA

Kenny, T J M and Enemark, S (1998) The growing importance of CPD, *Continuing Professional Development*, **1**, pp 154–63

Leary, M (1981) Working with biography, in *Management Self-development*, ed T Boydell and M Pedlar, Gower, Farnborough

Lewin, Kurt (1957) Action research and minority problems, in *Resolving Social Conflicts*, ed K W Lewin and G Allport, pp 201–16, Selected papers on group dynamics, Harper & Brothers, New York

Loynes, C, ed (1998) *Outdoor Management Development*, Adventure Education, Cumbria

Maslow, A (1954) *Motivation and Personality*, Harper & Row, New York

Maslow, A (1968) *Towards a Psychology of Being*, D Van Nostrand, New York

Miles, J C and Priest, S (1999) *Adventure Programming*, Venture Publishing, USA

Mortlock, C (1978) *Adventure Education*, Keswick Ferguson, London

Pedler, M and Boydell, T (1981) *Managing Self-development*, Gower, Farnborough

Pedler, M and Boydell, T (1999) *Managing Yourself*, Lemos and Crane, London

Priest, S (1998) The influence of instructor type on corporate adventure training program effectiveness, in *Outdoor Management Development*, ed C Loynes, pp 47–49, Adventure Education, Cumbria

Quinn, W (1999) The essence of adventure, in *Adventure Programming*, ed J C Miles and S Priest, pp 149–51, Venture Publishing, USA

Redington, C (1983) *Can Theatre Teach*, Pergamon Press, London

Reece, I and Walker, S (1997) *Teaching, Training and Learning*, Business Education Publishers Ltd, London

Rogers, C (1969) *Freedom to Learn*, Charles E Merrill, Columbus, OH

Symons, J (1994) Understanding and analysing outdoor (management) development programs, *Journal of Adventure Education and Outdoor Leadership*, **11**, pp 6–12

Woodall, J and Douglas, D (2000) Winning hearts and minds: ethical issues in human resource management, in *Ethical Issues in Contemporary Human Resource Management*, D Winstanley and J Woodall, pp 116–36, Macmillan, London

Index